Alona Shestopalova

From Screens to Battlefields
Tracing the Construction of Enemies on Russian Television

UKRAINIAN VOICES

Collected by Andreas Umland

44 *Konstantin Sigow*
   Für Deine und meine Freiheit
   Europäische Revolutions- und Kriegserfahrungen im heutigen Kyjiw
   Mit einem Vorwort von Karl Schlögel
   Herausgegeben von Regula M. Zwahlen
   ISBN 978-3-8382-1755-0

45 *Kateryna Pylypchuk*
   The War that Changed Us
   Ukrainian Novellas, Poems, and Essays from 2022
   With a foreword by Victor Yushchenko
   ISBN 978-3-8382-1859-5

46 *Kyrylo Tkachenko*
   Rechte Tür Links
   Radikale Linke in Deutschland, die Revolution und der Krieg in der Ukraine, 2013-2018
   ISBN 978-3-8382-1711-6

47 *Alexander Strashny*
   The Ukrainian Mentality
   An Ethno-Psychological, Historical and Comparative Exploration
   With a foreword by Antonina Lovochkina
   Translated from the Ukrainian by Michael M. Naydan and Olha Tytarenko
   ISBN 978-3-8382-1886-1

The book series "Ukrainian Voices" publishes English- and German-language monographs, edited volumes, document collections, and anthologies of articles authored and composed by Ukrainian politicians, intellectuals, activists, officials, researchers, and diplomats. The series' aim is to introduce Western and other audiences to Ukrainian explorations, deliberations and interpretations of historic and current, domestic, and international affairs. The purpose of these books is to make non-Ukrainian readers familiar with how some prominent Ukrainians approach, view and assess their country's development and position in the world. The series was founded, and the volumes are collected by Andreas Umland, Dr. phil. (FU Berlin), Ph. D. (Cambridge), Associate Professor of Politics at the Kyiv-Mohyla Academy and an Analyst in the Stockholm Centre for Eastern European Studies at the Swedish Institute of International Affairs.

Alona Shestopalova

FROM SCREENS TO BATTLEFIELDS
Tracing the Construction of Enemies on Russian Television

Bibliografische Information der Deutschen Nationalbibliothek
Die Deutsche Nationalbibliothek verzeichnet diese Publikation in der Deutschen Nationalbibliografie; detaillierte bibliografische Daten sind im Internet über http://dnb.d-nb.de abrufbar.

Bibliographic information published by the Deutsche Nationalbibliothek
Die Deutsche Nationalbibliothek lists this publication in the Deutsche Nationalbibliografie; detailed bibliographic data are available in the Internet at http://dnb.d-nb.de.

ISBN (Print): 978-3-8382-1884-7
ISBN (Ebook [PDF]): 978-3-8382-7884-1
© *ibidem*-Verlag, Hannover • Stuttgart 2024
Alle Rechte vorbehalten

Das Werk einschließlich aller seiner Teile ist urheberrechtlich geschützt. Jede Verwertung außerhalb der engen Grenzen des Urheberrechtsgesetzes ist ohne Zustimmung des Verlages unzulässig und strafbar. Dies gilt insbesondere für Vervielfältigungen, Übersetzungen, Mikroverfilmungen und elektronische Speicherformen sowie die Einspeicherung und Verarbeitung in elektronischen Systemen.

All rights reserved. No part of this publication may be reproduced, stored in or introduced into a retrieval system, or transmitted, in any form, or by any means (electronic, mechanical, photocopying, recording or otherwise) without the prior written permission of the publisher. Any person who commits any unauthorized act in relation to this publication may be liable to criminal prosecution and civil claims for damages.

Printed in the EU

Contents

Foreword by Nina Jankowicz 7

Introduction 11

Part I: How to Create an Enemy
The Enemy as a Social Construct 17
    "We" and "Our" Enemies 20
    Do Objective Threats and Real Enemies Exist? 25
    The (Un)Changing Face of the Enemy 32

The Role of the Media in Constructing Enemies 45
    Constructing Enemies at Home 47
    Enemies on Export 59
    The Potential for Enmification in News Coverage of
    Conflicts 70

Part II: Russian Media and Russia's Wars
Russian Media Reality: Autocracy, Control, Wars 77

Russia and Ukraine: Interplay of Geopolitics and Colonialism 93

Part III: Methodology
Standardized Content Analysis 105

Discourse-historical Approach 111

Part IV: Preparing for the War on Channel One Russia and RT
Tracing Russian Hostile Communication 117
    When Negative Depiction Turns into Strategic
    Enmification 126
    Differences in Enmification on Channel One Russia
    and RT 137
    Evolution of Enmification Over the Analysed Time
    Period 144

> The Recipe of Fear and Hatred 155
>> Russia's Communication Strategies 155
>> Same Enemies — Different Enmification Patterns 164
>> The Road to Demonization and its First Fruits 170

> Conclusion: Autocracies Learn from Each Other 189

> References 195

> Annex 233

> Index 245

Foreword

In early 2023, after a long travel hiatus due to the COVID-19 pandemic, I packed into a baroque ballroom in downtown Brussels with hundreds of other academics, researchers, bureaucrats, and diplomats for the launch of a new European Commission report on "Foreign Information Manipulation and Interference" or "FIMI", a new acronym the body was introducing to help coalesce the international community toward action against what it had previously deemed, interchangeably: disinformation, hybrid warfare, propaganda, and fake news.

As a speaker at the conference, I was engaging with the online conversation about the event and started to notice harassing messages appearing in my Twitter replies and email inbox. One alleged I was a Nazi and leered, "We're watching you."

Where were these messages originating from? Of course, any European Commission-sponsored event is likely to attract some criticism or conspiracy theorists, but nothing in my notifications or a quick search on the web seemed to indicate any adversarial attention.

Just then, the moderator answered my question: RT — formerly Russia Today, Russia's international broadcasting arm, known for amplifying all manner of falsehoods and even extremist content — had shared the livestream of the event. I tried to look up their tweet, but couldn't find it; a few months earlier, after Russia had launched its full-scale invasion of Ukraine, the EU had taken the step of banning RT within the borders of the bloc. Even its Twitter feeds were inaccessible.

The path to that decision had been long and circuitous. Since the American presidential election of 2016, RT had occupied a special place in the Western consciousness. At once blamed for electing Donald Trump and birthing Russian disinformation in and of itself, RT became the embodiment of a "Russian troll" in media outlet form. Few journalists, policymakers, or citizens sought to learn more about the reality of the coverage RT broadcast or its effects.

As is typical, Western interest in RT and other Russian media came with a certain degree of hubris, focused only on the effect of Russian propaganda and falsehoods on Western government. It was described as the sole and most grievous vector of Russian interference in the American electoral process, a stature it almost certainly did not deserve; more surreptitious means of communication, including online influence campaigns, likely were more effective than their "mainstream media" counterparts, at least in the Western context. The influence of Russian autocracy-controlled media and online environments echoing them within the audience of millions inside Russia as well as Russians living abroad was not even mentioned: it was off the radar of most of the decision-makers and experts for decades.

Then came the full-scale invasion of Ukraine, and as images of Ukrainian civilians fleeing the war filled most of the airwaves, some Western governments took the decisive step of coming down hard on RT, banning it in the EU. Broadcast service providers like DirecTV dropped it within a week of the full-scale invasion. At that time and up until now, Channel One Russia has been informing millions about Russia's full-scale war against Ukraine, supporting it and calling it nothing more than a 'special military operation'.

As Alona Shestopalova argues in From Screens to Battlefields: Tracing the Construction of Enemies on Russian Television, RT and its domestic counterpart Channel One Russia had a nefarious role to play ahead of the full-scale Russia's war in Ukraine: fertilizing the informational ground and creating enemies of Ukrainian politicians and the Ukrainian people. For anyone who has ever wondered "what exactly does Russian television do that's so bad? Is lying illegal now?" Shestopalova lays out precisely the dehumanizing, enmifying arguments that RT and Channel One Russia broadcasters made to turn their audiences at home and abroad against Ukrainians, their leaders and those that were searching for safety.

Where others did a cursory examination, relying on only a few headlines or a short time period, Shestopalova does much more. She examines all RT and Channel One Russia weekly news stories relating to Euromaidan, Russian annexation of Crimea and the first months of the war in the Donbas over 42 weeks, demonstrating that over time, those actors that were portrayed negatively were more likely to be understood as enemies over time. The channels "offered their viewers black-and-white news coverage creating a clear dichotomy between positively depicted Russian and Russia-affiliated actors and negatively depicted Ukrainian and Western actors", Shestopalova writes. They regularly eschewed covering events that might be viewed as critical of Russia to instead promote narratives that hostilely portray Western powers, and more importantly, Ukraine.

"As early as eight years before the beginning of the full-scale Russian-Ukrainian War," Shestopalova explains, "Ukrainian political actors were the main targets of Russian state-controlled enmification compared to other actors including Western ones, and that Ukrainian actors were already being demonized and dehumanized." This had effects not just within foreign audiences targeted by RT; Shestopalova finds that Channel One Russia, the flagship domestic news broadcaster, was even more extreme in its coverage than its international counterpart: where RT had to soften its rhetoric so as not to scare off Western viewers living in pluralistic media environments, Channel One Russia was free to lie and obfuscate as it chose.

Sceptics, look no further than this case study to understand the role disinformation and propaganda can play; months into a full-scale war that many are convincingly arguing is part of a genocide against Ukrainians, the ground was fertilized and prepared by encouraging Russians to be more accepting of violence and human rights abuses against those that they perceive as enemies.

Given that broad-based rejection of Russia's war in Ukraine from ordinary Russian citizens would make it much less likely to continue, Shestopalova's work underlines how critical it is that policymakers and communicators continue to attempt to pierce the Russian filter bubble and not just successfully deliver information to Russian audiences, but ensure that they trust that information as well. Similarly, ensuring that external audiences consuming high quantities of Russian state-sponsored media are receiving quality, trustworthy content is critical—otherwise audiences in the Global South, for instance, where information about the war in Ukraine stems primarily from Russian and Chinese sources, will be more likely to buy into Russian lines about the war. It is research like Shestopalova's that will take us from broad brushstroke reactions that miss some of the biggest harms that campaigns like Russia's can perpetrate.

Nina Jankowicz, author of
How to Lose the Information War: Russia, Fake News, and the Future of Conflict?

Introduction

I'm writing these lines in 2024, more than 800 days after the beginning of Russia's full-scale war against Ukraine. Today, Russian missiles and artillery systems attack Ukrainian cities, towns and villages. It was also happening yesterday and the day before yesterday. In the territories occupied by Russia, the occupation authorities torture and kill civilians. Millions of kids wait for their fathers and mothers to come back home: numerous civilians joined the Ukrainian army to prevent the invading Russian army from reaching their homes. Multiple cases of killings and rape by Russian soldiers in formerly occupied Bucha have already been uncovered. The world also already knows about hundreds of graves in the forest in Izium and multiple torture chambers established during the Russian occupation of Kherson. The Ukrainian army managed to push the Russian army from the Northern regions of Ukraine, from most of the Kharkiv region and the right bank of the Dnipro river in the Kherson region. Hundreds of Ukrainian settlements are still under Russian occupation. The world still does not know the complete picture of Russian crimes committed in occupied Mariupol, Donetsk, Crimea, etc. The International Criminal Court issued arrest warrants for the Russian president and Russia's Commissioner for Children's Rights for their roles in the deportation of Ukrainian kids to Russia. Nowadays, scientists and lawyers discuss possible framings of Russia's actions in Ukraine as genocide.

I did not know all of these would happen when I started working on this book.

It was at the end of 2018. What did I know back then? That Russia and Russia-controlled forces occupied approximately 7% of Ukrainian territory. That more than a million civilians had to flee from those territories to other regions of Ukraine, among those civilians were indigenous inhabitants of Crimea—ethnic Crimean Tatars—many of whom were forced to leave their homes after the Russian occupation. I knew that a long wall in the city centre of Kyiv had an uncountable number of photos of Ukrainian soldiers and volunteers killed since 2014 and that sooner or later, Russia will launch a full-scale invasion.

Was I shocked on the morning of February 24, 2022? Yes, shocked but not surprised. By that time, I researched the construction of enemies on Russian TV long enough to avoid being surprised.

I submitted the dissertation that later formed the core of this book in 2022, shortly after the onset of Russia's full-scale invasion of Ukraine. When I received the initial documents proving the successful defence, a representative from my university's faculty asked me when I had changed the research topic to make it so relevant in the context of the ongoing Russia's war against Ukraine. I replied that this had been the research topic of my doctoral dissertation from the very beginning, and that I had started working on it a couple of years before 2022, observing Russia's attempts to instil hatred and fear towards Ukraine and Ukrainians through state-controlled hostile communication. For the faculty member that reply was surprising, for me it was clear that the hostile communication against Ukraine was omnipresent on Russian TV long before February 24, 2022.

When I started working on the construction of enemies on Russian TV, both my topic itself and my research questions seemed a bit too alarmist to many. Luckily, there were also people who supported my understanding of the case and my theoretical idea of revisiting the concept of enemy and the construction of enemies—the significant topic from the turbulent past—and were eager to see fragments of the analysed data that were relevant for the autocracy-controlled construction of enemies in the 21st century.

Due to the mood of those years, I had to proceed cautiously, taking one step at a time. The academic standards required avoiding building any arguments on statements like 'everybody knows that Russia is …' and substantiating every single interpretation of research finding. I am extremely glad that I had to take that path.

Because of what I explained in the previous paragraphs, from today's perspective, some of the observations and conclusions of this book might seem too obvious to argue. However, even if we feel that we know something by heart, to make it solid, someone has to sit down and document how exactly we have come to those conclusions based on findings — not on beliefs, feelings or general knowledge. This is what I'm doing in this book: systematically tracing the construction of enemies on Russian TV during the Euromaidan, occupation of Crimea and the first five months of the war in Donetsk and Luhansk regions of Ukraine to explain how it helped Russia to make the full-scale war against Ukraine possible.

As early as 1945, the Constitution of the United Nations Educational, Scientific and Cultural Organization stated "[t]hat since wars begin in the minds of men, it is in the minds of men that the defences of peace must be constructed" (p. 1). However, almost 80 years later, there are still numerous wars around the world, one of them in the centre of Europe. Each of those wars repeatedly brings up the question of how exactly a situation arises in which people take up arms to attack and kill those whom they see as enemies. I try to answer this question using the example of Russia's full-scale war against Ukraine.

The book consists of four parts. In the first part, the reader will not see many references to Russia's war against Ukraine as Russia's atrocities in Ukraine are only a new manifestation of what hatred and fear lead to for millennia. To understand this manifestation better, I take a step back to conceptualize the very ideas of us vs. them, enemies, hatred and fear, as they are those leading to wars and genocides at all times with the help of respective mass communication.

Only after revisiting and updating the most fundamental concepts of the topic, I dive deep into the second part, examining Russian media and their role during previous Russia-led wars of recent decades with the focus on wars against Chechnya and the war against Georgia. The second half of this part is focused on Russia's aggression against Ukraine, its chronology and possible framing. In particular, I argue why the understanding of Russia's war against Ukraine cannot be complete without understanding its imperial and colonial nature.

The third and fourth parts are entirely devoted to the hostile Russian communication in the context of Russia's aggression against Ukraine. In these parts, I explain how exactly I've analysed the Russian state-controlled news coverage of the Euromaidan, occupation of Crimea and the first five months of the war in Donetsk and Luhansk regions of Ukraine, reveal my main findings and put them in the context of further developments in an attempt to explain how we found ourselves where we are now and where we might be going if other autocracies learn from Russia's experience.

An important note on terminology has to be made: throughout the book, I refer to the new stage of Russia's invasion of Ukraine that started on February 24, 2022, as Russia's full-scale invasion, Russia's full-scale war, full-scale Russian-Ukrainian War, etc. to underline that the war has not started on that day. On the contrary, by that time almost a decade has passed since the beginning of Russia's invasion of Ukraine including the occupation of Crimea and the war in Donbas. As the time frame of the news coverage I analyse includes Euromaidan, Russia's occupation of Crimea and the first five months of the war in Donbas, I refer to that period (November 2013 to September 2014) as the Russian-Ukrainian conflict. Notably, I avoid using the word 'conflict' or 'crisis' in this book when discussing the period after February 24, 2022. The reason for this is that nowadays, Russia tends to use these words in its international communication to downplay the scale of its war against Ukraine, despite the fact that it has already become the deadliest war in Europe since the end of World War II.

Part I
How to Create an Enemy

Part I

The Enemy as a Social Construct

To understand how to construct an enemy, one must start with the question of why human beings and the entire social reality can be seen as constructs. Otherwise, it becomes difficult to comprehend why the formation of hostile or friendly attitudes is also a constructivist practice that is rarely rational. For this reason, I begin with a concise overview of the core ideas of constructivism. This overview will aid in better understanding the construction of enemies in people's minds.

The starting point of constructivism as a theoretical framework is that there is no objective social reality understood the same way by everyone (von Glasersfeld, 1982; Wendt, 1995; Pörksen et al., 2011; Onuf, 2013).[1] Even if everyone had the same information about social events, we would still see things differently. This is because each person perceives the world uniquely. Specifically, our individual socialization experiences give us different outlooks on the same things.

Traditional socializing agents like families, schools, religious institutions, and the mass media teach us how to see and engage with the social world (Oppenheimer, 2005). These agents cannot have the exact same impact on everyone because they are quite diverse themselves. Together, they shape what is called "cognitive maps" in our minds (Herrmann & Fischerkeller, 1995). These cognitive maps help us simplify information about social reality. They allow us to categorize events, facts, or individuals in our personal perception of the world by labelling them as positive, negative, dangerous, and so on. Throughout life, we reflect on our upbringing and reproduce these cognitive maps, though often with changes.

---

1   Here and further in the book, the surnames and years in brackets denote the surnames of authors of the texts (such as scientific articles) I used while working on a respective fragment of my book and the years denote when the mentioned texts were published. You can see the full list of references at the end of the book.

This mechanism of attitude creation is strengthened by our self-perception, values, and interests, and is inseparable from them. Obviously, each person's identity, values, and interests are also unique and are socially constructed (Grusky & Szelényi, 2011; Gregg, 2012). Their formation begins with infants' first social interactions and, more or less intensively, lasts throughout their whole life (Feinman, 1992). As can be seen, any human being is a textbook social construct in terms of their perception of self and the world around them.

The consumption of information about social reality also has constructivist elements determined by human features (Hacking, 1999; Demeritt, 2002). This could be explained in the following terms. There are facts, but even when faced with them directly, we consume them along with other facts. Then, we put them into a broader context—in other words, we make sense of the facts by assigning particular meaning to them. The next unavoidable step is to reduce information, i.e. to decide which facts are more important than others, and this requires even more cognitive effort. As a result, we form our own understanding of an issue using the above-mentioned cognitive maps. It is clear that in such conditions, our understanding is a priori far from being objective (Eisenberg, 1995).

Selecting some facts and ignoring others distances us from what is indeed happening over there, but it is the only way of perceiving a complicated and multifaceted world that is impossible to embrace fully (Lachman et al., 2015). Partly, the selection is made for us by media outlets performing the role of mediators between the audience and the facts. They make decisions about what we should know and what not (Bennett, 1990). Media outlets organize thousands of events into the media agenda and only then a recipient comes into play to customise, select, and reduce the information further.

At the same time, media companies also do not simply mirror reality. They inevitably transmit only versions of reality while telling us stories about the world (Pörksen et al., 2011). The best journalistic practices seeking objectivity try to work with facts instead of opinions, frame information neutrally and give word to all conflicting sides if they exist. From a positivist perspective, such an approach would be considered as objective (Wien, 2005). However, "the truth" is never the whole truth, "the importance" of an event is not an objective criterion, and the problem of balance is even more complicated. Journalists face it whenever they try to decide which proportion of conflicting ideas should be in their work: 50:50? Proportionally, considering the weight of the arguments in the public discussion? Or is it enough just to mention that there is another view of the issue?

After the invention of the photo-camera and its advent to journalism, there were hopes that it would finally show the world as it was. The idea "do not tell me — show me" looked persuasive. Professional photographers were considered technicians rather than storytellers, people "pushing the button" rather than interpreters of reality (Brennen, 2010). Those hopes vanished when it became clear that photos are not objective either. Factors such as the usage of different perspectives or attention to different details contributed to the diverse framings of the same issues (Woo, 1994; Bowers, 2008).

Therefore, we have examined the arguments for the constructivist essence of humans as well as of the information created and consumed by them. The third element to consider is social interactions. Wendt writes that "a fundamental principle of constructivist social theory is that people act toward objects, including other actors, on the basis of the meanings that the objects have for them" (1992, pp. 396–397). Thus, the interaction between humans or social groups is based on the information they possess about each other.

A limitation (or maybe an advantage) of the fact that humans acquire information only through the frames of their world perception becomes decisive when it comes to the dimension of international interactions. States are created by humans and their imagined communities — nations (Anderson, 2006). Therefore, the subjectivity of humans is transmitted to macro and mega levels influencing inter-state interactions; the inconsistency between "reality" and people's perceptions of it becomes even more striking. That is if we accept the postulates of epistemological constructivists who believe that reality exists independently of those who try to understand it (Raskin, 2002).

Thus, humans and international relations, as well as all intermediate elements between them, can—and will in this work—be viewed from a constructivist perspective. Human self- and world-perception, information that makes humans unite into communities, those communities and their identities, and, lastly, information about other communities used to create interaction strategies, are all social constructs. Further, this chapter examines how the constructed identities and interests of political actors lead to the perception of other actors as enemies.

"We" and "Our" Enemies

The concepts of "we" and "others", denoting groups with different identities, had already been used in social sciences more than a century ago (Sumner, 2007). Yet in the 1950s, a new stage of in- and out-groups research began—scholars became interested in the connections between group self-perception and social conflicts (Rinder, 1954; Rose, 1960; Himes, 1966). In the beginning, it was quite widespread to qualitatively analyse real-life conflicts, but that approach did not provide answers to the question of why people actually start hating and fearing each other.

The solution was sought in a series of social experiments devoted to the interaction between in- and out-groups (Sherif, 1958; Ferguson & Kelley, 1964). The grand aim of those experiments was to understand which factors made people from one group discriminate against people from another group and express enmity towards them (Tajfel, 1970). Interestingly, the experimental studies mentioned above have shown that the mere fact of dividing people into groups is already enough for a slightly hostile attitude. Moreover, that pattern was evident even if experiment participants were aware that the group categorization was made randomly (Billig & Tajfel, 1973).

Despite some critique of those studies highlighting their ignorance of the impact of competition (Rabbie & Horwitz, 1969), oversimplification of intergroup interactions, and underestimations of socio-cultural factors (Yamagishi et al., 1998), there were numerous later attempts to replicate the experiments considering different mediating variables (Brewer & Silver, 1978; Mullen et al., 1992; Fischer & Derham, 2016). For instance, scholars were trying to understand if factors such as self-esteem (Abrams & Hogg, 1988), cultural biases (Yuki, 2003) or the migrant status of certain group members (Rubin et al., 2014) were influencing intergroup interactions. The research referenced above has moved the topic at hand beyond the borders of Social Psychology and contributed to the formation of Social Identity Theory (SIT) (Brewer, 1979; Tajfel, 1979; Hogg, 2000; Turner, 2010).

In a nutshell, SIT claims that different social groups have different identities, those identities could be activated by some means, and the mere existence of an in-group provokes its members to be prejudiced towards an out-group (Stets & Burke, 2000). Both communication and International Relations scholars have benefited from SIT as it has given them a foundation for intergroup interaction research.

At the same time, it is not only scientists who make use of the psychological patterns described by SIT. Among the main communicators constantly underlining the group's identity are political actors. For them, it is hard to avoid group categorization as politicians often appeal to some particular social group. The practice of political communication shows that an in-group could be created based on formal criteria such as citizenship, in which case it is possible to avoid the creation of an out-group. The examples of this widespread method are, for instance, the following addresses: "My fellow citizens" (Merkel, 2018); "Dear Ukrainians" (Zelensky, 2019), and so on.

Formally created in-groups (as in the above-mentioned examples) are sometimes granted extra features that could strengthen their pride and group identification: "We will never forget that we are Americans and the future belongs to us. The future belongs to the brave, the strong, the proud and the free" (Trump, 2019). There is no particular out-group named in this statement but, as the speaker says that being American means being "brave, strong, proud and free", this implicitly suggests that an abstract out-group does not possess these characteristics (the future belongs to us, not to the others). It is also possible to unite people into a single in-group in the cases when multiple and diverse groups are actually present: "There is no liberal America and a conservative America. There is the United States of America" (Obama, 2012). Or another example of a similar communicative strategy: "Wherever we live, whoever we are, we all share the same responsibility – to make our planet great again" (Macron, 2017).

In- and out-groups could also be created based on other criteria such as religion, social status, ideological preferences, etc. Such categorization is less formal as it allows individuals more freedom to decide which groups to relate to, which ones not to, and what meaning to attribute to those group identities (Stets & Burke, 2000). As a result, diverse group identities overlap in one human shaping a subjective personality structure. German citizen, father, Muslim, teacher – all these elements constitute the identity of many people but the mix of in-group identifications within one individual and the uneven strength of those identities is unique in each particular case.

All identities are social constructs formed under the influence of numerous factors. However, political actors also often deliberately influence people's group identities (Ehrkamp, 2006; Kallis, 2015). A vivid example illustrating the political impact on group identity is the dual treatment of Muslims in today's world.

On one hand, extremist leaders attempt to radicalize the Muslim religious identity by associating it with Islamist political goals (Gunn, 2003; Rabil, 2011). For example, in a BBC interview, an Afghan militant named his in-group and aligned it with radical Islamist views: "Muslims are thirsty for Islamic Caliphate in the world" (BBC, 2014). Such statements not only distort the perception of Muslims by non-Muslims but also create a dilemma for non-radical Muslims. They might feel compelled to align with Islamist goals or risk being excluded from the Muslim in-group despite the fact that the proposed in-group characteristics apply solely to Islamists, not Muslims. Consequently, reducing the entire Muslim group to its minor radical faction (Islamists) confuses identities.

On the other hand, some politicians (e.g. right-wing populists) frame Muslims as a dangerous out-group (Kallis, 2015). One of them, Hungarian prime minister Viktor Orban, talks about the need "to defend Christian nations against immigration, which [...] led to the virus of terrorism" (Al Jazeera, 2019). By spreading such messages, politicians instigate fear toward Muslims among the population. Consequently, Muslims face Islamophobia that results in a confrontation in different spheres of life (Allen, 2007; Wheatley, 2019).

These two examples demonstrate that stigmatization and its consequences are not solely experienced by out-group representatives. Being involuntarily assigned to an in-group can also provoke frustration among individuals who do not share some of the declared group attributes or do not feel part of that in-group at all. This rejection of an imposed group identification turns an individual from a representative of the in-group to one of an out-group.

As highlighted above, group categorization is often accompanied by the emergence of bias and prejudice, which manifest in the distortion of incoming information about the out-group's features and actions. This, in turn, increases bias even more, creating a vicious circle. A series of studies featuring five-year-old children have shown their tendency to accept positive information about in-group members and negative information about the out-groupers (Dunham et al., 2011). Adults can even feel joy when something bad happens to the members of the out-group (Combs et al., 2009). However, categorization—even when it goes along with bias and prejudice—is still not enough for confrontation (Castano et al., 2002). The others have to be perceived as dangerous for the in-group members to feel threatened. In the theory of international relations, such an actor—one who is "viewed by someone with hostility" (Silverstein, 1992, p.145) and "is judged as a threat" (Eicher et al., 2013, p. 129)—is called an enemy.

Then arises the question of why an actor could be perceived as threatening. In contrast to the realist approach in International Relations, Rousseau argues that information regarding the actor's affiliation to the in-group holds greater importance in determining whether they are viewed with hostility than knowledge about their military potential (2006). Consequently, even an actor with substantial military power could be regarded as a friend if they are perceived as "one of us". Buzan extends this argument further by asserting that non-material factors are also significant when considering an out-group actor (2009). He contends that, in the post-Cold War era, the absence of a military threat does not guarantee security (Buzan, 1997). In essence, an enemy may pose a threat not only due to their military might but also by challenging the actor's interests by limiting their authority or causing humiliation on the international arena (Hast, 2014; Wolf, 2019).

Therefore, based on the literature discussed above, it can be concluded that the enemy is someone who threatens an actor's sense of security. However, an actor cannot have a clear understanding of the boundaries of their security until they know what their interests are (Adler, 1997). That, in turn, is impossible before an actor has a clearly constructed in-group identity. Putting it the other way around, the following scheme can be drawn:

Identity – Interests – Security – Threat – Enemy

(Wendt, 1992; Adler, 1997; Rousseau, 2006; Buzan, 2009; Onuf, 2013). Importantly, each of the elements in this scheme can only be shaped on the basis of the previous one. Most of the time, changes in international relations are not crucial and do not lead to a change in the starting point of the scheme—the actor's identity. So, even if extraordinary situations occur between political actors, they just need to adjust their behaviour in the new circumstances. This makes the described scheme relatively stable.

However, the given sequence is not fully linear and, in exceptional cases, changes in the last element can lead to changes in the first element. These would be situations that make the actor's identity irrelevant and create a need for a new one. For instance, when your existential enemy "dies" you cannot stay the same either, as hostility towards them was a significant part of your own identity. When the threat is gone, and the interests are secured, there is no need for protection and resistance anymore. This is what happened in international relations with the collapse of the USSR. As Wendt describes it, "Without the Cold War's mutual attributions of threat and hostility to define their identities, [...] states seem unsure of what their 'interests' should be" (1992, p. 399).

Thus, "we" and "our" enemies are strongly interconnected. First, because an enemy is always someone's enemy. There are no societies or states evil or dangerous in their essence — these features can only manifest themselves in relation to someone and in someone's perception. Second, by changing themselves, "our" enemies also change "us", as a political actor's identity and self-perception — to a great extent — depends on who their enemy is. So, as long as states have identities, interests, and the sense of being or not being secure, there will be threats and enemies around.

The contemporary world is replete with hostile attitudes between political actors and with conflicts, including violent ones. But are these enemies real, and are the threats faced by political actors objective? These are the main questions of the next section.

Do Objective Threats and Real Enemies Exist?

Among the first scientists who conceptualized the problem of the objectivity of threats were representatives of the so-called Copenhagen School (CS). They argue that there are no objective problems, and that any element of public discourse successfully framed as a threat may actually turn into a threat in the public eye (Buzan et al., 1998). Such an approach has shifted the focus of attention from the so-called "real" (military) threats to why people believe that something is threatening. It has also broadened understanding of the security agenda itself. According to CS, lifestyle, values, people's religious beliefs and their present and future welfare can also be seen as threatened (Wæver, 1995). This new view has expanded the boundaries of security to cover areas that have never previously been associated with it. Among those are, for example, societal and environmental threats that have found their place in the security discourse and become its traditional elements (Canefe, 2008; Trombetta, 2010; Karafoulidis, 2012; Schuilenburg, 2015).

Along with the new boundaries of security, the understanding of what or who could be threatening has also been widened. To address this issue, CS has introduced securitization—the concept describing how an "issue" becomes a "security issue" and how political actors consolidate public opinion against the "enemy" (Fierke, 2015). Despite its wide acceptance, securitization received various criticisms from international relations scholars. That is why I decided to focus here not just on the concept itself but on its critique, too. This will help to generate more ideas and form a deeper comprehension of the threats' objectivity dilemma.

Securitization theory claims that any topic has its place in the public agenda, ranging from non-politicized to securitized (Buzan et al., 1998). This range identifies how important the issue is, who is responsible for dealing with it and which measures should be taken. According to Buzan and colleagues, "non-politicized issues" are routine; they lie outside of political discourse, and are under the full responsibility of the public. In turn, "politicized issues" are the liability of the state, which is expected to use all legally approved measures to solve them. Politicized issues are still quite common in everyday political processes. The last type is "securitized issues", and they occupy the most extreme spot in the securitization range (Buzan et al., 1998). Only a few issues are placed there, and all of them are seen as threatening to the public and the state.

The issue's status is rarely stable. It can shift from non-politicized to politicized or even securitized. The shift is mostly performed by politicians and decision-makers who are the usual political communicators (Wæver, 1995). According to Wæver, the main condition required for such a shift is the respective communication, the so-called "speech act" that would successfully articulate the problem as threatening (1995). The effectiveness of the communication depends on the strategy chosen by politicians to convey the issue's status to citizens.

To include an issue in the security agenda, politicians should "present [it] as an issue of supreme priority" (Buzan et al., 1998, p. 26). Similarly, to persuade the public that a certain problem is urgent, communicators should first prove that the threat in question is existential and that the mere existence of the state/nation/community is in danger (Williams, 2003). If it works and the audience is convinced, the securitization is successful (Balzacq,

2005). According to the logic of the CS, without successful securitization, situations are not perceived as dangerous, and the actors causing those situations are not seen as enemies.

By increasing the importance of an issue, securitization also gives politicians the justification for extraordinary actions (Floyd, 2015). This makes securitization an attractive political strategy (McDonald, 2008) because of its exculpatory effect: threats cannot be dealt with within "normal bounds of political procedure" (Buzan et al., 1998, p. 23). In addition, threats are often attributed to other political actors rather than being inanimate. Consequently, safeguarding against securitized issues frequently involves confronting these actors through extraordinary measures justified by a self-defence motto. In real-life international relations, these securitization scenarios often lead to violent international conflicts.

As pointed out above, threats and enemies are not objective a priori but only with respect to a particular actor. In turn, the paragraphs above show that what makes an issue problematic for an actor is also not objective but has its origin in political communication. Does this mean that conflicts arise exclusively because of politicians who tell people that there is a need to confront the danger? Critics of securitization theory do not agree with this view. They think that securitization overestimates the role of politicians' subjective fears and interests in the process of creating enemies and argue that not only politicians' speech acts are capable of bringing new security threats to the table (Knudsen, 2001; Wilkinson, 2007). Particularly, Knudsen writes that CS theorists reduce the matter of threats to domestic policy and agenda by believing that politicians play a central role in introducing threats to the public (2001). "The problem here is that this [securitization approach] serves to downgrade the significance of problems that exist out there—not just in the heads of politicians and decision-makers" (Knudsen, 2001, p. 361). However, it is not clarified which problems should be called "real".

Following Knudsen's logic, if an objective threat exists, it should be threatening for everybody regardless of their identity, interests, and understanding of security. In that case, it would be possible to define inherently threatening situations using some universal indicators. Furthermore, all actors should agree that they are threatened when being placed in such a situation. The most extreme kind of threat is an existential one as it challenges not only the actor's interests but their existence — for instance, a death threat. So, could the threat be called "objective" and an actor causing this threat a "real" enemy in a situation threatening someone's life?

Mostly yes, but even in such cases, exclusions are possible. Consider the episode from the world-famous novel *The Three Musketeers* by Alexandre Dumas. While reflecting on his life's miseries, the French guard d'Artagnan concludes that as a Catholic, he cannot shoot himself; what he can do is to go and fight the outnumbering Englishmen until they kill him. Is the threat coming from the Englishmen objectively? Formally, yes: they possess some level of enmity towards d'Artagnan (as he is French) and there is a real chance that they might kill him. On the other hand, being initiated into his motives, it is possible to conclude that Englishmen are not his enemies: they may indeed pose a threat to the French in general, but their hostility towards d'Artagnan actually helps him implement his plan. Thus, even the presence of a death threat does not always signify the existence of a "real enemy".

It should be easier to define objective indicators of threat when it comes to international relations since the system of international relations is more formal than interpersonal relations. Is it possible to say that a threat is objective if it jeopardises the state's existence? Securitization theorists describe an existential threat to the state in terms of the loss of sovereignty, territory, and autonomy, which are the main characteristics of statehood (Buzan et al., 1998). So, can the situation be identified as one with an 'objective' threat if a country possessing statehood risks losing it? CS scholars would likely disagree, as per securitization theory, suggesting that the risk of losing statehood must initially be presented as a concern for the public. Conversely, some critics cited earlier in this discussion of the securitization approach might argue that the threat of losing statehood represents a scenario where the threat "exist[s] out there — not just in the heads of politicians and decision-makers" (Knudsen, 2001, p. 361).

Austria's Anschluss by Nazi Germany in 1938 gives a prominent example in favour of CS scholars' argument. It illustrates the possible ambiguity in the assessment of a situation that, at first sight, looks quite unequivocal. Before the Anschluss, Austria was a fully fledged state, so did Austrians see the threat of the annexation as an existential threat and did they perceive Nazi Germany as an existential enemy? The prompt to the answer lies in the reaction of Austrians to the annexation. Historians underline that, despite some degree of resistance, there was no massive wave of counter-actions against the Anschluss among Austrian citizens (Rauscher & Suppan, 2016). This case shows that citizens can perceive the loss of statehood in a non-dramatic light if it is framed as non-challenging for them. They could even support it if they are persuaded that the new circumstances could give them a chance to elevate their self-perception instead of being humiliated. In the case of Austria, the bigger in-group that included both Germans and Austrians was revitalised on the basis of ideas from the 19th century and the time right after the collapse of the Habsburg Monarchy (Ritter, 1975). This group had common constructed enemies (e.g. Jews), a common understanding of threats and, to some extent, a similar identity—all these elements were intensively promoted by Nazi state propaganda.

At the same time, securitization of threats and enemies, based on appeals to Austrians' unique identity, appeared not to be enough to mobilize people against "the enemy". As a result, the event was not seen by many Austrians as external aggression. However, those people who, for whatever reason, did not share the proposed "German identity", did not support the Anschluss. Statistics show that the lowest support for the Anschluss was in the "provinces with the strongest sense of Austrian identity: at one extreme rural Roman Catholic Tyrol (0.70 percent); at the other, working-class Red Vienna (0.59 percent)" (Bukey, 2000, p. 39). Compare these figures to the more than 99 percent support in Lower Austria, Styria and Burgenland (Bukey, 2000). So, what could have been seen as an objective threat for the state was seen by many of its citizens as a new possibility.

Undoubtedly, both of these examples—those of d'Artagnan and Austria—are rather exceptions than samples of the traditional perception of threats. However, they show that it is hard to determine even minimalist indicators of threat objectivity when perceptual elements come into play. Therefore, even if one does not accept the securitization theorists' logic according to which threats and enemies are non-objective essences, the opposite cannot be claimed either.

One way to distance oneself from uncertainty regarding the objectivity of a threat is to focus on situations that are commonly accepted as threatening. One of the founding documents of modern international law, the United Nations General Assembly's Resolution 2625, declares that in international relations, threatening actions are those that challenge the state's territorial integrity and political independence (United Nations General Assembly, 1970). Although these criteria are also debatable, they provide at least some point of reference for what a threatening action is. However, something widely accepted as a threat is not the same as an objective threat. Therefore, the CS logic can still be followed even when the concept of "widely recognised threats" is used.

Despite the fact that political practice often confirms the assumptions of CS about the nature of threats, there are two aspects that deserve additional attention in this context. First, securitization theorists argue that domestic politicians and decision-makers are the main agents of securitization (Wæver, 1995; Buzan et al., 1998). However, such an approach ignores the impact of non-domestic political actors even though in today's globalised world, borders do not stop the flow of information and national political elites are not able to fully control the national security agenda (Eriksson & Giacomello, 2006). Second, by focusing on communication coming from political elites, CS ignores the role of other political communicators, for instance, media outlets that play an indispensable role in the transmission of information and security agenda-setting (Sanders, 2009). Williams highlights the necessity to pay attention to the role of media outlets in the securitization process even more specifically; he argues that it is impossible to fully understand how issues of low public interest suddenly become issues of supreme priority without scrutinizing "media images", as well as "mediums, structures, and institutions of contemporary political communication" (2003, p. 512). In the second chapter of this book, I will focus on this problem more closely.

An additional aspect is the relation between the construction of threats and the construction of enemies, which is open to discussion. Following the logic of securitization, enemy-making could be seen as a variation of securitization: while securitization is the process of constructing threats out of ordinary political issues, enemy-making is the similar process but directed at political actors instead of political issues. This is the view I apply further in the book. The word *enmification* is used in this study as the term giving a descriptive name to the process of constructing enemies (Rieber & Kelly, 1991, p. 6).

Therefore, I accept the general idea of CS that communication has a central role in the securitization (and enmification) process. However, like some critics, I also see the need for broadening CS comprehension of communication through incorporating media outlets and other relevant actors into the model. I likewise subscribe to the idea that media outlets of other countries, as well as other communicators from abroad, can have an impact on the national security agenda.

To summarize this section, theoretical considerations and the examples provided demonstrate that the existence of "objective" threats and "real" enemies is questionable, if not unprovable. This point brings us back to constructivism where perception is a crucial element of reality, and the problem is something that a certain actor sees as a problem. This theoretical premise will be used throughout the whole book. Although enemy-related topics have received close scientific attention for decades, the issues of the universal research strategies and of consensually accepted terms are still unresolved. It is hard to do research on one's actor's enemies at least because there is little factual—not perceptual—information at one's disposal. Although enemies themselves may not be objective and "real", the construction of enemies in the eyes of the public may lead to real confrontation.

Moreover, Hoffmann and Hawkins (2015) argue that the cruel image of the actor held by the public is the main component required for any conflict to occur. Thus, actual conflicts are among the real-life outcomes of successful enmification campaigns. In the light of this, the next section of this theoretical chapter aims to look at the existing research dedicated to the enemies of various conflicts of the past. Just as the history of humankind, or any region/country, can be presented as a chain of positive developments, it can also be seen as a never-ending conflict with constantly changing enemies. Studies of those conflicts are exactly the source of unique information about the evolution of the "enemy" concept. Besides, attention to the outcomes of enmification campaigns of the past helps us to understand those currently underway more deeply.

The (Un)Changing Face of the Enemy

A large number of studies in political science, communication, and psychology examine enemies in the international arena. Most frequently, violent conflicts are the main stimulus motivating researchers to study hostile attitudes between political actors, with some conflicts used as research cases more often than others. The beginning of the 20th century brought WWI, which was the most destructive conflict until it was followed by the even more violent WWII, which, in turn, resolved into the protracted and world-splitting Cold War. Humankind spent the whole 20th century either in preparation for one of these wars, or in attempts to build a new world, making new friends out of old enemies. Therefore, it is to be expected that these three grand conflicts constitute the historical axis of the 20th century reflected in the enemy-related academic literature. These "copybook" cases extend knowledge about enmification as well as about its social and political consequences (Silverstein, 1989); they serve not only as illustrations of theoretical ideas but also as sources for them.

As already noted above, political actors can stimulate conflicts by constructing enemies for the public and the underlying politically motivated reasons for enmification remain relatively unchanged over the course of time. However, the circumstances leading to conflicts may vary dramatically. The same is true for the methods used in the process of enemy creation: against the background of technological developments, they are becoming more and more advanced. Therefore, each conflict is the unique story of enmity and hatred full of highly valuable details that constitute the current conceptual understanding of the enemy.

Notwithstanding rich historical data, there are still many blind spots in the domain. For example, there is a lack of systematic knowledge about enmification campaigns even when it comes to the most crucial conflicts of the past, not to mention the absence of a separate branch of research that would consistently study enemies. Among rare attempts at systematization would be a couple of pages by Schleifer, where he explores the usage of propaganda for enmification purposes in the conflicts of the 20th century (2012, pp. 107–109). Schleifer's attempt at systematization is extremely valuable despite its brevity, as he refers to the demonization of Germans during WWI, hatred towards Jews before and during WWII, and Third Reich information campaigns against the USSR after the actual termination of the Molotov-Ribbentrop agreement. Schleifer (2012) also takes note of the USA's hostile communication about the Japanese during WWII, the Koreans during the Korean War, the Vietnamese in the context of the Vietnam War, and the Iraqis during the First Gulf War, etc.

The following pages are another attempt at systemizing the existing scientific knowledge about the enemies constructed in the past. In particular, I provide a deliberately non-exhaustive literature review of the most crucial conflicts of the 20th–21st centuries with a special focus on the enmification features and on shifts in the scientific understanding of enemies.

***

At the beginning of the 20th century, a simplified approach to defining enemies prevailed in both law and politics. The still-relevant question of threat perception used to be answered in quite a formal way: an obvious manifestation of hostility — the state of war — was seen as the most important criterion of enmity existence (Warren, 1918). Both WWI and WWII, occurring in a time frame of thirty years, made this view widely accepted — it is hard to pay attention to less evident manifestations of hostility while in the midst of a war or at risk of one.

Another problem faced by politicians and scientists at that time was how to interpret wars: either as interstate confrontations, when states fight each other by means of military power, or as international confrontations, when "all the subjects [citizens and their units] of the one [state] are considered to be at war with all the subjects of the other" (White, 1900, p. 397). In other words, is the war a battle only between armies or between all the citizens of the involved sides? This theoretical obscurity becomes quite significant when it comes to real-life confrontations. It creates a further dilemma: should the civilians of the hostile state be viewed the same way as its soldiers? If so, should they be treated accordingly?

According to Turlington, during WWI, courts as well as the majority of researchers on international law viewed war between nations as the war between all citizens of those nations: "The whole nation [...] must be reconciled to submit to one common fate" (1928, p. 270), the formal reason justifying such an approach is that "the government at war is the representative of the will of all the people and acts for the whole society" (Turlington, 1928, p. 270). Such logic is partly right, but it ignores the issues of political participation and the level of democratization of the states at war. In light of this, labelling people "enemies" based exclusively on their "hostile nationality" seems far from perfect, but this very idea was applied during WWI.[2]

This approach then affected the lives of the so-called "enemy aliens" — people of "hostile nationalities" temporarily or permanently living in states that were at war with the countries of their national origin. They faced personal limitations, confiscation of property, and imprisonment (Kempner, 1940). The philosophical principle "war is a relation between states in which individuals are

---

[2] This dilemma has transformed, but it remains relevant nowadays, including in the context of the Russian-Ukrainian War. For example, should Russian civilians supporting Russia's war against Ukraine be viewed with hostility?

enemies only accidentally, not as men or even as citizens, but simply as soldiers" (Turlington, 1928, p. 270) was ignored by all the conflicting sides despite its formal incorporation into international law.

It is not a flawless approach either to consider interstate conflict merely as a fight between "their" and "our" soldiers. This does not include various groups that are at least potentially dangerous: civilians from a hostile state whose sons are fighting against "our" sons, making those civilians desire "our" defeat; millions of citizens of enemy states who pay taxes used for the production of arms; those of "our" citizens who sympathize with the enemy; spies of all sorts—"an (invisible) army of 30,000 Prussian spies was as much a Prussian 'army' as (the visible and much larger) 'fighting army' [. . .]" (Forster, 1917, p. 132), etc.

So, if the formal approach, when nationality is seen as a criterion of enmity, is imperfect, what would a more appropriate solution look like? Should a more balanced approach justify certain social groups potentially being seen as hostile (e.g. all groups, except for the soldiers of the enemy state), or should it add new social groups to the "list" of enemies (e.g. "our" citizens who sympathize with the enemy)? And what would be the rules for such in- or exclusion? The discussion among scholars and politicians seemed to be in a deadlock until the political reality showed that none of the previously existing ideas was capable of solving the problems that emerged ahead of WWII and as it progressed. As Robinson puts it, "international law was no more prepared for the dynamics of the present war than was the Maginot school of military strategy" (1945, p. 216).[3]

Despite international awareness of repressions against its citizens by the Third Reich, it was not easy to deny the nationality-based approaches to the definition of enemies. Yet, the gradual shift to the less radical treatment of people with hostile nationality and/or citizenship was evident starting from the late thirties. An example of this trend was, among other things, the positive attitude to the citizens of the former Czechoslovak Republic, occupied by the Third Reich. Those people shared the formal characteristics of

---

[3] Robinson refers to the Maginot Line—an ineffective French line of fortification that was intended to deter the German invasion in WWII.

enemy aliens but were not viewed as such by British and French law (Kempner, 1940, p. 444). The decision was based on the assumed loyalty of Czechoslovaks to the allies. However, the same positive treatment was not automatically extended to the numerous German and Austrian refugees—they had to convince authorities of their loyalty. Only six months after the beginning of WWII, British tribunals categorized thousands of Germans and Austrians based in Britain into three groups: "enemy aliens", "friendly aliens", and "subjects with special restrictions" (Kempner, 1940, pp. 445–446). The least dangerous group was "friendly aliens" who were allowed to stay in Britain without any restrictions. According to Kempner, 86.7% of the examined cases ended up in that category.

So, due to the political features of WWII, the "fundamental spiritual loyalties of a person" became much more important than "the formal facts" (Kempner, 1940, p. 452). In the middle of the 20th century, the enemy evolved from a formal category into a more complicated scientific concept closely connected to the political attitudes of human beings, and this approach prevails among scholars today. A "contemporary enemy" is not an actor capable of doing something bad to "us" but one who wishes to. This again brings us back to the constructivist example of Wendt: "500 British nuclear weapons are less threatening to the United States than 5 North Korean nuclear weapons" (1995, p. 73).

***

The whole 20th century was a time of international unions created *against* rather than *for* something: the fear of Nazism attempting to enslave humankind, Communism threatening to destroy Western civilization, Americanism aiming to become a global hegemon, Islamism striving to create a worldwide caliphate. What unites these "-isms" is that they have been considered dangerous by many political actors and, driven by this fear, those actors united into groups and alliances against them. Such a collective reaction to a perceived threat is nothing new. History has seen numerous joint military campaigns, such as the confrontation between the coalition of Christian states and the Ottoman Empire, or the common efforts of the European monarchies against the French Revolution, to mention just a few. The same is happening today as well: unions are no less influential then before and security remains a team game at both state and individual levels (Kelsen, 1948; Young et al., 1987).

The direction and intensity of hostile and friendly attitudes between various actors are deeply permeated by notions of collectivity and interdependence. When we know that an actor hates the same actor as we do, we consider them our friend as we share a common enemy. Moreover, our shared hatred towards another actor tends to generate positive feelings between us. The reasons for this lie on the plane of human psychology: "If I know nothing about the reason why another person dislikes my enemy, I might assume that we dislike him for the same reasons and, therefore, that we share similar beliefs and attitudes" (Aronson & Cope, 1968, p. 8). This psychological mechanism justifies the popular statement "the enemy of my enemy is my friend" and allows further inferences: "the friend of my friend is my friend; the friend of my enemy is my enemy; the enemy of my friend is my enemy" (Lee et al., 1994, p. 354; Heider, 1946). Extrapolation of these observations to the sphere of international relations explains the structure of international security, which consists not only of the relations between pairs of states but of complicated interactions between the whole spectrum of actors (Lee et al., 1994).

From this perspective, the system of international relations is nothing other than blocs of enemies and friends. These friendly and hostile actors constitute enmity networks—formal or informal unions where a group of actors has shared feelings of fear and hatred towards another actor and, simultaneously, a certain degree of positive feelings towards each other (the definition is based on Network Theory, see Borgatti & Halgin, 2011).

The current state of international affairs formed after the end of the Cold War is also characterised by enmity networks. However, they are not as indisputable and stable as during the Cold War when the confrontation between the Eastern and Western Blocs determined international interactions for decades. As a part of the Cold-War system of international relations, a state from one Bloc could not cooperate closely with a state from the opposite Bloc, otherwise the whole logic of international security would be violated. The opposite Bloc (as a collective actor) was the principal enemy; there was no greater threat to one Bloc's security than the other Bloc's actual or possible hostile actions (Holt & Silverstein, 1989).

After the collapse of the USSR, the international situation is not so strictly predefined but rather complex, flexible, and context-dependent (Wright, 1999). It is quite widespread that a pair of states share an understanding of some elements of their security but resist each other on the other "fronts". For example, both the United States and Russia were fighting Islamic State (IS) in Syria but supported opposite sides in the confrontation between the Syrian government and opposition. When it comes to United Nations resolutions related to Syria, even the broader networks become visible. For instance, it is common for China and Russia to mutually block collective resolutions proposed by supporters of the Syrian opposition. The system is certainly less flexible again after the onset of Russia's full-scale invasion of Ukraine, but the present-day system of international relations remains much less stringent than that of the Cold War era.

Despite numerous cases proving that enmity networks result from shared enemies, it is also important that the already existing networks are capable of reinforcing the existing hostile attitudes and generating new ones. Therefore, acquiring a new enemy on the international arena also means acquiring new friends, and this rule works the other way around as well (Lee et al., 1994). Therefore, even the fact of having friendly ties with a state can make an actor become involved in a confrontation with enemies of that state. Collective sanctions, vetoes, and military campaigns are often manifestations of this "secondary" or "indirect" enmity having emerged in and been transmitted through one of the existing networks.

***

In the international arena, nations are represented by political leaders, making the latter the primary targets of enmification. A study conducted among Polish school pupils during the WWI German occupation showed that children were inclined to make German leaders "the goal of their special hate" (Baumgarten & Prescott, 1928, p. 310). Although the collected responses are often simple-minded, they illustrate the importance of the leaders' image in the perception of the hostile nation: "I wish that they would hang Wilhelm and his minister up high by the feet, burn them on fire, and that lightning would strike them" (Baumgarten & Prescott, 1928, p. 310).

As early as the beginning of the 20th century, the leaders of hostile nations had already been listed as enemies in British law: "State or Sovereign of a State at war with his Majesty [is an enemy]" (Parry, 1941, p. 164). Such a juridical claim remains true. Moreover, political leaders are often believed to be responsible for the beginning of conflicts and their consequences. Ottosen calls this "the scapegoat effect" and argues that "in the cases of Ceausescu, Khomeini and Saddam Hussein [. . .] the blame for violation of international law, human rights, etc., is partly explained through the personal characteristics of the leaders involved" (1995, p. 109). In the perception of the in-group, hostile leaders often personify all the threats coming from the enemy. One of the striking examples of the demonization of the enemy's leader is the portrayal of Ariel Sharon in Palestinian caricatures: "Sharon was described [. . . as] a monster, a drinker of children's blood, a sadist who enjoys the sufferings of Palestinians" (Schleifer, 2012, p. 119). So, while analysing the hostile framing of political actors, it is important to pay attention to the enmification of "their" political leaders.

Another important aspect is the role of the in-group leaders in enmification which, just like securitization, is often performed by them. In situations of uncertainty — for instance, during conflicts, statements by "our" politicians become especially important for the public (Holsti, 1967). People start listening more carefully to those who are believed to be better informed of potential threats. In addition, it is hard to ignore the leader's enmifying messages, at least because these statements are usually well-covered by the media and widely discussed among citizens. Thus, "our" political leaders are often among the first to showcase hostile attitudes towards particular "others". However, in the era of new technologies and borderless information, "our" leaders' attempts to construct an enemy may hit on the rebound; therefore, the outcomes of each enmification campaign are hard to predict.

Therefore, the accounts of enemies made by "our" leaders, as well as the accounts of hostile leaders themselves, have always been important components of hostile communication. And the usage of such portrayals is becoming increasingly sophisticated, not least due to constantly developing technologies. Is it just technologies changing the face of the enemies over time, or have we started thinking differently about them?

***

While bringing up a child, adults try to protect it from threats from the outside world. In the beginning, it is enough to keep a baby away from danger. This task becomes harder as an infant gets more physically and mentally active. As a result, parental control over a child's life diminishes year by year. That is why it is crucial to teach children how to recognize danger and how to protect themselves from it. Being social animals, people need to be protected not only from natural but also from social threats. Therefore, via their upbringing, children adopt the fears of their parents and inherit their family's hostile stereotypes.

Goldschmidt and colleagues studied two Native American tribes — Yuki and Nomlaki — that were fighting each other (Goldschmidt et al., 1939). The confrontation was the business of many generations, and this was even cemented at the semantic level: the tribe's name "Yuki" meant "enemy" in the language of Nomlaki (Goldschmidt et al., 1939). Basso gives another example of transmissive enemy images: she writes that even not being sure of the existence of the so-called "bushman", indigenous people were transferring stories of danger from generation to generation, so that "virtually every adult had a repertoire of [. . .] stories" about a mystical enemy kidnapping people of the tribe (1978, p. 692). Indeed, we do not have to encounter the enemy face-to-face in order to have a hostile image of them. The interviews with the Polish school pupils who lived in the time of the WWI German occupation show that even before any contact with German soldiers, children were afraid of them: "When the Germans entered Warsaw I had a very great terror of them because I pictured them to myself as giants and bad men" (Baumgarten & Prescott, 1928, p. 306).

Does this mean that adults' behaviour prior to and during conflicts influences their children's attitudes to the involved sides? The following statements from the above-cited article are in favour of this assumption. In answering the question "What do you wish for your enemies?", Polish children mostly desired them harm: "I wish for my enemies that they should die of hunger and that they should catch malaria" (Baumgarten & Prescott, 1928, p. 310). However, in schools known for more liberal worldviews, the children's answers were quite different: instead of wishes for death, diseases, and hunger, children from those schools wished that "the enemies would change into friends, I wish that the whole world would be like that so that they would all love each other", moreover, even those children who named enemies explicitly had significantly different wishes towards them "I wish for my enemies, that is the Germans, that they would become better" (Baumgarten & Prescott, 1928, p. 310).

The above-listed hostile attitudes cannot be exclusively credited to the fears of the families. Children share not only the unique fears of their parents and other relatives, but, to some extent, the hostile attitudes widespread in the societies they live in. In the beginning, the process of acquiring societal stereotypes is indirect. Family, the main socializing actor of early childhood, shares societal hostile attitudes and transmits them to the children. Later, when children start to interact with "outsiders" independently, the direct consumption of societal hostile beliefs begins. As for societies, the factor of the free circulation of information is believed to play the main role in the occurrence and maintenance of hostile images (Oppenheimer, 2006). Therefore, the question of politically controlled media is closely connected to the psychology of enmification.

Today, the role of balanced information in the (de)construction and transmission of enemy images is hard to overestimate.

WWI constituted the point in time when states started systematically using propaganda for political goals, primarily for the motivation of their own soldiers and demotivation of the hostile ones (Schleifer, 2012, p. 107). Only a couple of decades after, the usage of propaganda became pervasive in totalitarian states with controlled media. Here, enmification was simplified by the prohibition or suppression of any alternative information. The Ministry of Propaganda founded in the Third Reich was a political reaction to the growing potential for psychological warfare. The sophisticated information attacks of the Third Reich were adjusted for specific political aims and various audiences. Hostile communication varied in topics, targets, and intensity but the main aim—the formation and maintenance of the desired public opinion—stayed unchanged (Malay et al., 2018).

The next shift in the features of psychological warfare took place during WWII when German and Austrian refugees became volunteers in the psychological battle against the Third Reich. The formal approach to the definition of enemies became not only inhuman but ill-conceived: "highly qualified enemy aliens in England, refugees from Germany and Austria become a particularly powerful propaganda menace by speaking against their native land over stations of the British Broadcasting Corporation" (Kempner, 1940, p. 454). Therefore, regulations from previous times—when aiding an enemy was only seen in terms of giving them material goods or supporting them physically in the fight—were put under question (Loane, 1965).

Although psychological warfare effectively assisted the military effort, it was not properly reflected in national and international law during or right after WWII. Even after the Korean War, when an American citizen—a radio orator of North Korean prison camps—was prosecuted by the US court, one of the arguments against his offence was that "making a speech was not aiding the enemy with any [material] 'thing'" (Loane, 1965, p. 75). This statement became part of the final sentence despite the authorities' intermediate conclusion that psychological influence on masses had "become as important as arms, ammunition, and guided missiles" (Loane, 1965, p. 76). As a result, the conviction was based on the fact that the accused person was "communicating, corresponding or holding any intercourse with the enemy" (Loane, 1965, p. 76) instead of a direct accusation of psychological warfare. However, examples of when people involved in enmification were convicted for their actions are also known, and not just from the Nuremberg trials. The cases of Rwandan journalists and an artist who were accused of provoking mass killings (Gendron, 2012) are additional illustrations of the power of psychological influence.

Thus, some psychological characteristics of enmification — such as the transmissibility of enemy images and its dependence on information flow — remain unchanged. Nevertheless, the role of the collective psychological state of the public has become more important over the last century. Supportive "hearts and minds" turned into a political necessity in the international arena, especially in the context of violent conflicts, as it is a successful enmification campaign that motivates people to confront the enemy by any means including a physical fight. The next chapter will unravel the practical dimensions of enmification, delving into the influence of the media on constructing enemies within diverse political regimes.

The Role of the Media in Constructing Enemies

In ancient Athens, the demos exercised democracy directly without delegating power to political representatives. Decisions regarding any problems of the polis were to be made by all free adult males — by citizens, each of whom possessed political power. Similarly, each of the citizens had a right to become a rhetor — a speaker who could address the crowd by proposing, supporting, or confronting particular political solutions to the community's problems (Yunis, 1996). This meant that, in Athens, political communicators had more political power than actual decision-makers because rhetors were capable of influencing public support for any issue, which meant that they had influence over final decisions via direct democracy. Later, in the time of feudalism and absolute monarchies, when wide political participation played a much smaller role in politics than the power of tradition and the rule of heredity, the need for communicating politics to the public became less important. Therefore, it is no wonder that the ancient interest in the ways of affecting public opinion through political communication should have been revitalised together with the beginning of democratization processes and strengthened further after the introduction of universal suffrage.

Since then, citizens in numerous states have gained the right to influence politics through choosing political representatives in free elections. In order to make informed electoral choices, the public has to be aware of the political process (Dahl, 1992; McNair, 2000). As a result, balanced and unbiased information about politics is a necessary condition for the existence of democracy (Sanders, 2009). Thus, from the normative perspective, the media of democratic states is supposed to perform watchdog journalism that checks and balances all three branches of political power by informing the public about them (Entman, 2010). But what exactly is the role of the media in the real political process? This question has been asked and answered many times by the most prominent scientists in the field. The spectrum of answers is very wide and includes the following: the media is capable of acting as political institutions (Cook, 1998), political actors (Page, 1996), or actors of political communication (McNair, 2018).

The same uncertainty characterises the extent of the media's influence on politics. On the one hand, the importance attributed to the media in the electoral process may be overestimated, at least because its direct impact on electoral preferences is said to be limited (Lazarsfeld et al., 1968; Finkel, 1993). On the other hand, examples like the Watergate scandal, the Clinton–Lewinsky scandal or Snowdengate that all began with publications in mass media show that the media is capable of influencing public support for particular politicians, challenging the policies of geopolitical players, making changes in international relations, or, in short, considerably influencing political process as a whole.

This influence becomes even more crucial when it comes to the public security agenda. The balance of negative and positive information about an actor in media coverage influences what the public attitude to this actor will be, whether this actor will be seen as hostile or friendly by the in-group, and how emotional this attitude will be (Shoshani & Slone, 2008). CS scholars studying securitization—the specific type of political communication—argue that appropriate communication is the central element required for any issue to be securitized (i.e. included into the security agenda). Critics of CS accept this idea but add that not only politicians and political groups are actors when it comes to securitization, but that media outlets also have this role (Williams, 2003). The same logic could be applied to the process of enmification, as enmification is, in a sense, a "securitization" of political actors, not issues. Based on the above arguments, I assume that media outlets are actors of enmification, and I will use this assumption further throughout the book. The general goal of this chapter is to analyse the existing research and generate new ideas regarding the role that media outlets play in the enmification process.

Constructing Enemies at Home

The role of media outlets in the enmification process and the frequency of enmifying messages in media texts is determined by factors such as the degree of media outlets' political and economic dependence, freedom of speech, and pluralism. All together, these factors predetermine the place of media outlets between two extremes: media outlets as independent watchdogs chasing enmification, and media outlets as speakers of their commanders whose role is to provoke hatred towards their opponents.

However, the level of media freedom—that includes the above factors—varies not just in states with different political regimes. Even the democracies of Europe and North America are painted in different colours on the maps of the World Press Freedom Index: from a very light peach colour for the freest Scandinavian countries, Portugal, etc., to an intense yellow for the United States and some of the post-communist EU-countries of Central and Eastern Europe where journalists are facing more pressure (Reporters Without Borders, 2021).

There are also numerous red and black countries on the map of the Press Freedom Index. In those countries, media outlets are dependent on the ruling elites, the political regimes of most of them can hardly be called democratic because of the restrictions of freedom of speech, the absence of free compatible elections, and the limited distribution of political power into branches. The empirical part of this book is focused on the performance of two TV channels controlled by a non-democratic political regime. Therefore, it is to be expected that the hostile communication of autocracies is at the centre of the study at hand. Nevertheless, here in the theoretical chapter, significant attention is also paid to the risks of enmification in established democracies. First of all, such an approach is aimed at creating a point of reference that is especially useful for readers who are well-informed about the features of media performance in free information environments. In addition to this, attention to the differences in hostile mass communication in democracies and autocracies helps us to focus on the question of how the political regime of a country in which mass media operates influences hostile communication campaigns aimed at its public.

***

Each country has its own media system characterized by the combination of unique features (Hallin & Mancini, 2004). Moreover, even in different models of democracy, the desired gold standards of media performance are understood slightly differently (Strömbäck, 2005). Therefore, to make more general assumptions on the enmifying role of media outlets in democracies, let us imagine a country where media outlets are free and do not have any intention of constructing enemies for their audiences. As system failures are still possible in a democratic political system and free media environment, even such conditions cannot guarantee that an enemy will not be constructed and that media outlets will not be involved in this process. The reasons that may lead to unintended enmification in free media environments have not been systematically conceptualised yet despite their impact on the quality of media performance. That is why I explore the separate factors that may contribute to enmification in democratic countries. These questions are touched upon in the following literature: McNair, 2000; Nossek, 2004; Abraham and Appiah, 2006; Lasorsa and Dai, 2007; Correa, 2009; Kalogeropoulos et al., 2015, etc.

In democratic states with a market economy, the media functions within the competitive information market. There is usually no great pressure on the media from the ruling elite, but often there is pressure from sponsors and advertisers who will not accept criticism from the media they fund (Thomas, 2017). The information market itself enforces its own freedom and diversity: each media outlet has to fight for the attention of its consumer. This characteristic is remarkably strong among media outlets functioning online – they are constantly competing for the number of views and clicks (Munger, 2020). However, press, radio, and television also have to compete for their recipients more than ever: traditional types of media are also influenced by the constant supply of information that is deepened by the Internet and widespread usage of social media, especially by the youth (La Ferle et al., 2000).

In such circumstances, "just" providing the audience with information of excellent quality is not always the winning strategy for media outlets. Earlier research revealed that scandalizing and negative information has more chance of gaining the attention of the public (Patterson, 2000; Soroka, 2006). The study of newspapers in 28 EU member countries has shown this trend towards scandals and negativity — media outlets "generate clicks not through quality content but rather, in nearly half the cases, through catchy, provocative and sensationalist [...] headlines" (García Orosa et al., 2017, p. 1261). One of the factors explaining such a trend is that negative media stories about threats and dangers are subconsciously seen by the recipients as more applicable to their real lives than positive media stories (Green et al., 2004).

Even independent media outlets that are financed by public funds are tempted to share negative information about political actors and "bad news" about social reality, as the attentional bias of the audience in favour of negative and distressing information is too strong to resist (Field, 2006). The absence of "catchy negative" news may cause the loss of the audience but the presence of it entails the risk of encouraging an unfavourable attitude towards negatively depicted actors. Positive depictions often have a limited persuasive effect unlike negative ones, which tend to provoke non-favourable attitudes towards negatively depicted actors among the audience (Smith & Searles, 2013). Therefore, the pressure of the media market creates a risk of enmification due to the fact that one of the ways to keep the attention of the audience is to fulfil the recipients' demand for negative information which, in turn, may have enmifying outcomes (Entman, 2010).

The next risk on the way to unintended enmification is rooted in the free media's role as a platform for political discussion. In an attempt to keep the public informed about the political process, the media strives to provide all political actors with fair access to their audiences. However, politicians may use this opportunity differently. Political actors that have deeply integrated enmification techniques in their usual communication strategy may use the very same strategy when they are invited to the news or talk-show rooms.

In her study, Wodak (2015b) claims that politicians may use the media as a platform to reach a broader audience with their radical messages, the covert denial of the Holocaust in the UK and Austrian media by the leader of a political party and a presidential candidate respectively are just a couple among numerous other examples of this. Surveys also show that the more time individuals spend watching TV, the more anti-immigrant beliefs they share, and this pattern is also seen in European countries with a relatively high level of media independence (Jacobs & Hooghe, 2019). In a free media environment, media outlets are usually not politically motivated to contribute to fostering anti-immigrant attitudes among the public. However, not acting in a socially dangerous way is not the same as preventing others from doing so. Research into populism in ten European countries demonstrates that media outlets may fail in their "gatekeeping role" and give word to populist political actors transmitting enmifying messages (Wettstein et al., 2018).

Keeping enmification out of the gates seems to be easier in the press or in non-live broadcasts (Abbott & Brassfield, 1989) where there is a higher chance to "cut out" the enmifying message or frame it accordingly. However, the difficulty of keeping the balance between the role of societal watchdog and the role of the "enemy of the people", as populist political actors sometimes call mass media (Fawzi, 2019), remains. The need to inform the audience about the political process and about the actors involved in it may lead to the appearance of enmifying messages in media texts, even if media outlets do not create those messages themselves (Sanders, 2009).

The next stumbling block that may push free media into enmifying practices is the fact that media outlets including independent ones function in societies with certain traditions, societal norms, and stereotypes. When a media outlet shares negative stereotypes widespread in society and covers "sensitive topics" in line with them, it provokes the further deepening of prejudiced attitudes to stereotypically depicted groups (Koivula, 1999; Bonnes, 2013). For instance, it is negative stereotyping that leads to the overwhelming news coverage of crimes performed by Afro-Americans in the USA (Entman, 1992) or to the emphasis on the "un-Britishness" of British Muslims by the British national press (Saeed, 2007, p. 443). Such coverage makes both groups appear threatening by the recipients of the information. Therefore, the retranslation of negative stereotypical beliefs about particular social groups and actors may in fact be seen as an example of an enmifying practice even if those beliefs are accepted by some segments of society (Lester & Ross, 2003).

However, even when a piece of journalism is well-balanced, media outlets may still be accused of hostile coverage. The perceptual effect causing such situations is called the hostile media phenomenon (Vallone et al., 1985). The main prerequisite is that the audience should have a pre-existing biased view on the topic covered. Recipients that share non-objective attitudes concerning particular political issues do not see the balanced coverage of those issues as objective. In other words, if recipients have a view of an issue, all other views may look prejudiced and one-sided to them. Moreover, if two groups of people with conflicting views on the matter come into contact with the same news story, both groups would say that it is biased in favour of the opponents. This was the scientific conclusion of a study in which groups of pro-Israeli and pro-Arab recipients watched identical samples of television coverage of the Beirut massacre (Vallone et al., 1985, p. 577). Therefore, if media coverage is accused of bias that contributes to enmification, it is crucial to have the criticized content deeply analysed to see if it includes unbalanced or hostile messages, what are they, whether they are used sporadically or constitute some kind of a pattern, what could be the reason for such a pattern to appear, etc. Otherwise, even free media outlets that are trying to produce objective coverage may receive more critical feedback on their work than the fully controlled media of authoritarian regimes as there are fewer independent actors who are allowed to express critique in an authoritarian media environment. Below, I focus on enmification for an internal audience in states with a politically dependent media environment and on the role of politically controlled media in the enmification process. Therefore, our focus shifts to those countries that are coloured

red and black on the aforementioned world map of the Press Freedom Index.

***

Unlike in democracies, in autocracies, where governing is performed "by a single person or small group that has unlimited power" (Cambridge Advanced Learner's Dictionary & Thesaurus, 2022), the media is adapted to the authoritarian political system as the "press always takes on the form [...] of the social and political structures within which it operates" (Siebert et al., 1984, p. 1). As a rule, media outlets support the political systems of their home countries: in democratic states, mainstream media tends to support democratic rule, in authoritarian states, the authoritarian status quo.

More precisely, the task of the media in free environments is to inform citizens and help them to elect the government they would like; in contrast, the task of the state-controlled media is to "help" the public to "like" the current government. This task is performed by complimenting the ruling elite and blaming its opponents. To stay in power, each autocratic regime finds the suitable balance between the following two communication strategies: legitimizing themselves and delegitimizing everybody confronting them (Dukalskis & Patane, 2019). The latter may be successfully achieved by means of enmification.

If, in pluralistic democratic states, enmification is assumed to be a rare practice that is often unintended and mostly results from the failures of the system, in authoritarian states where the media is controlled, enmification is assumed to be conscious and strategic. Moreover, I suggest that enmification is not just the side effect of autocracy; on the contrary, successful enmification causes — or at least maintains — the authoritarian features of the political system, helping authoritarian regimes to survive. The following arguments support this assumption.

The attempts of the regime to adopt an individual to authoritarian political practice cause significant changes in their self- and in-group perception (Adorno, 1951). In authoritarian environments, political communicators including mass media articulate the idea that the interests of the collective (of the in-group as a whole) are of higher priority compared to the interests of individuals; individual rights and wishes are said to be less important than the interests of the collective. In line with this, the best self-realization of individuals is understood as their serving society (Siebert et al., 1984). Therefore, in authoritarian societies, the role of the in-group for its members and for the whole political system is bigger than that in democratic societies. After the first step is complete and people are persuaded of the supreme importance of the collective, it is essential to reinforce the desired framing of the identity and the interests of that collective to the public. Therefore, the emphasis on the shared identity and interests attributed to the in-group is another important component of mass communication in autocracies.

Having limited opportunities to develop self-identification freely, representatives of an authoritarian in-group replace it with the promoted in-group-identification. This challenges not just people's self-perception but also their perception of other people as unique individuals and provokes constant categorization of them into in- or out-groupers (Meer, 1955). Another social implication of exaggerated group categorization is the development of in-group narcissism (Fuchs, 2018). This phenomenon is claimed to be one of the consequences of radical and aggressive propaganda (Adorno, 1951), but even in cases of lighter media campaigning, glorification of the in-group results in the belief that those who belong to the in-group are better than those who do not (Vetlesen, 1994, p. 240). Moreover, even if the out-groupers have not done anything bad to "us", they are perceived as potentially dangerous rather than as potentially friendly, especially by people with authoritarian mentality. Maslow (1943) argues that people with authoritarian mentality have a very defined understanding of the promoted in-group identity and interests combined with the feeling of psychological insecurity, therefore,

> the authoritarian person lives in a world which may be conceived to be pictured by him as a sort of jungle [. . . inhabited by] animals who either eat or are eaten, who are either to be feared or despised. (pp. 402–403)

As a result, even if there is no particular political actor depicted as an enemy, all preparations for the acceptance of such a depiction have already been made: the sharper the collective identity is and the more concrete group interests are, the easier it is to believe that they have been violated, especially when the world is perceived as dangerous by default.

Along with the constant need for strengthening the basics of their authoritarian world perception, the regime also has to address the everyday challenges of political communication. Helping to fulfil this goal, controlled media typically try to maintain a "black-and-white" public agenda, which is the best basis for successful enmification. On the one hand, the media broadcast stories about the powerful and benevolent defenders of the nation—its political leaders—but on the other hand, tell stories about the cruel opponents of the regime—its internal and external enemies who are said to cause all the existing problems. Thus, devoted citizens influenced by authoritarian propaganda idolize their political leaders (Fuchs, 2018), do not tolerate critique towards the ruling elite (Meer, 1955) and apply "scapegoating"—a mechanism of ego-defence responsible for attributing the blame for the problems to abstract or concrete "others" (Glisk, 2005).

In authoritarian states where one-sided information provokes the audience to think about "others" in terms of hatred and confrontation, many people share such a point of view. Yet not all citizens of authoritarian states have an authoritarian comprehension of people and society (Geddes & Zaller, 1989), just as not all people who enjoy the benefits of democratic political rule are free of authoritarian values. When shared by the citizens of democratic states, authoritarian values may be the product of individual features and fears or may indicate the growth of the overall popularity of an authoritarian world-perception in a society. However, they may also be inherited from previous forms of political organization.

One example of the latter phenomenon is the presence of post-authoritarian elements such as scapegoating and stigmatization of "others" in the mentality of some citizens of the current EU-member states that were formerly members of the Eastern Bloc (Oppenheimer, 2006). Thus, even outside of authoritarian states, some people are more vulnerable to enmification than their "average co-citizens". Despite the overall social trends, these people tend to think about "others" in terms of threats and enemies. Moreover, even in democracies, political movements based on authoritarian values may exist and may try to share their enmifying messages, making use of the free media system.

Another point to be made here is that there is hardly a country where none of the popular media outlets have political motives. Above, the risks of enmification in an idealized free media environment were discussed. In those circumstances, mass media do not aim to construct a hostile attitude towards any political actors. This may really be true of some independent broadcasters (above all those that are funded by the public of democratic states); still, often, all the above-mentioned risks of unintended enmification are supplemented by some involvement of mass media in the struggle of its owners, sponsors, etc. for political power (Hallin & Mancini, 2004). However, even admitting that some media outlets in democratic states are influenced by political groups, it is still crucial to understand the difference in the enmifying potential of mass media in the pluralistic media environment and in the state-controlled media environment. This issue will be addressed more closely at the end of this part of the book in the context of media coverage of conflicts.

Furthermore, even if an enmification strategy has been applied by a media outlet, its political outcomes may be very different depending on the intensity and the level of aggression of the enmification campaign. Therefore, while being quite a concrete form of information influence, enmification can manifest itself differently. Let us imagine that one political actor was depicted as "other", their values were said to be different from "ours", while another political actor was depicted as our "mortal enemy", and it was said that there is—or may be—a fight between the two of us and only one survives at the end of it. Both depictions encourage the audience to see the negatively framed actors with some hostility, but the social consequences including the level of fear and hatred caused by those two depictions would vary dramatically.

Scholars use different wording to underline the gradation of danger that is said to come from the constructed enemy. Besides the "other" (e.g. Rieber & Kelly, 1991), "agonistic other", and "evil enemy" (e.g. Ivie, 2003), expressions such as "diabolical enemy" (e.g. Sande et al., 1989), "principal enemy" (e.g. Dillon et al., 1977), "foe" (e.g. Green & Bogard, 2012), and "mortal enemy" (e.g. Kernan, 1943; Orleans, 1971) are used. Therefore, attempts to distinguish levels of enmity attributed to an actor could be found in the literature. Still, to my best knowledge, there is no fully fledged typology capable of classifying hostile actors of varied degrees of enmity even though such a tool might help to predict and compare the societal outcomes of the particular enmification campaigns even before they are seen in a societal dynamic between representatives of in- and out-groups.

As argued above, the form and intensity of enmification messages that may be detected in mass media differ depending on the political regime in which media outlets operate. Changes in the global and internal political situation also influence these aspects. Coverage of conflicts is of special interest in this context, as the mass media of both information environments risk shifting to higher levels of negativity while reporting on conflicts—especially violent ones. Still, it is important to remember that the imagined "starting points" from which shifts begin dramatically differ for mass media in democracies and in autocracies as do the communication goals of independent and of politically-controlled media outlets.

***

Violent conflicts and crises fall into the category of "catchy negative", at least because conflicts commonly constitute a newsworthy element of social reality. Even when the home country of the media outlet is not involved in the conflict, there is still a risk of producing a black-and-white representation of it in simplified stories that are likely to be of greater interest to the audience (Moeller, 1999). The heroes and villains of such black-and-white stories may be either unknown (e.g. impersonal characters) or known (e.g. real actors involved in the conflict being covered). For example, in the following excerpt, the heroes are named and the villains are kept nameless: "The dashing French doctors and American Marines rescued the starving [. . .] but the evil warlords stole away the chance for peace and prosperity" (Moeller, 1999, p. 13). In the case of natural disaster, media outlets can simply report on the heroes fighting it, but in the case of international conflict (when conflicting actors are known), the successful positive framing of one side automatically decreases support of the other side.

The second and more challenging scenario is when an ally of the media's home country is involved in the international conflict being covered. Allies are believed to have similar values and goals. Therefore, the wish to support the side of the conflict that is more similar to "us" may cause biased coverage.

The third and most challenging case that may stimulate the media to perform enmification is when the media's home country is one of the conflicting sides. In such a case, free media has to make hard choices regarding the coverage of political elites' failures, enmification of the hostile party or parties, and coverage of acts of aggression made by "our" side, etc. Mostly, media outlets in the liberal democracies of Western Europe and North America do not face this challenge, as most of those countries have not been involved as the main party in a violent conflict for many decades. Nevertheless, there are exceptions.

Studies of US media coverage revealed that at least in the time frame from the Vietnam War to the Gulf War, there were enmifying messages about various political actors not only on US international broadcasters but in the relatively free or at least pluralistic national mass media as well. Researchers have also touched upon the reasons why such strategies were adopted by certain media outlets. Scholars point to the fact that it was not the political dependence of the media but the overall political situation in the country that made mass media cover the conflicts in a certain way. They argue, for example, that in the early stages of the Vietnam War, there was no overall political debate on the war itself. Instead, "there were debates in Congress over certain tactical questions — whether the military should have greater freedom in selecting bombing targets", this state of affairs was mirrored by the mass media, and when the consensus broke down, media outlets started to cover it (Hallin, 1984, p. 20).

Some of the US media outlets can be seen to perform enmification in the case of hostile political leaders such as Khomeini, Gaddafi, Hussein, etc. The US media also frequently seeks to justify the interventions and external aggression of the US forces by framing international threats as principal ones for US citizens (Kamalipour, 1997; Powell, 2011). All in all, numerous books and scientific articles focus on the topic of the unbalanced media coverage of the conflicts in which the USA took part. Those works were written by US and international scholars and journalists during and after those conflicts (Hallin, 1984; Stabile & Kumar, 2005; Aday, 2010). However, a combination of factors such as media pluralism on the one hand and the existence of free competitive elections on the other presumes that being covered by pluralistic media, the actions of politicians managing the conflict influence the number of votes they get in the next elections. This would not be the case in authoritarian countries where media outlets are under centralised state control, so no alternative view on an issue or an actor reaches a broad audience, and where no free elections are possible.

In fact, a decentralized media system plays a crucial role not only in the prevention of enmification. It even has the potential to democratize a society that shares all the above-discussed authoritarian features that make people vulnerable to enmifying practices. This idea finds support in the example of the post-totalitarian transformation of Germany after the fall of the Nazi regime. Unlike in the German Democratic Republic (East Germany) where media remained under the centralized control of the state after the end of WWII (Zipser, 1990), in the Federal Republic of Germany (West Germany), responsibility for media performance shifted from the national to the regional level. This decentralization of the media is believed to be one of the important elements of the denazification of West Germany (Erk, 2003). Among the results of the policy was the liquidation of the state institution controlling media performance and the further creation of a media system where the strategic enmification of "others" on a national level is prevented by its very structure. There are too many independent outlets acting in the media arena to take control over them easily and to make them demonize "others" in favour of the ruling elite.

The role of the media in enmification for an internal audience differs depending on the political regime and the level of the media's political dependence. But what about the international broadcasters of democratic countries that are financed by the state? It is not acceptable for democratic political elites to "brainwash" their own internal audience in favour of the current ruling elite, but how about the external audience? What is more important in this case: the democratic essence of a home state, or the dependence of the broadcaster on the acting government? A similar question could be asked about the international broadcasters of authoritarian states making coverage for an audience from democratic countries. In other words, how do political regimes in the home country of an international broadcaster influence their enmifying practices? All these questions will be addressed in the following section dedicated to enmification for an external audience.

Enemies on Export

Together with diverse educational and cultural programmes, international information influence is considered to be an essential element of public diplomacy (Gilboa, 2008). Unlike traditional interstate diplomacy, public diplomacy is not communication between governments but the communication of the government of one state with the public of other state(s) (Signitzer & Coombs, 1992). Created to communicate domestic politics to foreigners, international broadcasters fulfil their part of this state-given task.

Technical developments in recent decades have made international broadcasters available on various devices to audiences in foreign countries all around the world. Unlike the North Korean authorities that have total control over media and allow no Internet access for their citizens (Ko et al., 2009), other governments are unable or unwilling to supervise the flow of information in their countries. This leads to the accessibility of various broadcasters of other political actors for the domestic audience of dozens of countries, helping international broadcasters to reach their minimalistic goal of having access to the desired audience.

While the independent media of democratic countries are the societal watchdogs who balance the influence of ruling elites, international broadcasters are created to extend this influence beyond state borders. Despite having a different role, international broadcasters often take the form of mass media—above all radio and TV channels in the languages of the targeted audiences. In the case of international broadcasters, a mass-media-like appearance facilitates the objective dictated by the state—to perform concrete information influence that is desired by the state (Wood, 1994).

In certain circumstances, political actors and national media outlets may perform enmification, as can international broadcasters. The main formal criterion for such an ability is to deliver information about politics to a broad audience, and international broadcasters meet this criterion. In line with this, I consider international broadcasters to be (potential) actors of enmification for international audiences. Further in the chapter, I focus on the role of enmification in the fulfilment of governmental goals abroad. However, before moving further, I will briefly demarcate international broadcasters, and mass media more precisely.

International broadcasters and mass media outlets may be very similar in appearance. For example, a first glance at a 24-hour news channel on a screen does not reveal whether it is an international broadcaster or a national media outlet. Nevertheless, as mentioned above, the tasks assigned to them are opposite and the audiences targeted by them are different. The goals and the audience are the main—if not the only—universal criteria that can be applied to distinguish independent media from international broadcasters. The reason for this is that additional features such as state financing are not a universal characteristic of all international broadcasters, just as the state or public financing of a media outlet does not always make this outlet dependent on the state's interests (Price et al., 2008). As for the goals, international broadcasters have more in common with the domestic media outlets of authoritarian states than the domestic media outlets of autocracies have in common with the domestic media outlets of democracies. Unlike the independent media outlets that are believed to do their best to make the coverage as unbiased and balanced as possible, international broadcasters and controlled media outlets often aim to frame the actions of their commanders favourably and the actions of those who challenge their commanders unfavourably.

Speaking of the goals of international broadcasters more generally, it is necessary to underline that public diplomacy and international broadcasting as an element of it are often confused with propaganda. Scholars point to the fact that the term "public diplomacy" appeared "in the United States in the 1970s as an alternative to propaganda, which had negative connotations, and as an umbrella label for the U.S. government's international information, cultural relations and broadcasting activities" (Gregory, 2008, p. 275). Nevertheless, propaganda techniques that are commonly used by international broadcasters cannot be seen as their distinctive feature, since these techniques are widely applied not just by international broadcasters but also by other media outlets, especially by state-controlled media outlets in autocracies. Therefore, the only layer where the two do not overlap is the targeted audience: internal for controlled mass media and external for international broadcasters.

***

Public diplomacy aims to influence the external public in a way that is fruitful for its home state. Therefore, international broadcasters that are capable of performing information influence are a tool of soft power that is widely used on the international arena (Nye, 2008). Despite the unlimited variety of interests, usage of international broadcasting by different political actors helps them in achieving the international goal common to all of them — to gain public support for the home state outside of its national borders.

By analogy with the legitimation of the elites vs. delegitimation of their opponents (Dukalskis & Patane, 2019), there are two main ways of gaining public support abroad: "Making the Audience Love Us" vs. "Making the Audience Hate Our Enemies". The first one is positive framing of "our" own actions/beliefs/attitudes/values (Gilboa, 2008; Rawnsley, 2015) and the second one is negative framing of the actions/beliefs/attitudes/values of "others" (Brdar & Vukovic, 2006; Połońska-Kimunguyi & Gillespie, 2016). Looking back at the beginnings of international broadcasting in the Cold War era, one notices that its main focus was informing the audience from the opposite Bloc. As blaming enemies is not always the best strategy while communicating with citizens of hostile states, "[t]he idea was to provide the public in the target society with more balanced information on one's own country to counter the domestic propaganda of the target society's government" (Gilboa, 2008, p. 69). Such a policy illustrates the application of the first of the two communication strategies given above. Put more precisely, the given way of using international broadcasting to manage a state's national reputation abroad is a two-step process. First, it helps to create a (more) positive attitude towards "us" among the public of the hostile state, second, the improvement in public opinion makes the government of the enemy-state less hostile towards "us" (Gilboa, 2008, p. 57; Wang, 2006).

Psychologically, positive information about the enemy dilutes its hostile image and weakens the motivation for defence and confrontation (Holt & Silverstein, 1989). Cognitive self-defence mechanisms are strong and often able to decline any non-negative knowledge about the enemy, nevertheless, positive and highly emotional information about the enemy tends to activate empathy and sympathy towards them (White, 1991). Therefore, it may cause a weakening of the enemy image through the replacement of the hostile perception by a more balanced view of the (former) opponents.

The German soldiers in Remarque's "The Road Back" are terrified when they meet better equipped American soldiers. The tension is high despite the fact that both of the groups are on the way back home from the battlefields after the end of WWI. How shocked they are when they learn that one of the friendly-looking Americans speaks perfect German and lived in Dresden prior to the war. A couple of minutes later, the two soldiers—a German from Dresden and this American—are chatting like old comrades, talking about the Elbe river and wondering why they had been fighting each other. A couple more minutes later, the soldiers of the two units are communicating with gestures and swapping bread and cigarettes in exchange for small souvenirs from the battlefields.[4] This short summary of the episode from Remarque's novel explains by itself why his books were burned on the squares of Nazi Germany. In this scene, representatives of the fighting sides simultaneously learn that their enemy "has a human face". It contributes to the changes in their perception of each other; those changes are so strong that both groups question the necessity of the war between them.

From this point of view, the communication strategy of telling positive stories about "us" to the enemy-audience looks even more attractive. However, even states applying it to influence the hostile audience may appear vulnerable if they do not simultaneously "protect" their citizens from receiving positive information about the enemy, especially while the conflict with them is ongoing. The methods employed in the "war for hearts and minds" during the Cold War included both elements—international broadcasting for export and blocking external international broadcasters at home. The superpower that failed to deprive its public of alternative information lost the war: "[w]ith the help of Western radio and television broadcasts, people under communist rule developed a certain image of the West, which arguably contributed to the fact that they did not defend their regimes at crucial moments in 1989–91" (Mikkonen, 2010, p. 771).

In contrast to the first strategy of public diplomacy, when actors want to persuade the world of their benevolence, enmification as the core of the second strategy lies in sharing negative infor-

---

[4] Notably, a similar exchange is hardly possible—for example, between the perpetrators and survivors of genocide.

mation about "others". Research shows that this second communication approach is more successful when it comes to changing attitudes to political actors: negatively framed nations are more often seen in a bad light than those positively framed are seen in a good one (Wanta et al., 2004).

As has been discussed earlier, enmification is more likely to be applied by mass media while covering conflicts. This pattern works for international broadcasters, too: it becomes notably strong when the home country is involved in the international conflict, becoming almost complete when the conflict is violent.

While blaming enemies is not a new technique, in the past, its main task was to mobilize soldiers to fight. Therefore, it has been widely used to influence internal audiences during various violent conflicts. Atrocity propaganda — the specific term for extreme forms of blaming "others" (Robertson, 2014) — refers not only to the mobilizing information campaigns of WWI, to which it is applied most frequently, but also to the instances of telling stories of the enemy's terrible crimes in the more distant past: examples include the conflicts in England in the 17th century (Read, 1938) or the Balkan Wars in the Ottoman Empire (Çetinkaya, 2014). Blaming the enemy, including the usage of atrocity propaganda, was focused on the internal audience for centuries as the technical possibilities of reaching a distant audience were limited. This remained the case until the invention of short waves that made global broadcasting possible (Wood, 1994, p. 2).

Along with the growing importance of non-material factors in conflicts and the decreasing number of direct violent conflicts between the main geopolitical actors, blaming the enemy moved beyond the boundaries of violent conflicts and entered the field of conflicts for "hearts and minds". The Cold War was such a global conflict of worldviews and values, but the structure of the international relations system that was constituted of two Blocs fettered political actors and limited the wide usage of enmification in international broadcasting (Gilboa, 2008).

The end of the Cold War and the changes in the structure of International Relations destroyed this limitation and made interstate relations within and beyond international unions more complex and flexible. Nowadays, enmity networks are not linear and do not always help to give the evident and universal answer to the question of who is whose enemy. Detailing of interests and a widening of security's boundaries on the one hand, combined with a less-strictly structured system of international relations on the other hand, enables the creation of new alliances even if their members oppose each other on other matters. Such a status quo causes the latent but constant "war of all against all" that may lead to the golden age of enmification as a prevailing technique of international broadcasting. Not all international broadcasters apply this strategy. Still, interstate information attacks including the deliberate negative framing of geopolitical opponents are among the features of global information warfare.

***

Unlike nuclear power that is too strong and destructive to be regularly used in international conflicts, information campaigns are widely employed prior to, during, after, and without connection to violent conflicts. As a result, adherence to the methods and tools of information warfare (IW) became one of the important features of modern international relations.

As a concept, IW is not limited to international relations only. IW goes from stealing personal cyber data for further blackmailing to fulfilling international information campaigns to gain public support abroad (Jones et al., 2002). Actors of IW are also very diverse including amateur and professional hackers, armies of bots and trolls paid by the state, non-state or individual actors, etc. Any actor influencing data or performing information influence could be listed here. Therefore, the media and international broadcasters are among the actors, too.

Within the frame of international relations, the era of information warfare is believed to have started at the beginning of the 1990s. The Gulf War is often called a significant watershed in this regard. It not only showed the potential of new information technologies in achieving geopolitical goals but also revealed the vulnerability of states that are not ready to defend themselves from the threats of the information age (Eriksson, 1999).

Being a broad phenomenon, IW is used by political actors in various ways. Libicki (1995) approaches this topic with high technological sophistication and lists seven different forms of information warfare. Although the terms used and the proposed classification of the forms of IW are open to discussion, the paper remains up to date and contributes to the development of the IW domain that still has no unified terminology. Libicki points to the forms of IW that include: the physical destruction of the information infrastructure of the enemy that can be carried out not just by means of hard power tools (like bombs) but also using "soft-kill weapons" such as computer viruses (Libicki, 1995, p. 11); the captivity of the information infrastructure of the hostile by means of intelligence-based systems and further usage of it; usage of the newest cryptographical techniques to secure their own data and unscramble the data of the enemy, and so on (Libicki, 1995).

All the techniques mentioned above are the creations or updates of recent decades that have changed the entire face of international conflict. All of them are widely used as high-technological supplements for military warfare, many are aimed at disabling the material weapons of the hostile party in one way or another. Other forms of warfare listed in the paper cited above, such as hacker and cyber warfare, can also be helpful during or prior to military conflict, but unlike the previous forms of IW, these two are often performed by state and non-state actors independently of any military confrontation as they focus on data that is not necessarily connected to the military (Libicki, 1995; Bellamy, 2001). Psychological warfare is also a form of information confrontation, but a specific one that turns information itself into the weapon. This is one of the oldest forms of IW that was already in use long before the advent of global information warfare.

Unlike cyber-attacks or implantation of computer viruses that have recently been introduced to the domain of international relations, psychological warfare has a history of thousands of years. However, with modern technologies, weaponized information may be spread not just by dropping flyers from hot air balloons over hostile or enemy-occupied territory (Wilkin, 2017). Currently, it may also be done secretly by hiring a hundred trolls to write social network comments glorifying or blaming whoever the sponsoring actor wants. As has been claimed by scientists and practitioners, the ease of information influence over the masses today has brought the entire population—all citizens—into international conflicts. It has turned all of them into supporters or opponents of one of the fighting sides or at least into viewers of the battle (Jones et al., 2002).

To become even more efficient in such circumstances, public diplomacy often takes the form of "individual diplomacy": in the time of traditional diplomacy, information went to the offices of foreign diplomats; then—after the introduction of public diplomacy—to the millions of foreign homes; currently, political messages from abroad may appear in the personal news feed of a foreigner, moreover, with the help of algorithms, this information will correspond to the preferences and interests of a particular individual (Shestopalova, 2022).

Studies of personalized psychological campaigns performed by ISIS on social networks have shown that ISIS has quite an effective propaganda strategy that helps them win the support of thousands of people regardless of their nationalities. The personal approach used by numerous ISIS recruiters on Twitter and other social media strengthens the recipients' Muslim group identity and motivates them to join the global jihad—the collective fight of all so-called "faithful Muslims" for the Islamic caliphate—or at least turns them into sympathizers of ISIS and jihadists (Ferrara, 2017; Lara-Cabrera et al., 2017). Looking at ISIS propaganda, it is easy to distinguish which of the two public diplomacy strategies has been chosen: "to love us" or "to hate our enemies". The messages they spread are not about the actor's attractiveness. Their messages are composed of the three enmifying steps: you are one of us, we are in danger, let's fight our enemies (Farwell, 2014).

ISIS is not the only actor that uses new technologies for political goals and is also not the only one who uses enmification for political purposes. However, the specifics of Islamists' goals that are closely connected to the physical fight make enmification prominent in the messages they spread. Those political actors that have more advanced technical potential and more funds to finance information warfare also use the Internet and social networks to gain public support abroad. The difference in their communication goals makes the enmification strategies of different actors very variable, from the call to the physical destruction of the enemy to a selection of facts that prevent recipients from associating themselves with the hostilely framed side of the distant conflict.

Information warfare between countries or the information attacks of one country against another may not be accompanied by any kind of open (e.g. military) confrontation. Therefore, it may be hard even to understand who is seen as an enemy by the actor who is paying for an information attack. From this angle, the coverage made by international broadcasters — constituted of well-structured units of information — may be a very rich source of knowledge about the information interests of the broadcasters' home country.

Nowadays, the market of international broadcasters that perform international information influence is very diverse, just like the home countries of those broadcasters. Most of the main players in the information warfare arena are the heavyweights of international relations such as China, France, Germany, Russia, the United Kingdom and the United States. Each of them has one or more international broadcasters including China Global Television Network (CGTN, formerly CCTV International), France 24, Deutsche Welle (DW), RT (formerly Russia Today), the BBC World Service and Voice of America (VOA) respectively. The arena is mainly controlled but not completely occupied by international broadcasters that are affiliated with the main geopolitical actors. Among the exceptions is Al Jazeera — a broadcaster founded and funded by Qatar, however, this channel is often positioned as the global voice not of Qatar but of the Arab world. Not all international broadcasters are owned and financed by state actors; the most well-known privately funded broadcaster is CNN International — a USA-based broadcaster owned and operated by a private company.

The traditions of media performance within the home states of the broadcasters mentioned above are very different and determined by the features of those states' political systems. In line with this, I suggest that even the financial or administrative dependence of international broadcasters on the state's government do not make the international broadcasters of, for example, Germany and Russia equal in their enmifying attempts: the acting governments of the two are also very different, as are their communication goals in regard to their internal and external opponents. Hundreds of scientific papers have been written about the information influence of international broadcasters mentioned in the previous paragraph (e.g. Zöllner, 2006; Nye, 2008; Samuel-Azran, 2013; Fiedler & Frère, 2016; Zhu, 2022). Some of these papers analyse the glorifying or enmifying practices performed by these channels or the information influence of these channels in the context of international conflicts. However, the existing scientific literature about international broadcasters does not allow them all to be placed into one system of axes in order to apply a universalized set of criteria to compare the chance that (some of) those international broadcasters will perform enmification campaigns in accordance with the communication goals of those political actors with which they are affiliated.

At the same time, in her book about the global market of international broadcasters, Geniets (2013) conceptualizes three groups of broadcasters based on their level of editorial freedom. According to Geniets, CGTN and RT constitute the first group of international broadcasters: their coverage is highly dependent on the government, therefore they transmit the point of view approved by state authorities; VOA and France 24 occupy the middle position that "promote a US- and French-centric view of the world, but appear editorially much more independent from their governments than CCTV [CGTN] and RT" (p. 69); the international broadcasters from the third group—BBC, DW, and CNN are claimed to be even more independent and trying to cover the events and frame political actors more objectively than the broadcasters from previous groups (Geniets, 2013).

Therefore, two of the international broadcasters mentioned — those of the least democratic countries, China and Russia — are said to be the most dependent on the states' authorities, which can be explained by the features of media performance in autocracies. Therefore, these two international broadcasters are the most likely to perform enmification of actors hostilely perceived by their governments. However, to state that these two broadcasters are the two doing it most often and most aggressively, at least one more detail is needed — the clarification of whether these broadcasters follow a hostile strategy of public diplomacy.

The scholars studying CGTN claim that "to know us is to love us" is the main strategy of the channel and that the channel is the state's information tool created mainly to inform the world about China (Rawnsley, 2015). Zhang (2011, p. 57) also claims that Chinese international broadcasters promote China as a great power but underlines their "non-threatening and non-confrontational manner". According to Wang, the goal of CGTN is to hide China's negative side and build a positive image of the country abroad in order to gain a more positive public opinion, to receive more loyal treatment from foreign governments and therefore deepen international economic cooperation with them (2020, p. 3). Closer attention to the Russian international broadcasting strategy is paid in the following parts of this book — both theoretically and empirically — as generating new insights on this topic is one of the aims of this monograph.

The Potential for Enmification in News Coverage of Conflicts

It is an axiom of cognitive psychology that the process of obtaining new information about a topic is much faster and easier than the process of changing existing beliefs and attitudes about it (Lachman et al., 2015). In this context, international 24-hour news broadcasters frequently covering distant and unknown events are unique tools used for the purposes of public diplomacy: having limited knowledge, their audiences are often unable to verify the depiction of political actors and, as a result, have no other option than to believe in what is said and shown about them (Gilboa, 2008). This cognitive mechanism is a universal one; therefore, the news coverage of distant and unknown events activates this mechanism not just among the foreign audience of a state's international broadcaster but also among the internal public informed by domestic mass media.

Due to their higher degree of political dependence, the mass media and international broadcasters of autocracies are more likely to use this cognitive mechanism for the benefit of the ruling elites than media outlets that are not dependent on political actors. The mass media and international broadcasters of autocracies are, in general, more likely to cover news in line with the communication goals of the acting government than the mass media and international broadcasters of democracies, which is a well-researched aspect of mass communication (e.g. Becker, 2004; Stier, 2015; Chin, 2018).

Even though news coverage is said to have some impact on the audience's perception of the topic covered, along with this advantage, news coverage has some weaknesses compared to other forms of information influence, for example, as a rule, news coverage is believed to have a non-prolonged effect on the audience (Gilboa, 2008, p. 72). However, due to its psychological influence on the public, successful enmification based on news coverage could be an exception: the successful introduction of hostile depictions leads to the negative perception of hostilely depicted actors and creates enemy images that are self-fulfilling, self-reinforcing, and transmissible once rooted in society (Oppenheimer, 2006).

As discussed in the first theoretical chapter of this book, enmification can be seen as an instance of securitization, however, unlike the latter, enmification is aimed at presenting not issues but actors as the matter of security concern (Wæver, 1995). To do so, actors of enmification should construct a feeling of threat and danger coming from the enmified actor, which, in turn, requires a construction of a crisis. When viewed in this context, news coverage of a conflict — which is a crisis situation by definition — is a special communication situation making the successful enmification of the hostilely framed political actors even more likely.

Analogous to the conditions for successful securitization, successful enmification also requires positioning the danger coming from the hostile political actor as an issue of supreme priority (Buzan et al., 1998, p. 26). Thus, for enmification to be successful, a conflict or crisis used as a basis for the hostile portrayal of an actor should receive the close attention of communicators including mass media and international broadcasters (Williams, 2003). The close attention of media outlets to any topic is exercised through the respective setting of their agendas and is reflected in the significant share of their coverage devoted to this topic. It is known that the increased attention of media outlets to a certain topic influences the public agenda regarding this topic by increasing its role in the eyes of the public (e.g. McCombs & Shaw, 1972; Ghanem et al., 2009). Earlier studies of international news coverage have shown that the media agenda also influences the public agenda when it comes to the security-related topics, moreover, news coverage about conflicts as well as negative coverage have a much stronger agenda-setting effect (Wanta & Hu, 1993; Wanta et al., 2004; Besova & Cooley, 2009).

Furthermore, media outlets performing enmification might be eager to pay special attention to those events of the conflict that are said to reveal the (alleged) negative and dangerous characteristics of the actor the ruling elites want to portray as an enemy, helping media outlets to construct a better-defined negative portrait of the enemy (Oppenheimer, 2010). In order to canalize all the negative feelings of the audience receiving the enmifying messages and to contribute to the construction of enemies, even those particular events should be framed in accordance with the general line of enmification, as it is the news frame that offers recipients a certain "organizing idea" of a news story, "suggesting what is at issue" (Gamson & Modigliani, 1989, p. 3).

To illustrate the importance of framing for either a positive or a negative portrayal: vultures (birds of prey that feed on carrion) do not receive much of a positive evaluation in popular culture. However, this does not necessarily have to be the case: in the Netflix documentary series "Animal" devoted to birds of prey, the narrator predominately tells the viewers about positive characteristics of vultures, e.g. that they never kill other animals or that their role is indispensable as they help to control the population of disease-spreading insects.

The same logic applies to the strategic negative portrayal of political actors involved in conflicts: the precise framing of separate events from the conflicts covered and adjustment of the news coverage to fit with the general line of enmification is what helps to turn an ordinary actor into an enemy in the eyes of the public. When discretionary setting the media agenda and the politically motivated framing of events is exercised simultaneously, actors performing enmification do not necessarily have to rely on disinformation techniques in the process of constructing enemies. It might be enough just to cover those events of the conflict that are in line with the desired enmifying patterns and to frame those events accordingly. The possibility to abstain from intense disinformation and still be able to perform politically motivated enmification might be especially attractive for those international broadcasters of autocracies that broadcast for the audience living in media environments with a free flow of information, i.e. where disinformation can be uncovered.

Thus, international news about conflicts is the well-suited basis for successful politically motivated enmification due to the following factors: first, the cognitive mechanisms securing the influence of the new information on the viewer; second, conflicts, especially violent ones, offer actors performing enmification a ready-to-use setting needed for the successful creation of the notion of crisis; third, the news coverage of conflicts has a strong impact on the public agenda; fourth, the discretionary strategy of setting the media agenda helps media outlets to focus (only) on those events of the conflict that are in line with the communication goals of the political beneficiary of the enmification campaign; fifth, news coverage of conflicts allows media outlets to precisely work with separate events of the conflict and to frame each of those events in a way that secures the desired hostile portrayal.

As a result, when the politically motivated news coverage of the conflict is done systematically, it might significantly undermine the audience's comprehension of the very logic of the conflict, its developments as well as the role of different political actors involved in the conflict's developments. The general acceptance of Russia's full-scale war against Ukraine by the Russian public allows suggesting that this was exactly what happened to a lot of viewers of Russian state-controlled TV. In the next part of the book, I explain how it is possible and whether there are any discernible differences compared to Russian news coverage of Russia's wars of previous decades.

Part II
Russian Media and Russia's Wars

Part II

Russian Media Reality: Autocracy, Control, Wars

The decades following the collapse of the USSR have shown that the fifteen states once coexisting under the totalitarian rule of the Soviet regime have chosen very different directions for the development of their media systems (e.g. Richter, 2008; Lysenko & Desouza, 2014; Rollberg & Laruelle, 2018). Diverse levels of press freedom in those states are among the fruits of those developments. For example, in the 2021 international ranking of press freedom, Estonia[5] was in the 15th place, right after Germany and Canada, and higher than such liberal democracies as Austria or Australia (Reporters Without Borders, 2021). In contrast, in accordance with this very ranking, Turkmenistan[6] was in the 178th place: the situation regarding press freedoms in this country was worse than in China, for example, and only slightly better than in North Korea. Russia was in the 150th place in the 2021 ranking, which was close to Central Asian autocracies such as Kazakhstan and Uzbekistan—the 155th and the 157th places respectively (Reporters Without Borders, 2021). In 2023, a year after introducing de facto war censorship, Russia was in the 164th place: around 30 places below the abovementioned Kazakhstan and Uzbekistan and 85 places below Ukraine (Reporters Without Borders, 2023). Even this basic information about media freedoms in those countries makes the attempt to find significant overarching characteristics applicable to media systems of all independent states formerly occupied by the USSR quite challenging. This general observation is also true for the attempt to define the common (post-)Soviet characteristics of the information environments in those states. Moreover, even comparing

---

5 This country, the same as Latvia, Lithuania, some parts of Ukraine, etc. was occupied by the Soviet Union in 1939 after the agreement on mutual non-aggression between the USSR and the Third Reich was signed.
6 Territories of this country were taken under the full control of the USSR in the mid-1920s after the defeat of the movement of Muslims of Central Asia who were fighting for their independence against the Red Army.

the media system of the Soviet Union with the media system of Russia shows that the post-Soviet frame might be somewhat misleading, as since the collapse of the USSR, "Russia has adopted a neo-authoritarian media system that has more in common with similar non-democratic systems around the world than with the Soviet system" (Becker, 2014, p. 191).

During most of its history, the Soviet Union was a totalitarian state with ideological censorship limiting mass communication to the flow of information that was fruitful for the regime (Ferguson, 1998; Linz, 2000; Becker, 2004). In contrast, in the years before the full-scale invasion of Ukraine, Russia was an autocracy limiting the flow of information that was critical towards authorities (Litvinenko & Toepfl, 2019). However, there is a consensus on the matter that media performance was more independent from the pressure of authorities in the final years of the Soviet rule (after the announcement of glasnost) compared to Russia under the presidency of Putin (Becker, 2004; Oates, 2016; Lipman, 2018). Thus, the shift in recent decades to the somewhat greater pluralism of information was not linear. The following paragraphs turn to the main developments of the Russian media system in the post-Soviet period in more detail. Where applicable, those developments are looked at in the context of the media coverage of wars fought by the Russian Federation in the last three decades. Such an approach helps to provide a closer analysis of the literature offering useful insights for the further empirical analysis of the news coverage of the Euromaidan, Russia's occupation of Crimea and the first months of the war in Donbas.

To a great extent, the politically-relevant pluralism of the Russian media system in the first post-Soviet decade was secured by the existence of the oligarch-owned NTV channel—"the only fully private television network to obtain a virtually nationwide broadcast reach" (Belin, 2002, p. 19). For instance, this major TV channel critically covered the brutality of the First Chechen war (1994–1996)—a Russian military campaign trying to take control over the territories of the unrecognized Chechen Republic of Ichkeria seeking independence from Russia. Lipman and McFaul (2001, p. 119) cite the public opposition to the war caused by its pluralistic coverage, especially prior to the presidential elections of 1996, as the reason why the then Russian president Yeltsin withdrew the Russian troops and ended the war.

In the years following the First Russian-Chechen War, Russian authorities began to limit the pluralism of non-state-controlled media, which resulted in less independent, i.e. less critical, news coverage. These changes were also reflected in the news coverage of the active phase of the Second Chechen War (1999–2000), which was much less balanced than the coverage of the First Chechen war; for example, information about victims among Chechen civilians and the atrocities of the Russian army in Chechnya were often hidden from the wider Russian public, while some media outlets, e.g. the state-affiliated Krasnaya Zvezda, dehumanized and demonized Chechens (Askerov, 2015, pp. 18–20). Like many smaller media outlets, the two major TV channels RTR (nowadays known as Rossiya-1) and ORT (nowadays known as Channel One Russia) offered their audiences predominately positive coverage of the actions of the Russian authorities in Chechnya as well as a predominately positive portrayal of Russian authorities in general, including in the context of the 1999 parliamentary elections and 2000 presidential elections (Becker, 2014).

NTV, which continued to cover the second war against Chechnya and other actions of Russian authorities (including newly elected Putin) with criticism, was taken under the control of "Gazprom-media" in 2001, with the same fate awaiting the whole "Media MOST" holding, which owned NTV (Lipman, 2018). However, these changes in the media environment did not receive much attention from the Russian public: Lipman (2018, p. 44) referred to a poll from 2001 showing that approximately four percent of Russians saw the "squelching" of NTV as an event challenging media freedom in Russia; while by 2006, almost three quarters of Russians either did not remember "the NTV affair" or were "indifferent to its outcome" (Gehlbach, 2010, p. 84).

Just a couple of years later — during the Russian-Georgian War (August 2008) — NTV, along with Channel One Russia and Rossiya, supported the official Russian framing of this war as a peacekeeping operation on the part of the Russian army aimed at preventing ethnic cleansing and protecting Ossetians from the aggression of Georgia (Akhvlediani, 2009, p. 364). The Russian-Georgian War was not studied by communication scholars as closely as the Russian-Chechen Wars. One possible reason for this is that the Russian-Georgian War did not last long, so there was not much media content about the war to analyse.

As a result of the war, Georgia lost control over almost 20% of its territory; the self-proclaimed independence of Abkhazia and South Ossetia was only recognized by several countries, including Russia, Venezuela, Syria. The Russian-Georgian War significantly influenced the security landscape of Eastern Europe by "broaden[ing] the scope of concerns [about Russia's possible aggressive actions] to Russia's other neighbour states, especially Ukraine" (Allison, 2008, p. 1145). Despite causing those regional changes and despite becoming "arguably the most serious crisis in Russian–Western relations since the end of the Cold War", shortly after the end of the Russian-Georgian War, the global system of international relations more or less returned to its pre-war shape (Antonenko, 2009, p. 259). At the same time, Thornton claims that not everything in regard to the global system of International Relations remained unchanged, even on the Russian side: the Russian-Georgian War was one of the landmarks where Russian authorities decided to launch reforms helping them to use the tools of modern warfare more efficiently than their opponents; Thornton states that as a result of the steps undertaken, Russia became "more capable" than NATO in information warfare (2015, p. 40).

Whether it was motivated by the course of the Russian-Georgian War or not, in the 2010s, the active usage of information warfare against its neighbours and beyond became a characteristic of Russian international influence. The examples of Russian interference in the internal politics of Western European and North American countries by means of communication are well studied (e.g. Badawy et al., 2018; Baines & Jones, 2018; Tenove et al., 2018; Burrett, 2020); numerous studies about disinformation worldwide are based on the cases of Russian disinformation campaigns (e.g. Lanoszka, 2019; Karami et al., 2021).

In contrast, the information influence of Russia on its neighbours is not so well researched. As argued above, the media environments of Russian neighbours formerly occupied by the USSR, as a rule, do not have much in common, but there is an exception: all of those states are still somehow affected by Russian information influence, which is "a sore point of all post-Soviet media environments" (Rollberg & Laruelle, 2018, p. 11). Russia had significant information influence in Ukraine as well, including after the Euromaidan. Among other means used, this influence was exercised through TV channels controlled by Viktor Medvedchuk, a close ally of Russia's President. (Yanchenko et al., 2023).[7]

One of the elements of Russian information warfare of recent decades is targeted information influence on ethnic Russians and Russian-speaking people living in states neighbouring Russia: this influence is strong not just in traditional media environments (e.g. TV channels) but also in digital ones (Shestopalova, 2022), and is said to be among the factors significantly assisting Russia during conflicts with its neighbours (Ehala, 2009; Thornton, 2015).

Besides exerting international information influence on its neighbours and beyond, in the 2010s, Russian authorities have also reacted to internal challenges to the stability of the regime: most importantly, in 2011–2012, authorities responded to the protests for fair elections in Russia by taking the Russian information environment under even stricter state control than before. Elites focused on reducing the influence of "leadership-critical" voices by somewhat restricting the flow of the critical information on the Internet and, simultaneously, by creating and/or supporting uncritical digital environments (Litvinenko & Toepfl, 2019).

---

7 As of the beginning of Russia's full-scale invasion of Ukraine, Medvedchuk was under house arrest as a suspect in a treason case. He escaped from house arrest several days later but was detained by Ukrainian authorities. In September 2022, Russia agreed to exchange him for numerous Ukrainian prisoners of war, including high-ranked Azov fighters—commanders of the defence of Mariupol's steel plant Azovstal.

As for traditional media, due to the greater politically-relevant influence of TV compared to other traditional types of media (e.g. radio or press), the content of major Russian TV channels was taken under tough state control in the first years of Putin's presidency. As discussed above, this is also true of the formerly more balanced NTV channel: "NTV, like other national TV broadcasters with news programming, was tightly controlled so nothing unexpected or unpleasant for the Kremlin would ever appear on air" (Lipman, 2018, pp. 44–45). As a result, the Russian authorities managed to establish a media system in which state-controlled TV—the dominant medium—transmits messages that are fruitful for the regime, while state-controlled digital media reinforce those messages, making them appear even more convincing to Russians (Alyukov, 2021).

Communication scholars studying the Russian media environment argue that despite the restrictions and the state control over various media outlets, Russians have a choice of which media to follow and which information to believe in (e.g. Szostek, 2018; Shirikov, 2021). However, a relatively small proportion of Russians consumed anything except for state-controlled information, for example, a nation-wide poll held by the Levada Center in 2016 revealed that 87% of Russians never watched TVRain,[8] while the everyday / almost everyday audience of this channel was smaller than 1%; similarly, 83% of Russians never listened to Ekho Moskvy,[9] while the everyday / almost everyday audience of this radio station was close to 1% (Levada Center, 2016). Shirikov (2021) explains this with the findings of a survey revealing that the supporters of the Russian regime tend to underestimate the influence of the authorities on state-controlled outlets and to see those outlets as more reliable than the outlets critical towards the regime. While the findings of another study of media consumption among Russians reveal that even those representatives of Russian youth who see state-controlled TV as propagandistic and do not watch it regularly tend to

---

8   Non-state-controlled TV channel.
9   This radio station was owned by Gazprom-media, but it was relatively balanced compared to major Russian media outlets, especially TV channels.

reproduce the "overarching strategic narrative which state television conveys" (Szostek, 2018, p. 68).

Thus, the Russian media system faced significant changes in the period after the collapse of the USSR. While during the 1990s, the wider Russian public sought for and enjoyed some pluralism, in the decade presiding Russia's full-scale invasion of Ukraine, this was not a feature of Russian society and media system as a whole: even though more or less independent media outlets still functioned within the Russian media system in 2013–2014, the majority of Russians learned about the Euromaidan, Russian occupation of Crimea and the first months of the war in Donetsk and Luhansk regions of Ukraine not from those outlets but from Russian state-controlled TV.

As argued above, the Russian media system was highly dependent on the Russian authorities even before the beginning of the Euromaidan. However, in the midst of the Euromaidan and shortly before the occupation of Crimea by Russia in early 2014, further changes occurred that helped the elites to secure the reporting they desired on the events of the conflict and beyond. For example, in January 2014, major TV providers began to disconnect TVRain from broadcasting networks. Lipman (2018) explained the situation with the channel in the following terms: "[it] came under an orchestrated public attack" after the channel's website posted a poll about the Nazis' siege of Leningrad during WWII (p. 53). The disconnection of the channel under the pretext of the poll was not directly linked to the events in Ukraine. An independent Russian journalist Kolesnikov rather explains it by the fact that TVRain reported on Navalny's investigations about corruption among Kremlin officials but underlines "that the timing of the campaign against Dozhd [TVRain] is also probably affected by the current unrest in Ukraine, which has deeply worried the Kremlin" (Weir, 2014). Additionally, in February 2014, the general manager of the radio station Ekho Moskvy was changed after more than twenty years. On March 12, 2014, Galina Timchenko, editor-in-chief of the popular Russian online media outlet Lenta.Ru, was sacked after ten years working in this position, and was replaced immediately by the "pro-Kremlin editor" (Dobre, 2015, p. 56) a couple of days after the outlet published an interview with one of the leaders of the Right Sector;[10] still, there is no officially recognised connection between this interview (as a pretext for replacing the editor) and her replacement. In October 2014, together with several former journalists of Lenta.Ru,

---

10 The Right Sector is a Ukrainian far-right organization that took part in the Euromaidan; as of March 22, 2014, it also refers to a Ukrainian far-right political party, and, as of July 2014, one of the volunteer battalions taking part in the violent conflict in Donbas. First, it is important to explain the reasons why the Right Sector decided to join the pro-EU Euromaidan protests as, in general, far-right organizations are rather sceptical towards the EU (Szöcsik & Polyakova, 2019; Lorimer, 2021). One of the main reasons is connected to the (anti)imperialist element of the Russian-Ukrainian conflict: "The most obvious explanation for the Ukrainian far right's ardent participation in the EuroMaidan may be found in the primary goal shared by all Ukrainian nationalists, radical and moderate alike: to liberate Kyiv from the Kremlin's hegemony", therefore, as the closer connection to the EU could weaken Russian influence on Ukraine, representatives of Ukrainian far-right movements including the Right Sector supported the signing of the Association Agreement with the EU and the Euromaidan protests following the decision of the then government to suspend the signing (Shekhovtsov & Umland, 2014, p. 60). The polling data showed that 91.8% of people taking part in the Euromaidan were not members of any NGO, movement, or political party; 3.9% reported that they were members of a political party, while the Right Sector was not a political party back then. Thus, people affiliated with the Right Sector were among the less than 5% of people affiliated with *all* the spectrum of various Ukrainian NGOs and movements taking part in the Euromaidan. For further details, see: Maidan-2013. (2013). Kyiv International Institute of Sociology (KIIS). https://www.kiis.com.ua/?lang=eng&cat=reports&id=216&page=1&y=2013. Despite the relatively small share of representatives of the Right Sector among the protesters, the organization became quite famous at the end of the Euromaidan and thereafter. In a journalistic piece, the unexpected popularity of the Right Sector is explained as follows: "Experts agree that the group owes its popularity to Russian propaganda, which tried to build a public case for the Russian annexation of Crimea and the demonization of Kiev [Kyiv] by painting the Right Sector as a powerful neo-Nazi force determined to take over Ukraine." (Kozlowska, 2014). Despite the attributed popularity, the Right Sector was not successful as a political project. In the parliamentary elections in October 2014, the Right Sector received 1.81% of votes which was not enough to win any seats in the Ukrainian parliament (The Central Election Commission of Ukraine, 2014). In fact, after the Euromaidan, no far-right political party received enough votes to be elected to the Ukrainian parliament, while before the Euromaidan (as a result of 2012 elections), the far-right Svoboda party was represented there. Shekhovtsov and Umland (2014) suggest that after the success of the Euromaidan and the resignation of the pro-Russian authorities, the far-right parties, aiming to balance the influence of the pro-Russian forces in Ukrainian politics, lost their electoral popularity among Ukrainians.

Timchenko created a new online media outlet called Meduza, based in Latvia. Unlike Ekho Moskvy, which was controlled by "Gazprom-media", or Lenta.Ru, which was owned privately, Novaya Gazeta — another independent outlet — which was established by journalists in the first half of the 1990s and was controlled by them in 2013-2014, continued to work independently during the period of the Euromaidan, occupation of Crimea and the war in Donetsk and Luhansk regions, as it did during previous violent conflicts waged by Russia, e.g. during the Chechen Wars.[11]

In its reporting about the events in Ukraine, Novaya Gazeta paid close attention to the involvement of regular Russian military units in the violent conflict in Donbas; for example, journalist Elena Kostyuchenko (2015) conducted an interview with a Russian soldier who fought against the Ukrainian army near the Ukrainian town of Debaltseve (Donetsk region) at the beginning of February 2015, his battalion alone included hundreds of other Russian soldiers equipped with dozens of tanks.[12] As for the general tone of the Novaya Gazeta's reporting, Russian researchers Kazakov and Shestov (2016, p. 148) conclude that Novaya Gazeta was even more critical towards the Kremlin than The New York Times, especially when it came to assessing the role of Russia in the violence in Ukraine.

Despite the restrictions of the first months of the Russian-Ukrainian conflict (i.e. in 2013-2014), TVRain, Ekho Moskvy, Novaya Gazeta, Meduza, and other more or less oppositional media outlets continued to function within the Russian media environment. However, all of them had quite a limited influence on Russian public opinion, which can be explained by the small attention by the Russian public. In March 2022, after the beginning of the full-

---

11 For example, Novaya Gazeta's journalist Anna Politkovskaya (one of the most famous Russian journalists killed in recent decades) was closely reporting on the Second Chechen War, as was Dmitry Muratov, who was editor-in-chief of Novaya Gazeta for many years. Even though Novaya Gazeta continued working despite the circumstances, five of its journalists working on the most sensitive topics such as Chechnya, corruption in Russia, neo-Nazi in Russia, etc. were killed (Slavtcheva-Petkova, 2018).

12 The military successes of Russia-backed troops near that town were the major reason behind Ukraine signing the Second Minsk Agreement.

scale Russian-Ukrainian War, all those outlets were blocked in Russia. TVRain and Ekho Moskvy paused their work, while some of their journalists fled from Russia fearing threats;[13] Novaya Gazeta and some of its journalists did the same. Later on, the new outlet Novaya Gazeta Europe was created in the EU; Meduza's editorial office, which was established in Latvia back in 2014, continued to work and could be accessed from Russia with the help of VPNs.

In contrast to the above-mentioned oppositional media outlets critical to the Kremlin, numerous pro-Kremlin media outlets supported Russia's position in the conflict and official Russian framing of the conflict in 2013 and thereafter. Additionally, along with state-controlled traditional media outlets, Russian elites actively promoted pro-Kremlin framing of the conflict in the new media environments. For example, the state-sponsored international online disinformation campaigns on social media included the activities of so-called trolls who, "under fake identities", praised Russian and Russia-affiliated political actors and criticized actors opposing Russia's interests (Mejias & Vokuev, 2017, p. 1034; Golovchenko et al., 2018; Hjorth & Adler-Nissen, 2019). At the same time, a study of the opinions of Russian social media users about the Russian-Ukrainian conflict revealed that the conflict-related discourse in the new media was largely similar to that on Russian state-controlled TV: the "fascist" frame was the prevalent one in the context of the Russian-Ukrainian conflict both in the social media users' posts (Twitter, VKontakte, and Zhivoi Zhurnal) and in the news coverage of Channel One Russia (Gaufman, 2015, p. 141). The findings of Gaufman's study are in line with the findings of the above-mentioned study by Szostek (2018), revealing that even the Russian youth – a segment of Russian society that was not actively watching TV and was more active in new media environments than other demographic groups – was reproducing the dominant narratives from Russian state-controlled TV channels. Two of those state-controlled

---

13 For details, see: Glavred «Dozhdja» Dzjadko Soobshhil Ob Ot'ezde Iz Rossii Posle Blokirovki [Rain's Editor-in-chief Dzyadko Announced His Departure from Russia After the Blocking]. (2022, 3 February). RBC. https://www.rbc.ru/politics/02/03/2022/621f7a4e9a79470e6a0764c9

TV channels—Channel One Russia and RT (former Russia Today)—are discussed on the following pages.

Roman and colleagues (2017) interpret the post-Maidan international rankings of civil liberties in Ukraine and in Russia as follows: scholars state that in Ukraine, the situation generally improved "after its former authoritarian president, Viktor Yanukovych, fled the country", while the "civil liberties rating further plummeted in Russia" after the beginning of the Russian-Ukrainian conflict (p. 362). Speaking more precisely, the conflict caused a further limitation of freedoms in Russia but those changes did not make much difference for Russian state-controlled media outlets including Channel One Russia. The latter had even intensified its influence while focusing on the events in Ukraine at the end of February 2014, Russian columnist Melman described the extreme attention of Russian TV to Ukraine by writing "there is a feeling that we live in Ukraine".[14] Moreover, in 2014, Channel One Russia launched new politically-relevant programmes, e.g. the project Time Will Show (Vremya pokazhet) discussing political topics in a simple and casual way, which also was largely focused on Ukraine.[15] Therefore, unlike the situation on oppositional media outlets already facing significant negative changes in the first months of the Russian-Ukrainian conflict (in 2013–2014), the situation on state-controlled Channel One Russia at that time was rather stable. One of the main reasons for this stability was the fact that long before 2013, this channel was known for its support of Russian authorities (Lipman & McFaul, 2001).

The channel was launched in 1995 under the name Russian Public Television (ORT), and was renamed Channel One Russia (Pervy Kanal) in 2002.[16] However, even in 1995 the channel was not

---

14 Melman, A. (2014). Udarennye Majdanom [Hit by the Maidan]. Mk.Ru. https://www.mk.ru/social/tv-week/article/2014/02/27/991655-udarennyie-maydanom.html
15 Time Will Show. (2022). Channel One Russia. https://www.1tv.ru/shows/vremya-pokazhet
16 For details, see: Pervy Kanal. 20 Let v Jefire [Channel One. 20 years of Broadcast]. (2015). 1tv.Ru. https://www.1tv.ru/20years/

new for its viewers: it was broadcasting on the TV frequencies previously occupied by the so-called Ostankino's Channel One—the major Russian TV channel of the first half of 1990s; Ostankino's Channel One, in turn, was created in 1991 to replace the First Programme of the Central Television of the USSR (Mickiewicz, 1988; McNair, 1996).

After the announcement of glasnost, Soviet TV including the First Programme of the Central Television was no longer under the strict ideological censorship of the Communist Party; still, it did not become independent and balanced. The same can be said of the successors of its TV frequencies—Russian Public Television (ORT); for example, as of 1995—shortly after the beginning of the First Chechen war—it was "uncritically reproducing the government's versions of events" instead of criticizing Russian authorities and "reporting the realities of the conflict" (McNair, 1996, p. 494).

Channel One Russia's news programme—Vremya (i.e. time)—has a similar history: it is a successor of the Soviet news programme Vremya. In the book about TV in the USSR, Mickiewicz (1988, p. 10) called censored Vremya "the country's most important program" and revealed that in accordance with Soviet authorities, Vremya was the main source of news for 90% of Soviet citizens. Vremya remained the most important news programme on Channel One Russia, while this channel was the main source of news for almost three quarters of Russians (Levada Center, 2017a). In general, in March 2014—during the analysed time frame of the Russian-Ukrainian conflict—90% of Russians consumed news via TV (Levada Center, 2017b). Therefore, in analysing Vremya's news coverage made by Channel One Russia, we are examining the dominant voice of the dominant news-making actor in the Russian media system. The significant influence of Channel One Russia's news coverage on Russian public opinion about the Russian-Ukrainian conflict was the main reason for the choice of news coverage made by this channel for the empirical analysis of enmification.

Importantly, being a de facto successor of the First Programme of the Central Television of the USSR and producing the widely-recognized Vremya programme, Channel One Russia was a popular source of news for a multi-million audience outside Russia, first and foremost for ethnic Russians and Russian speakers in countries neighbouring Russia (Vihalemm et al., 2019; Juzefovičs & Vihalemm, 2020). The channel and its main news programme were popular in other parts of the world too, e.g. among Russian-speaking people in the USA "who number more than 850,000" (Burrett, 2020, p. 12) and Germany. Channel One Russia was also widely watched in Ukraine, especially prior to the beginning of the Russian-Ukrainian conflict but also thereafter, up until it was blocked. The list of Russian media blocked in Ukraine also includes other state-controlled Russian TV channels, online media outlets, social media platforms, etc. (Decree of the President of Ukraine №133 / 2017, 2017)

While Channel One Russia has a dominant position as a source of news for the Russian internal audience, the role of RT in informing people outside Russia is incomparably smaller. At the same time, scholars affiliated with Western institutions pay noticeably more attention to RT than to Channel One Russia: researching RT is easier for many of those scholars due to the absence of the language barrier, moreover, as it is widely known that RT's activities influence the public in Western countries, scholars from those countries pay attention to RT's performance there (e.g. Kragh & Åsberg, 2017; Carter & Carter, 2021; Yatsyk, 2022).

RT is a Russian international broadcaster that was created in 2005 under the name Russia Today and was aimed at favourably portraying Russia abroad; however, based on the findings of their study, Elswah and Howard (2020) argue that since then the channel's aims have changed:

> RT was an ambitious public diplomacy project that was initially established to present a positive image of Russia to the world. However, the dynamics of the channel's news production changed considerably during the Russia–Georgia conflict in 2008. Since then, RT has worked to encourage doubts about the West, its media, agenda, and values, epitomized in its slogan "Question More." (p. 625)

In 2009, Russia Today was renamed RT, which might have helped it to somewhat distract the audience from the channel's affiliation with Russian authorities (Nassetta & Gross, 2020). Year after year, the project developed: Carter and Carter (2021) specify that since 2005, RT's budget has increased tenfold. Currently, RT has several channels and websites in different languages including English, Spanish, and Arabic, targeting different segments of RT's audience, while RT International, a Moscow-based TV channel, broadcasts for its English-speaking audience all around the world. Still, the channel's influence in hosting countries remains limited, which the channel is said to work around by focusing on broadcasting information that disrupts the media systems of hosting countries rather than on information directly transmitting Russian narratives abroad. This feature of RT's broadcasting has also attracted close scholarly attention (e.g. Elswah & Howard, 2020; Wagnsson, 2022).

Even before the beginning of the Russian-Ukrainian conflict (in 2013–2014), RT was known for being highly dependent on Russian elites and for fulfilling their communication goals (e.g. Geniets, 2013). Kragh and Åsberg (2017), who analyse RT's performance and other Russian activities in the context of the security of hosting states (using the example of Sweden), reveal that after the beginning of the Russian-Ukrainian conflict, Russia's attempts to shift public opinion in Sweden and influence the decisions of the Swedish authorities "in a direction favourable or at least not harmful to the Kremlin" became considerably more extreme (p. 778).

As for the comparison between RT and Channel One Russia, earlier studies have shown that the fundamental narratives strengthening the Russian official framing of the Russian-Ukrainian conflict were similar on both channels (e.g. Unwala & Ghori, 2015; Mejias & Vokuev, 2017). Still, as Russian mass communication and public diplomacy are highly nuanced depending on the segment of the audience they address (Tupicyna & Nejmatova, 2008), it is especially relevant to compare the conflict-related news coverage of these two channels in more detail because it will allow us to address the Russian state-controlled enmification strategy more systematically.

Moreover, the comparison of RT and Channel One Russia is a study of largely similar communication actors. Thus, such a comparison will help to fully incorporate the new information about Channel One Russia into the system of existing knowledge about

Russian information influence because this new information about a less studied actor (Channel One Russia) will be directly linked with previously available knowledge about the better studied actor (RT).

The above-mentioned studies of RT reveal that the channel serves the political goals of Russian authorities, and this is also true of Channel One Russia. RT is widely criticized for its political dependence due to its potentially harmful influence on Western democracies. At the same time, Channel One Russia does not receive such negative attention despite the fact that this state-controlled channel is the main source of news for dozens of millions of Russians. Thus, what Russians learn about the Russian-Ukrainian conflict from Channel One Russia determines their understanding of Russia's aggression against Ukraine. This is an especially important issue when it comes to the construction of enemies.

After the beginning of the full-scale Russian invasion of Ukraine in February 2022, it became clear that a considerable number of Russians, if not the majority, support the invasion (Levada Center, 2022). In the light of those developments, the study of the enmification potentially performed by Channel One Russia helps to address the question as to whether the state-controlled coverage of the events of the first nine months of the Russian-Ukrainian conflict in 2013–2014 is in line with the Russian authorities' justification of the invasion in 2022.

As for RT, after the beginning of the full-scale invasion, the channel was blocked in the EU and the USA. Additionally, on February 23, 2022, i.e. right after Russia recognized the independence of the self-proclaimed "DNR" and "LNR", Margarita Simonyan — RT's editor-in-chief — was sanctioned by The Council of the European Union with the following reasoning:

> Margarita Simonyan is a central figure of the Government propaganda. She is also editor-in-chief of the English language television news network RT (Russia Today). Through her function, she promoted a positive attitude to the annexation of Crimea and the actions of separatists in Donbas. Therefore,

> she supported actions and policies which undermine the territorial integrity, sovereignty and independence of Ukraine. (p. 8)[17]

Therefore, the comparative analysis of the construction of enemies on the Channel One Russia and RT TV channels in the course of the Russia-Ukrainian conflict deployment is not just theoretically reasonable but also highly relevant for the ongoing full-scale Russian-Ukrainian War.

---

17 Council Decision (CFSP) 2022/265 of 23 February 2022 amending Decision 2014/145/CFSP concerning restrictive measures in respect of actions undermining or threatening the territorial integrity, sovereignty and independence of Ukraine. (2022). Official Journal of the European Union. https://bit.ly/3K76wAK

Russia and Ukraine:
Interplay of Geopolitics and Colonialism

Political and scientific discussions about the Russian-Ukrainian conflict (2013–2022) are largely focused on the clash between, on the one hand, the concept of the sovereignty of states and, on the other hand, the concept of the extraterritorial spheres of influence. The former is supported by international law and the latter by "the right of the strong". Voigt describes this clash as follows: "International law teaches us that all nations are equal. Politics makes clear that power is not distributed equally among states." (2015, p. 15) Despite the fact that the mere concept of spheres of influence contradicts the logic of international law and allows just a couple of states worldwide to enjoy their sovereignty, some political actors use power, including military power, in order to secure their extraterritorial influence (Sankey, 2020). The actions of those actors are conceptualized, for example, by the realist tradition of International Relations. In particular, within a realist frame, the so-called Ukrainian crisis beginning in 2013 is presented exclusively as a confrontation between the great powers over Ukraine, while the crisis is said to be predominately the fault of the USA, the EU, and NATO (Mearsheimer, 2014). The latter actors are said to have challenged Russia's strategic interests by considering closer cooperation with Ukraine in circumstances when the aim to keep Ukraine in the sphere of Russian influence was one of Russia's key interests (Wolf, 2019).

Scholars who find blind spots in the realist framing of the conflict argue that the sovereignty and agency of states that are not global powers are not just idealistic concepts but factors of international politics:

> [...] rejection of realist geopolitics as an analytical approach is also helpful for examining Ukraine as not just an object of big-power conflict, but as a subject whose domestic developments matter a great deal to the outbreak and eventual solution of the conflict. (Raik, 2019, p. 53)

Viewing Ukraine as a subject of politics allows us to pay attention not only to the geopolitical aspect of the Russian-Ukrainian conflict, which follows the well-known bipolar Cold-War logic, but also to analyse the aspects of the bilateral Russian-Ukrainian relations contributing to the beginning of the conflict.

From some points of view, even representatives of the realist tradition agree that the Russian-Ukrainian conflict is not just the challenge of the recent decades or the result of the eastward enlargement of the EU or NATO. This can be argued because as early as in 1993, Mearsheimer opposed the idea of the nuclear disarmament of Ukraine by pointing at the risk of Russian aggression against Ukraine:

> [a] nuclear Ukraine makes sense for two reasons. First, it is imperative to maintain peace between Russia and Ukraine. That means ensuring that the Russians who have a history of bad relations with Ukraine, do not move to reconquer it. (p. 50)

In other words, before the post-Cold-War enlargement of the EU and NATO, Mearsheimer was referring to the potential of war between Russia and Ukraine grounded in the history of relations between the two countries. Thus, the picture of the Russian-Ukrainian conflict would be incomplete if we looked at it only in the context of geopolitical changes after the enlargement of the EU and NATO. Since the time when Mearsheimer publicly opposed the idea of Ukraine's nuclear disarmament, referring to the risk of Russia's attempts to reconquer Ukraine, the latter gave up its (third largest) nuclear potential as well as got attacked by Russia.

After eight years of hybrid conflict (2013–2022), when some parts of Ukraine were occupied by Russia and in some others, Ukraine was fighting "separatists, who have Russian troops and weapons on their side" (Mearsheimer, 2015), on February 24, 2022, Russia began its full-scale invasion of Ukraine. The centuries-long history of Russian-Ukrainian relations makes some Ukrainians frame the beginning of the full-scale Russian invasion as the new beginning of "the eight years' Russian-Ukrainian War which lasts for centuries" (Zlobina, 2022). The following paragraphs offer a brief selective overview of the confrontational events and periods of the Russian-Ukrainian relations in order to put the Russian-Ukrainian conflict analysed into a broader historical context.

Centuries before the Moscow Principality was established, Kyivan Rus was the main centre of Eastern Slavs. This means Ukraine should not be viewed as a typical colony of the Tsardom of Muscovy and, later on, of the Russian Empire and the USSR (Schorkowitz, 2019). Still, the politics of tsars, emperors and General Secretaries of the Communist party towards Ukraine can be called colonial (e.g. Velychenko, 2002; Irvin-Erickson, 2021). Moreover, in general, there is a "continuity of colonial control from tsarist to Soviet times" (Schorkowitz, 2019, p. 117). Among the indicators of such colonial control, which lasted up until the collapse of the USSR, is the fact that even when it came to non-Russian "Soviet republics", the Russian *minority* dominated the non-Russian *majorities* of local nations (Chinn & Kaiser, 2019). Such a status-quo was often achieved by the means of occupation of territories and further oppression of locals.

To give just a few examples, in regard to Ukrainians, this oppression manifested itself, for instance, in the occupation and destruction of Baturyn, the capital of Cossack Hetmanate,[18] in 1708; in the establishment of the so-called Malorussian (i.e. little Russian) Collegium in 1722 — a Russian imperial administration aimed at ruling the territories of Cossack Hetmanate; in the occupation and destruction of Zaporizhian Sich in 1775, which by that time was the military and administrative centre of Ukrainian Cossacks and one of the last remaining spots of Ukrainian independence and self-governance; in the restrictions and/or prohibitions against the use of the Ukrainian language for various intellectual and cultural purposes e.g. Valuev Decree of 1863 or Ems Decree of 1876 (in which the Ukrainian language was also demeaningly called Malorussian — i.e. little Russian); in the artificial famine of 1932–1933; in the deportation and killing of numerous Ukrainian artists by the Soviet Regime (e.g. during the period of the so-called *Executed Renaissance*); in the mass systematic Russification of Ukrainians in the pe-

---

18   Ukrainian Cossack state.

riod after WWII, etc. These and similar events regularly caused violent conflicts between Ukrainians and Russians, which took the form of Ukrainian independence movements. For example, when the independent Ukrainian republic was defeated by the Russian Red Army,[19] some military units of Ukrainians continued guerrilla resistance against Soviet Russia (e.g. on the territories of Kholodnyi Yar where the fights for independence lasted until 1922).

Control over all the numerous national entities was important for the stability of Russian colonialism, but the case of Ukraine is somewhat special because control over Ukraine is an essential part of Russia's self-perception as an ancient pan-Slavic state and the centre of the so-called "Slavic civilisation" (Shevel, 2011). Moreover, Russia sees the roots of its statehood in the Kyivan Rus, thus, in order to secure the continuity of its statehood, Russia must have control over Ukraine (D'Anieri, 1997). Brzezinski (2006) puts it in a similar way by writing that the mere existence of a separate independent Ukraine turns Moscow's unique role as the only centre of Eastern European Slavs into the role of one of states with a large share of the Slavic population; Brzezinski also acknowledges the geopolitical relevance of the Russian-Ukrainian conflict: if Ukraine remains independent from Russia, the Russian aim of becoming the main political actor in the whole of Eurasia cannot be seen as realistic any longer (2006).

While addressing such risks, the centuries-long Russian imperial tradition tried to secure the dominance of the "older Russian brother" over the "younger Ukrainian brother" by presenting Russians (Velikorosy — i.e. Great Russians) and Ukrainians (Malorosy — i.e. Little Russians) as two parts of one big in-group — the big Russian nation — and by oppressing or eliminating those opposing such an understanding. The acting Russian president Putin also shares this idea: "I will never give up my conviction that Russians and Ukrainians are one nation" (Ria.ru, 2022).

Thus, both the denial of the geopolitical element of the analysed conflict and the denial of its colonial element might lead to

---

19 The army of the Russian Soviet Republic, and, after the creation of the USSR, the army of the USSR.

limitations in addressing this conflict's roots, course, and consequences (Bojcun, 2015). Still, despite the interplay of geopolitical and colonial factors outlined above, political actors involved in the conflict might try to reduce it to one of those factors depending on their communication goals. In such conditions, the study of enmification based on the events of this conflict is one of the ways to see whom those actors present as sides of the conflict, whom they try to portray as hostile and dangerous, and against whom they try to mobilize the public.

The Russian aggression against Ukraine is a complex, multidimensional, and highly politicised topic. Therefore, any attempt to propose a chronology of even its most important events could become a subject of critique; the same can be said about the very naming of the conflict and the time when it began. Still, to be able to move to the empirical analysis of enmification potentially performed by Russian state-controlled Channel One Russia and RT, there is a need to decide on at least some starting points and to provide the reader with at least a very general understanding of the course of the conflict. The following pages attempt to do so.

To begin with, most often, scholars from different disciplines call the events that started in Ukraine in November 2013 "the Ukraine crisis" or "Ukrainian crisis" (e.g. Mearsheimer, 2014; Bojcun, 2015; Goble, 2016; Laruelle, 2016; Lichtenstein et al., 2019; McGlynn, 2020). However, this is not the only option, for example, Härtel (2019) decides to use the formulation "Ukraine crisis" in his study but, simultaneously, underlines that this term is

> rightly criticized for creating the wrong impression that the conflict is mostly homegrown ('civil war') and that the events unfolding inside Ukraine from late 2013 onwards caused everything that followed. The author prefers the formula 'Ukraine-Russia conflict', but decided here to follow the scholarly mainstream for comparability reasons. (p. 87)

As for the formulation "civil war", calling the conflict thus is, first and foremost, widespread among Russian scholars, e.g. Buzgalin (2015, p. 331) uses such a term and adds that "[s]ince both Russia and the West (primarily the United States) are aiding the opposing sides only through financial help and by sending volunteers, the conflict can and should be described as a civil war". The term "civil war" appears to be the most widely used one in the Russian-language segment of the relevant literature (e.g. Kotlyarov & Puzyreva, 2014; Lazutin, 2015). In contrast, Czuperski and colleagues from the Atlantic Council (2015) analysing Russian involvement in the conflict argue that the conflict is of a "Kremlin-manufactured" nature and add that since 2014, Russia is, de facto, in a state of war with Ukraine, which can be concluded due to e.g. the involvement of Russian regular military units and commanders in the violent conflict, the supply of heavy weaponry into the war zone as well as cross-border shelling of the territory of Ukraine from the territory of Russia.

Despite acknowledging the involvement of Russia in the war in the Donetsk and Luhansk regions of Ukraine (2014–2022), in the context of this book, the term "Russian-Ukrainian conflict" is used instead of the term "Russian-Ukrainian War". This decision is based on a wish to include not just the military aspect of the conflict, but also its hybrid (first of all information) component. Moreover, the use of the term "Russian-Ukrainian conflict" allows us to include the period of the Euromaidan and the occupation of Crimea preceding the beginning of the violent conflict in Donbas in our analysis. For other examples of using the term Russian-Ukrainian conflict / Russia-Ukraine conflict, see Unwala and Ghori (2015), Veebel and Markus (2016), Juzefovičs and Vihalemm (2020), Alyukov (2021).

The selection of events to be recalled in the chronology of the Russian-Ukrainian conflict is also a subject of political discussions. Thus, it was decided to pay closest attention to those of the major events of the conflict that were somehow formalized by or reflected in national or international documents. In that segment of the literature about the Russian-Ukrainian conflict that is not exclusively focused on the military conflict in Donbas (2014–2022), the Euromaidan[20] is seen as the starting point of the conflict (e.g. Horbyk,

---

20 The title "Euromaidan" is a combination of words "Euro" (underlining the pro-EU essence of the protests) and the word "Maidan" — the shortened version of the name of Kyiv's central square, Maidan Nezalezhnosti (Eng. Independence Square), which is the traditional place of mass gatherings in Kyiv.

2015; Smith, 2016; Watanabe, 2017; Lichtenstein et al., 2019). Euromaidan — the months-long protest in Kyiv[21] and other Ukrainian cities — began on November 21, 2013, as a reaction of Ukrainian civil society to the official decision of the then pro-Russian Ukrainian authorities to suspend the signing of the Association Agreement with the EU. After the violent police dispersal of protesters staying on Maidan overnight on November 31, 2013, the focus of the protests shifted from being pro-EU to more anti-governmental while the protests became even more massive.[22,23] The anti-government protests lasted until February 22, 2014, when the Ukrainian parliament voted for the resignation of the pro-Russian Ukrainian president Yanukovych, who fled from Kyiv.

Approximately three weeks after the end of the Euromaidan, on March 18, 2014, Russia illegally annexed the Ukrainian Crimean Peninsula. Russian authorities claimed that the decision about the Annexation relied on the results of the so-called "referendum" held in Crimea on March 16, 2014; the sham referendum was not recognized internationally. In March 2014, the EU, the USA, Australia, etc. imposed the first round of anti-Russian sanctions.

In the middle of April 2014, after some local administrations in the Donetsk region of Ukraine were captured by Russian and pro-Russian forces (e.g. in Sloviansk), the Postmaidan Ukrainian

---

21 Here and further in the book, transliteration of Ukrainian names and toponyms is based on their official Ukrainian-language spelling (e.g. Kyiv, Kharkiv, Donbas). The exclusions from this general approach are the situations when those names and toponyms are used in the quoted fragments from Russian state-controlled TV, where their Russian-language spelling is used (e.g. Kiev, Kharkov, Donbass).

22 The use of force against protesters was a subject of investigation at the European Court of Human Rights. For details, see: Use of Force in the Policing of Demonstrations. Prohibition of Torture and Inhuman or Degrading Treatment (Article 3) (p. 9). (2021). European Court of Human Rights. https://www.ec hr.coe.int/Documents/FS_Force_demonstrations_ENG.pdf

23 In accordance with a poll conducted in December 2013 by the Kyiv International Institute of Sociology and the Ilko Kucheriv Democratic Initiatives Foundation, the most frequently named reason "which made people came out to the Maidan" was a "brutal beating of demonstrators at the Maidan on November, 30 night, repressions". For further details, see: Maidan-2013. (2013). Kyiv International Institute of Sociology (KIIS). https://www.kiis.com.ua/?lang=eng&cat=reports&id=216&page=1&y=2013

Authorities announced the beginning of the anti-terrorist operation (ATO). The official day of the beginning of the operation was April 14, but the decision about it was taken and announced on April 13, 2014. The middle of April 2014 is the starting point of the violent conflict in the Donetsk and Luhansk regions of Ukraine (also known as Donbas). In April 2014, the second round of anti-Russian international sanctions was imposed. Approximately one month after the beginning of the violent conflict, on May 11, 2014, the sham referendums for the independence of the so-called Donetsk People's Republic ("DNR") and so-called Luhansk People's Republic ("LNR") were held, the results of those sham referendums were not recognized internationally, just like the self-proclaimed independency of "DNR" and "LNR". More than seven years after the sham "independence referendums"—on February 21, 2022—Russia became the first member of the United Nations to recognize the independence of both of these self-proclaimed entities.

Three months after the beginning of the violent conflict in the Donetsk and Luhansk regions of Ukraine, on July 17, 2014, another major event occurred: the Malaysia Airlines plane (MH-17) flying from Amsterdam to Kuala Lumpur was shot down over Ukraine. The crash caused the death of the 298 people on board, and attracted intense international attention. Later on, the international investigation revealed that the plane was shot down by a Russian Buk missile system fired from Russia-controlled part of the Donetsk region (Toal & O'Loughlin, 2018). In July 2014, the EU, the USA, etc. began to impose the third round of anti-Russian sanctions, while the fighting continued.

The attempts to end the fighting in Donbas began in April 2014, when the Geneva Statement on Ukraine was agreed on. However, despite its aims, it did not result in the de-escalation. The same can be said about Poroshenko's peace plan proposed in June 2014. In general, the period between the middle of April 2014 and the beginning of September 2014 is called the most militarily active phase of the fighting in Donetsk and Luhansk regions of Ukraine before the beginning of Russia's full-scale invasion of Ukraine (Taradai, 2019). This phase lasted from the beginning of the violent conflict on April 13, 2014 to the signing of the so-called First Minsk Agreement (Minsk Protocol), which happened on September 5, 2014. The Agreement was signed after the massive counteroffensive of Russian and pro-Russian forces and deaths of numerous Ukrainian soldiers (primarily near the town of Ilovaisk).

One of the outcomes of the Agreement was the very first de facto involvement of Russia-backed separatists in the process of negotiations and the de facto formalization of the territories controlled by them, which occurred due to the need to document the demarcation line between those parts of the Donetsk and Luhansk regions controlled by Ukrainian forces and those occupied by Russian and pro-Russian forces (Åtland, 2020). The First Minsk Agreement declared the ceasefire along these lines; however, it was never fully held. In January 2015, a massive new escalation happened. After the months-long battle for Donetsk Airport, Russian and pro-Russian forces occupied it and proceeded to launch an offensive on the town of Debaltseve. The Normandy Format negotiations (Ukraine, Russia, France, and Germany) resulted in the signing of the Second Minsk Agreement on February 15, 2015, which was officially entitled "Package of Measures for the Implementation of the Minsk Agreements", aimed at proposing a roadmap for conflict management in the frame of the First Minsk Agreement.[24]

Åtland (2020) underlines that the Second Minsk Agreement was even less favourable to Ukraine than the First Minsk Agreement as it even more closely addressed Russia's goal to incorporate the Russia-controlled "republics" into Ukraine on Russian terms, and to use them to control Ukraine's foreign and domestic politics. However, both of the Minsk Agreements were rather pro-Russian as both of them were signed in moments of significant military escalation and advancement of Russian and pro-Russian forces, i.e. in a situation when for Ukraine the "most realistic alternative to a negotiated agreement [...] would have been a large-scale war" (Åtland, 2020, p. 137).

Despite the above-mentioned examples of the evidence of Russia's military involvement in the war, in both of the agreements,

---

[24] Package of Measures for the Implementation of the Minsk Agreements. (2015). Organization for Security and Co-operation in Europe (OSCE). https://www.osce.org/cio/140156

Russia was not officially called a fighting side, its influence on the self-proclaimed pseudo republics was not officially recognized either. Similar to the First Minsk Agreement, the Second Minsk Agreement never functioned as planned and was never able to even secure the ceasefire (Wittke, 2019). Despite this, the Second Minsk Agreement was the main document regulating the conflict up until February 21, 2022.

On February 21, 2022, Russia recognized the self-proclaimed independence of the so-called "DNR" and "LNR". At first, the exact territories of the Russia-recognized pseudo republics were not specified at all; later on, it was clarified that the whole territories of the Donetsk and Luhansk regions of Ukraine were recognized to be the territories of "DNR" and "LNR" respectively, despite the fact that Russian and Russia-controlled forces did not have those territories under their control at any period of the conflict.[25]

To sum up, the Russian-Ukrainian conflict was a years-long hybrid conflict involving various stages including the Euromaidan, the Russia's occupation of Crimea and the war in the Donetsk and Luhansk regions of Ukraine, which were followed by the full-scale Russian invasion of Ukraine on February 24, 2022.

Further in the book, I focus on the enmification performed by Russian state-controlled media between the beginning of the Euromaidan and the signing of the First Minsk Agreement as on the most dynamic enmification-related period laying the ground for everything happening later. That period was also the time of the most dramatic change in the rhetoric of Russian-state-controlled media in regard to Ukraine and Ukrainians (Khaldarova, 2021).

While the deep-seated fear and hatred towards Ukrainians as a distinct nation have roots that extend back centuries into the history of Russian colonialism and imperialism, this book aims to analyse the new seeds of the same plant sowed by Russian state-controlled media in 2013–2014. Today, the world sees the fruits of that fear and hatred in Russia's actions during the full-scale invasion of Ukraine.

---

25 In fact, Russia still did not manage to occupy the whole territory of Donetsk and Luhansk regions as of February 2024, almost two years into Russia's full-scale invasion.

Part III
Methodology

PART I

Standardized Content Analysis

Can an analysis of Russia's hostile communication based on data from 2013–2014 still be relevant when viewed from today's perspective?

The initial answer is "no". A decade has passed since 2014; today, very little can surprise us after all the atrocities the occupying Russian army has committed in Ukraine since the beginning of the full-scale invasion. Simultaneously, all the Russian soldiers abducting, torturing, and raping Ukrainian civilians, erasing Ukrainian settlements to the ground, castrating and beheading Ukrainian prisoners of war (and filming it) were not born like that. People justifying and cheering those actions were not born like that either. Nobody was. To understand what contributed into turning them into such people, we do have to look back.

In this and the following chapter of the book, I explain how I analysed the construction of enemies on Russian TV that occurred between the beginning of the Euromaidan and the signing of the First Minsk Agreement. I briefly show the most crucial parts of my methodology and only then move to the next part of the book to share the findings and make sense of them in the light of more recent developments of the war.

The methodology excerpts are rather technical but concise. The experience of discussing my research with people of different professions led me to retain the most crucial methodological fragments of my dissertation while turning it into this book. This is because non-academics showed genuine interest in aspects such as my approach to sampling (selection of data for analysis), codebook, main categories, etc. If you are a communication expert, a social psychologist, a lawyer, an investigator, a prosecutor of international crimes or anyone interested in seeing the systematic picture of Russia's hostile communication beyond the well-known anecdotal stories, I hope you find these excerpts particularly relevant.

Data. As explained in more detail in the previous part of the book, I chose two Russian state-controlled channels for analysis—

Channel One Russia (Pervy Kanal) and RT (formerly Russia Today). They were the dominant voices of Russian state-controlled news communication in Russia and abroad (respectively) at the time of the analysed dramatic shift in Russia's communication about Ukraine and Western countries. I examined weekly news programmes of Channel One Russia and RT. As for RT, two versions of each weekly news programme were considered: the first one broadcast at EU prime time (20:00 Western European Time), and the second one at US prime time (Atlantic Coast of the USA, 20:00 Eastern Time). This was done to check whether some differences in hostile portrayal and enmification were to be found in the two versions of the programme broadcast for different segments of RT's international audience.

For the standardized analysis, I took only those news stories broadcast during the 42-week period under analysis (November 2013–September 2014) that were related to the topics of Euromaidan, the occupation of Crimea, and the first months of the war in Donetsk and Luhansk regions of Ukraine. The duration of the selected video material was approximately 45 hours, with approximately 31 hours from the weekly news programmes of Channel One Russia, approximately seven hours from RT broadcast during EU prime time, and six and a half hours from RT broadcast during US prime time.

The total number of individual news stories selected from Channel One Russia was 328. Regarding RT, its weekly news could not be unequivocally divided into news stories due to the structure of programmes. Therefore, all fragments dedicated to the developments of the above-listed topics from one weekly programme were treated as a single news story.

Choosing the Approach to Analysing Enmification. I chose to focus on the content of the news coverage instead of analysing its trustworthiness because, regardless of whether true or fake, the news coverage has an impact on its viewers. This is especially true in the conditions of a non-free information environment where state-controlled media outlets are the main sources of information for most citizens. If two news stories attribute hostilely depicted actors with a similar degree of enmity, a fake news story would have a similar influence on viewers as a news story based on real-life events. Moreover, such an approach allows for a broadening of focus from disinformation only and also addresses other strategies applied by Russian state-controlled media to hostilely portray political actors confronting Russia's interests.

To be able to focus on the enmifying messages voiced by the channels analysed, after the general analysis of how frequently Russian TV covered events happening in Ukraine, I systematically identified information related to enemy-making in the transcriptions of all topic-relevant news stories. Consistent with earlier research of enemy-making and the understanding that a negative "other" often contributes to shaping a positive "self" (Rieber & Kelly, 1991), I documented both negative and positive assessments of actors involved in the covered events. Tracing the sources and patterns of positive evaluations also helped me analyse what proportion of positive evaluations was devoted to Russia and political actors supporting Russia's interests in the covered events.

Dissecting the Coding Units. To extract the relevant information, I have broken down the evaluation-relevant fragments of transcriptions into evaluation acts—statements from the media text attributing an actor with a positive or negative action or characteristic (Bednarek, 2006). The two required elements of an evaluation act were an indication of the actor and the information needed to draw a favourable or unfavourable evaluation of them. For example, the following statement negatively evaluated the EU by attributing it with adverse intentions: "probably Brussels hoped that by storm and onslaught it would be able to impose the desired position on Ukraine" (November 24, 2013, COR3, 00:14–00:19).[26]

---

[26] Here and onwards, the date represents the date when the quoted weekly news programme was broadcast. "COR" and "RT" denote the name of the quoted channel. In the given example, the number following "COR" is the quoted news story's number from weekly news programme broadcast by Channel One Russia on November 24, 2013. As for RT, news stories from RT EU prime are marked as RT1, news stories from RT US prime are marked as RT2. The timecode indicates the time when the quote was voiced during the respective news story.

The overall number of evaluation acts detected in all the analysed news stories was 3,723. 2,469 acts were identified in the coverage of Channel One Russia, 659 of RT EU prime time, and 595 of RT US prime time. The larger number of evaluation acts identified on Channel One Russia reflects the longer duration of weekly news programmes on that channel.

Evaluation acts were used as units of coding for the further analysis of the enmification campaign performed by Russian state-controlled media. The standardized content analysis of the data was performed on the basis of the codebook. It incorporated various categories and codes enabling the comprehensive and consistent documentation of evaluations voiced on the analysed channels.

Codebook. After creating a comprehensive database of detected evaluation acts, I came up with a systematic approach of analysing them. All evaluation acts from the analysed news stories were coded in accordance with the following codebook.

Table 1. Codebook applied for the standardized content analysis of the data

Category	Subcategory	Codes
VALENCE		Positive, Negative
MEANING		Manifest, Latent
EVALUATORS		Anchorperson, Journalist, Expert, Politician, Character, Other
THEMATIC FOCUS		Political, Economic, Human interest, Morality, Other
EVALUATED ACTORS	Negatively Evaluated Actors	Russian, Russia-affiliated, Other, Western, Ukrainian
EVALUATED ACTORS	Positively Evaluated Actors	Russian, Russia-affiliated, Other, Western, Ukrainian

Additionally, the above-listed groups of actors (e.g. Russian, Russia-affiliated, etc.) were detailed by lists of particular political actors evaluated in the analysed news stories as shown in the table below.

The political leaning of an actor played a major role in their group categorization. This decision aimed to facilitate quite a detailed and politically sensitive approach to the analysis of enmification or glorification of that actor in the selected news stories. All actors were grouped on the basis of their formal or informal political affiliations before the standardized content analysis was performed, i.e. the analysis itself did not have an impact on the group categorization.

Table 2. List of political actors coded in the process of standardized content analysis

Group of Actors	Actors
Russian	Russia (without specification)
Russia-affiliated	Pro-Russian Ukrainian Authorities (of the Euromaidan period); Yanukovych; Eastern Protesters; Eastern Militia; Special Police Force "Berkut"; Crimean Militia and Authorities; China; India; Brazil; Republic of South Africa; Belarus; Kazakhstan; Serbia; Party of Regions (after Euromaidan); The Eurasian Customs Union (EACU) and Eurasian Economic Community (EurAsEC); USSR; Other from Russia-affiliated actors
Other (non-affiliated)	International Humanitarian Organizations themselves; The International Court of Justice (ICJ); International Committee of the Red Cross (ICRC); Amnesty International (AI); Human Rights Watch; European Court of Human Rights (ECHR); International Monetary Fund (IMF); Organization for Security and Cooperation in Europe (OSCE); The United Nations (UN); Moldova; Georgia; Other from non-affiliated actors
Western	West itself; NATO; EU; USA; Obama; Germany; Merkel; United Kingdom; France; Poland; Latvia; Lithuania; Italy; Greece; Canada; Australia; Turkey; Western media itself; US media; European media itself; Polish media; French media; British media; German media
Ukrainian	Postmaidan Ukrainian Authorities; Poroshenko; Euromaidan Protesters; Right Sector (including Yarosh); Ukrainian Opposition (of the Euromaidan period); Indistinct/Other Ukrainian Authorities; Ukrainian Oligarchs; Kolomoisky; Ukrainian Civil Society and Religious Organizations; Ukrainian

Media; Ukrainian Insurgent Army (UPA) and Bandera; Ukrainian Volunteer Battalions

Importantly, the instances of negative information about an actor (e.g. a criticism of their actions) would not be enough to turn them into an enemy. In order to construct an enemy out of a neutral actor, the negative depiction of them must be intense, systematic, and unquestioned, transmitted in a communication situation where positive information about this actor is absent. In state-controlled media environments like those of autocracies, this is achieved by informing the public in the desired way, combined with preventing the public from reaching undesirable information. In contrast, in free media environments where nobody controls the discourse, political communicators are forced to react to messages contradicting their own, which they may do by dismissing undesirable information. Enmification might include dismissing positive evaluations of "others" and negative evaluations of "oneself" if they appear in the discourse for some reason. To check whether this approach was applied by the analysed TV channels, how intensively and whether there was a difference between Channel One Russia and RT in this aspect, each evaluation detected in the analysed data was checked for whether it was disproved in the same news story where it was voiced and was coded either as dismissed or as non-dismissed.

Discourse-historical Approach

Applying the methodology of the standardized content analysis described in the previous chapter allowed to understand a systematic general frame of who were the villains and heroes of the Russian state-controlled news stories about the events of interest: Euromaidan, Russia's occupation of Crimea and the first months of the war in Donetsk and Luhansk regions of Ukraine. This chapter explains the methodology of the second part of my research aimed at investigating the strategies helping Channel One Russia and RT to elicit fear and hatred in their audiences. In particular, the second part of the research is aimed at detailing the general systematic frame of Russian hostile communication by the features attributed to hostilely portrayed political actors, by the degree of enmity assigned to them, by the messages serving the enmification of those actors, by the precise periodization of the enmification campaign based on its changes, as well as by the understanding of particular means of mass communication used by Channel One Russia and RT in the process of enemy-making. All these nuanced aspects are captured with the help of a variation of critical discourse analysis (CDA), namely a discourse-historical approach (DHA).

Being a variation of CDA, DHA retains its major traits, above all in the attention to how discourse mirrors and co-constructs social structures (Reisigl & Wodak, 2001). For researchers using CDA, language is a form of social practice rather than a set of linguistic elements. The tradition of looking at language as "action in a social context" (Wodak, 1999, p. 186) makes all types of CDA valuable for studying enmification. This can be explained by the fact that enmification (as an instance of securitization) also suggests that successful "speech acts" are the main tools to make (regular) political actors appear threatening for the public (Wæver, 1995).

In addition to the universal features of all types of CDA, DHA has its own specific characteristics. Most of them are not distinctive characteristics of this type of critical discourse analysis, but in DHA they are more salient. In the context of analysis of Russian hostile communication, the most important of those characteristics is the close scholarly attention paid to background knowledge, including historical one. Russia, Ukraine, the EU, the USA, Germany, France and numerous other actors somehow involved in the events of interest have a history of hostile or friendly interaction with one another lasting for decades or even centuries. As a result, it would be beneficial for the study of enmification to be able to take the historical context that is referred to in the selected news stories into consideration.

Another point to underline is that enmification has the notion of *threat,* and the emotion *fear* at its core. In the light of this, DHA is also helpful in addressing fear-inducing discourses because of its potential to include relevant information about fears from the past in the analysis. As psychologists state, fear is often based on the "information transmitted through observation and instruction" (Murray & Foote, 1979, p. 489). Therefore, when something new that does not bring up any associations is said to be similar to something dangerous and fear-inducing from the past, there are high chances that the new and previously unknown situation/event/person would also be seen as threatening. In the case of international news reporting, similarities with events or periods from the past are mostly based on comparisons from world history.

To make the analysis more systematic, scholars using DHA have generated a set of clear tools helping to understand the discourse in-depth. Even though some variations are possible, among those tools are the following quite formalized discursive strategies (e.g. see Reisigl & Wodak, 2001, pp. 45-46; Wodak, 2015a, p. 8):

(1) referential/nomination strategy — what the portrayed actors are called and how they are categorized into groups;
(2) predication strategy — which characteristics are attributed to actors;
(3) argumentation strategy — how the evaluations of the actors are argued;
(4) perspectivization strategy — how the speaker is positioned in the communicated situation;
(5) intensification / mitigation strategy — whether the voiced evaluations are intensified or mitigated, for example, dismissed.

According to Wodak, "[discursive] [s]trategies refer to plans of actions that may vary in their degree of elaboration, may be located at different levels of mental organization, and may range from automatic to highly conscious" (Wodak, 1999, p. 188). Thus, when it comes to particular communicative situations, by analysing the usage of different discursive strategies, one analyses what exactly speakers do to achieve their communication goals.

Following the standardized content analysis described in the previous chapter, I analysed all detected evaluation acts and their context broadcast by Channel One Russia and RT in the 42-week period (November 2013–September 2014) using the five-discursive-strategies approach. I will not go deep into findings here and not list hundreds of quotes showing systematic use of each of the strategies by Russian state-controlled TV, but I will give a comprehensive interpretation of the main findings and illustrate them by brief relevant fragments from the analysed broadcast.

By including relevant fragments of the broadcast in the book, I want to give the readers a chance to get their own impression of the atmosphere and rhetoric on what is expected to be one of the most neutral elements of Russian television—news programmes. It is especially valuable when it comes to quotes from Channel One Russia (translated from Russian). Western experts often rightfully criticize RT for pushing communication goals of Russian regime outside of Russia, but they not always know how much more extreme the information Russians are consuming is.

Before moving further, it is important to remind the readers that my analysis of Channel One Russia's and RT's news coverage deliberately does not include a fact-checking component. There are numerous studies proving that Russia widely uses disinformation (e.g. see Khaldarova & Pantti, 2016; Hjorth & Adler-Nissen, 2019; Erlich & Garner, 2021). In contrast to those studies, in this book, I aimed at analysing the enmification performed by the analysed channels. No matter whether the enmifying messages were true or false, they were watched by the channels' audiences and had some influence on viewers' perception of political actors involved in the events of interest.

Part IV
Preparing for the War on Channel One Russia and RT

Tracing Russian Hostile Communication

The percentage of the airtime devoted to the topics of interest—Euromaidan, occupation of Crimea and the first months of the war in Donbas varied weekly from 0% (i.e. those events were not covered), to over 90% of the airtime in the weeks with the most intense coverage. About two-thirds of the overall airtime of the weekly news on Channel One Russia was devoted to the topics of interest, while on RT, developments of those topics took slightly more than one-third of the airtime of all its international weekly news during the analysed 42 weeks. Figure 1 specifies weekly changes in the attention paid to the conflict on the analysed channels.

Figure 1. Share of the airtime devoted to the events of interest in the weekly news programmes of the analysed TV channels. Channel One Russia (n = 42), RT Average (RT EU prime n = 41, RT US prime n = 41)[27]

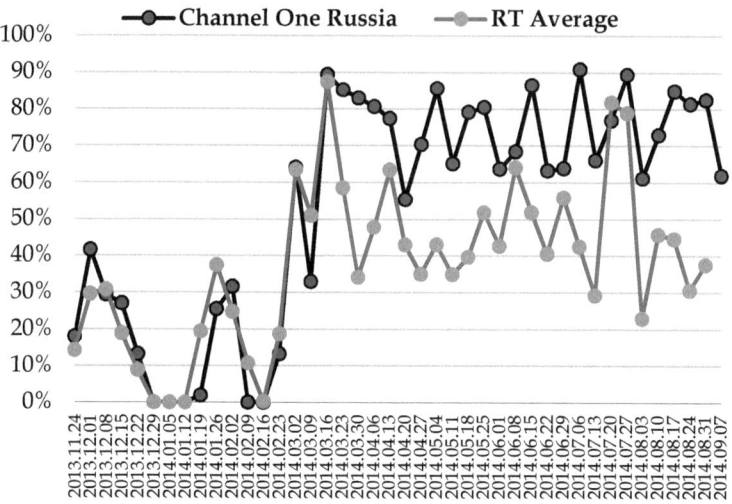

---

27 Weekly news programmes of RT EU prime and RT US prime broadcast on September 7, 2014 (42nd week) were not available on the Internet Archive website.

As can be seen, events of interest received noticeably less attention in the news programmes during the first 14 weeks compared to the rest of the analysed period. Even in the weekly news programmes broadcast on February 23, 2014 — the Sunday following the mass-shooting of protesters in the centre of Kyiv, the flight of President Yanukovych to Russia, and the change of authorities in Ukraine — coverage of the topic took less than 15% of the airtime on Channel One Russia and less than 20% on RT. On that date, the analysed weekly news programmes were heavily focused on the Winter Olympics taking place in Russia in February 2014. However, events that happened in Ukraine in February 2014 were referred to in the analysed weekly news programmes in the weeks and months following them. Russian politicians and journalists still continue referring to them ten years later.

Developments of the events of interest became the number one topic in the majority of the weekly news programmes analysed. On Channel One Russia, RT EU prime, and RT US prime, this was the case in 26, 29, and 30 out of the analysed weekly news programmes respectively.

Speaking of the number one topic, coverage of the events of interest on Channel One Russia may be split into two periods: the first one from the beginning of the Euromaidan up until the week prior to the so-called "referendum" in Crimea, and the second period beginning with the "referendum" up until the end of the analysed time frame. In the first 16 weeks, the events of interest were framed as the number one topic three times: (1) at the beginning of December 2013, after the forcible dispersal of protesters supporting the EU-Ukraine Association Agreement followed by mass rallies against the pro-Russian Ukrainian government; (2) at the end of January 2014, after the first protesters were killed; (3) at the beginning of March 2014, on the Sunday following the seizure of the Crimean parliament by Russian Special Operations Forces. Importantly, none of those turning points of the conflict were closely covered in the news on Channel One Russia. Instead of covering these events, the channel's headline topics were: (1) the possible negative effects of closer ties with EU; (2) the radicalism of the protesters and concessions of pro-Russian Ukrainian authorities;

(3) the readiness of the Russian army to be (potentially) used in Ukraine in order to "normalise the social-political situation", respectively.

In the remaining 26 weeks, the events of interest were a number one topic on Channel One Russia all the time except for April 20, 2014, June 22, 2014, and July 27, 2014. On April 20, 2014, the first news story covered Putin's annual live conference and the situation in Ukraine was still among the topics touched upon by the Russian president. On June 22, 2014, the first two news stories related to the anniversary of the Soviet-German part of the Second World War and commemoration of Soviet soldiers by Putin. However, the situation in Ukraine was also touched upon in Putin's comments regarding the anniversary. On July 27, 2014, the first news story was devoted to the celebrations of the Day of the Russian Navy. In other words, during this period, only Putin or military-related topics could push Ukraine-related news from the top place in Russian *internal* news agenda.

Attention to the events of interest on the two versions of RT coverage analysed cannot be easily split into the same two periods. Nevertheless, some details regarding RT are similar to those of Channel One Russia. The events of interest were not the number one topic on the eve of January 2014 and during the Winter Olympics (that shifted attention from Ukraine to sport-related matters in Russia in February 2014). In the weeks and months after the end of the Olympics, the analysed events were not the number one topic in RT's weekly news a couple of times when being replaced by events such as protests in Egypt and Turkey and bombings in Gaza.

The Table below shows the results of the standardized content analysis followed by notable details about some of them and discussion of those results in the context of Russian state-controlled hostile communication and further developments of the war.

Table 3. Summary of the standardized content analysis of the non-dismissed evaluation acts identified on Channel One Russia, RT EU prime, and RT US prime (n = 3538)[28]

Category Subcategory	Code	Channel One (n = 2392) %	RT EU prime (n = 606) %	RT US prime (n = 540) %
VALENCE	Positive	24 [a]	19 [a]	22 [a]
	Negative	76 [a]	81 [a]	78 [a]
MEANING	Manifest	31 [a]	35 [a]	33 [a]
	Latent	69 [a]	65 [a]	67 [a]
EVALUATORS	Anchorperson	17 [a]	36 [b]	39 [b]
	Journalist	50 [a]	24 [b]	23 [b]
	Expert	11 [a]	19 [b]	15 [b]
	Politician	16 [a]	16 [a]	18 [a]
	Character	5 [a]	3 [a]	5 [a]
	Other	1 [a]	1 [a]	1 [a]
THEMATIC FOCUS	Political	31 [a]	43 [b]	48 [b]
	Economic	7 [a]	6 [a]	6 [a]
	Human interest	5 [a]	5 [a]	5 [a]
	Morality	38 [a]	34 [a,b]	30 [b]
	Other	19 [a]	11 [b]	11 [b]
EVALUATED ACTORS Negatively Evaluated Actors	Russian	0 [a]	2 [b]	2 [b]
	Russia-affil.	1 [a]	2 [b]	2 [a,b]
	Other	1 [a]	0 [a]	1 [a]
	Western	22 [a]	27 [b]	28 [b]
	Ukrainian	52 [a]	49 [a]	46 [a]
EVALUATED ACTORS Positively Evaluated Actors	Russian	13 [a]	6 [b]	8 [b]
	Russia-affil.	7 [a]	6 [a]	8 [a]
	Other	0 [a]	1 [a]	1 [a]
	Western	2 [a]	2 [a]	3 [a]
	Ukrainian	2 [a]	3 [b]	2 [a,b]

---

28 Different letters (superscript) indicate statistically significant differences within each code according to Z-tests with adjusted p-values (Bonferroni method).

The findings of the standardized content analysis revealed that:

- The events of interest were covered in a predominately negativistic way both on Channel One Russia and RT: the number of statements negatively evaluating actors involved in those events was three times higher than the number of positive evaluations;
- Most of the evaluations were voiced by journalists and anchors of the analysed channels, as well as by the experts frequently invited to comment on the issues covered;
- On both versions of RT, the role of experts in voicing negative evaluations was significantly greater than on Channel One Russia. On RT, invited experts were often responsible for manifest statements negatively evaluating Western actors;
- Negative evaluations were often focused on morality. This tendency was especially strong on Channel One Russia: the emphasis on immoral actions and features of negatively depicted actors was the most frequent thematic focus of this channel;
- On Channel One and both versions of RT, there was a clear cleavage between positive evaluations towards Russian and Russia-affiliated actors on the one side and negative Ukrainian and Western actors on the other side;
- Coverage of the analysed conflict on Channel One Russia was more extreme — the difference between the most positively depicted actors (Russian) and most negatively depicted (Ukrainian) was greater than on RT;
- RT was more critical to Russian actors than Channel One Russia. RT was also significantly more critical towards Western actors;
- News coverage of RT was more pluralistic — there were more evaluations that did not fall in line with the overall picture. However, those evaluations were often dismissed in the same news stories where they were voiced. In contrast, on Channel One Russia, evaluations opposing the overall picture of positive and negative evaluations were less frequent and therefore less frequently dismissed.

The share of positive and negative evaluations in weekly news programmes was more or less stable even though the intensity of coverage of the conflict itself dramatically varied throughout the analysed period. The only news programme in which the number of positive evaluations was higher than the number of negative ones was the one broadcast on RT US prime on July 20, 2014[29]. This particular weekly news programme—the first weekly coverage after the downing of the MH-17 flight—is the exception to the general negativistic trend prevailing in all versions of the coverage throughout the analysed period. From the 12 positive evaluation acts identified in this weekly coverage, nine referred to Russian actors offering condolences and calling for an impartial investigation into the tragedy.

Evaluations of political actors on Channel One Russia and on the two analysed versions of RT were predominately latent, i.e. an interpretation of the evaluation acts was needed to make sense of them. The share of manifest and latent evaluation was similar on all channels: approximately one third of the evaluations was manifest, two thirds were latent.

Among all the weekly programmes with an average or above-average number of evaluation acts, there were just two programmes where the number of manifest evaluations exceeded the number of latent evaluations. Both of them were the weekly news programmes broadcast on RT EU prime. The first programme with predominately manifest evaluations was broadcast on March 16, 2014, and the second one on June 15, 2014. In the weekly news programme from March 16, 2014—the week of the sham referendum in Crimea—21 of 22 detected manifest evaluation acts were negative. They related to Ukrainian and Western actors (ten negative evaluations for each group of actors), as well as to the International Monetary Fund (one negative evaluation).

On June 15, 2014, the weekly news programme was broadcast a day after Russian and pro-Russian forces downed a Ukrainian Air Force Il-76, killing 49 people on board. By the middle of June 2014,

---

29 Only news programmes with an average or above average number of evaluations were taken into consideration for this particular calculation.

the downing of the plane was the single event with the most human casualties since the beginning of the war in the Donetsk and Luhansk regions of Ukraine. The event itself was not covered by RT. However, this event was one of the reasons for protests near the Russian Embassy in Kyiv. In their turn, the events near the embassy were closely covered by RT. Negative manifest evaluations towards protesters and Ukrainian officials taking part in events near the embassy constituted half of all negative manifest evaluations from the respective weekly news programme. The table below shows most frequent negative adjectives used by the analysed channels in their manifest evaluations during the analysed period (November 2013–September 2014).

Table 4. Top 5 most frequent negative adjectives identified within manifest evaluation acts on Channel One Russia, RT EU prime, and RT US prime (n = 1132)

Channel One Russia (n = 742)	RT EU prime (n = 211)	RT US prime (n = 179)
Punitive (карательный)	Violent	Deadly
Fascist (фашистский)	Controversial	Violent
Aggressive (агрессивный)	Notorious	Outrageous
Dangerous (опасный)	Dangerous	Dangerous
Scary (страшный)	Bloody	Wrong

In its turn, the figure below illustrates the overall balance of the evaluations identified in the analysed coverage. The balance was calculated as the difference between the number of positive evaluations and the number of negative evaluations for each group of actors respectively.

Figure 2. Balance of evaluation acts related to five groups of political actors involved in the events of interest. Channel One Russia (n = 2392), RT EU prime (n = 606), RT US prime (n = 540)

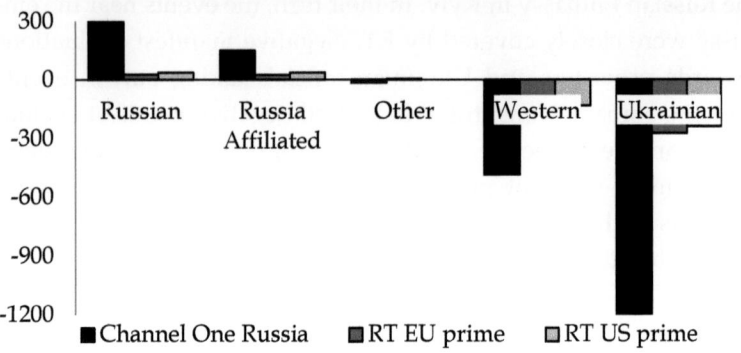

The figure reflects the overall prevalence of negative evaluations on all three versions of the coverage. As can be seen, the coverage of Channel One Russia was the most extreme — the difference between the most positively depicted group of actors (Russian), and the most negatively depicted one (Ukrainian) was the biggest. The analysis of weekly developments showed the peculiarity of evaluations on Channel One Russia in more detail: there were no weekly news programmes where the group of Russian actors had negative balance or the group of Ukrainian actors had positive balance.

Ukrainian actors were the most negatively evaluated throughout the whole analysed period. Negative evaluations of them account for approximately *half of all* non-dismissed evaluations detected in the coverage of the topics of interest. Western actors were the second most negatively depicted group: negative evaluations about Western actors account for approximately a quarter of all non-dismissed evaluations.

Based on the analysed coverage of Channel One Russia and RT, these five actors — the Postmaidan Ukrainian Authorities, the USA, Euromaidan Protesters, the EU and the Right Sector — are the top five most negatively depicted actors involved in the events of interest.

As mentioned above, the group of Western actors was negatively evaluated in the analysed coverage. Despite this, there were some exceptions when it came to individual actors. The balance of evaluations about Germany and France on Channel One Russia was positive, unlike for the whole Western group or the USA and the EU, which are among the most negatively depicted actors. Additionally, while on Channel One Russia, Germany and France are among the top ten most positively evaluated actors; on RT, those two actors were covered predominately negatively.

Evaluations of international organizations involved in the events of interest also differed on Channel One Russia and RT. The evaluations of those organizations were not frequent due to their limited role in the events of interest. Still, while on RT, organizations such as the European Court of Human Rights, the International Criminal Court, Amnesty International, the Organization for Security and Co-operation in Europe, etc., were either not mentioned or covered positively; on Channel One Russia, the balance of evaluations about these international organizations was negative.

Last but not least regarding the evaluations of particular actors is the depiction of different media, above all Ukrainian and Western. While on Channel One Russia, the balance of evaluations for Ukrainian media is more negative than for Western media, the opposite is true on RT. Both groups — Ukrainian and Western media — are among the most negatively depicted actors on the respective TV channels: Ukrainian media is among the top ten most negatively depicted actors on Channel One Russia, while Western media is among the top ten most negatively depicted actors on RT. The degree of negativity in the depiction of Ukrainian media on Channel One Russia and in the depiction of Western media on RT is similar to the negativity towards NATO on those TV channels respectively.

When Negative Depiction Turns into Strategic Enmification

In short, the analysis revealed that Channel One Russia and RT used enmification while covering the events of interest. This conclusion can be reached by combining existing literature on enemy-construction with the features of the analysed coverage, in particular: (1) Most of the evaluations identified in the news programmes were one-sided — some actors were evaluated almost exclusively positively, others almost exclusively negatively; (2) Evaluations that were not in line with the overall evaluative patterns were often dismissed; (3) One-sided depictions of the actors were kept stable during the analysed period; (4) The black-and-white depictions allow a clear dichotomous division of the evaluated political actors into a positive in-group and a negative out-group.

Studies of enemy construction argue that any in-group is seen as inherently positive and the mere exclusion from it is already the indicator of, at least, mild enmification (Harle, 1994; Leyens et al., 2001; Vuorinen, 2012). Thus, an outsider is already seen in bad light or, as the religion-rooted idiom states, "whoever is not with us is against us". In the case of the analysed coverage, enmified actors were not just outsiders, they were systematically depicted as actors with a negative impact on the specific situation.

Various reasons may lead to enmification. Enmification of some degree may appear under different circumstances; it is not only a distinctive element of non-free media environments where it supports ruling elites by blaming their internal and external opponents. Therefore, saying whether the enmification is strategic and/or politically motivated requires addressing its roots and causes.

Unlike situations when enemies are constructed out of actors that are seen as threatening purely by the regime, enmification may also be used to dispraise actions that are widely seen as threatening and hostile, e.g. those classified as such in line with international law (Bassiouni, 1979). Therefore, when enmification takes place in the media, it is not always exclusively a politically driven campaign; it may also be an instance of a systematic negative evaluation of actors in response to their illegal actions.

Enmification identified in the analysed coverage of the events of interest was not driven by the logic of international law. Although not all the events of interest qualify for legal analysis, in some cases, when legal analysis classified actions of some particular political actors as those violating international law, actors performing those actions were not evaluated negatively in the analysed news programmes. On the contrary, they were often praised for those actions. For instance, while covering the Russia's occupation of the Ukrainian Crimean Peninsula, Channel One Russia and RT evaluated Russian actions positively — as those restoring the safety of locals, achieving historical justice, and establishing an international balance of power (Gardner, 2016; Strycharz, 2020). At the same time, legal analysis of the Crimean events from February–March 2014 clearly identifies three points: that "in the absence of any severe human rights violations against the Russian speaking minority there is no room for an intervention for humanitarian reasons" (Marxsen, 2014, p. 374), that the Russian official framing of Crimean "secession" from Ukraine as a case of self-determination is legally incorrect (van den Driest, 2015), and that the use of Russian military forces in Crimea prior to and after the Annexation qualifies as international aggression against Ukraine (Cwicinskaja, 2017).

These three points show the legal reasons for enmifying Russian actors for the occupation of Crimea, and enmification could have been justified using formal, widely recognised arguments. Instead, Russian state-controlled TV channels constructed enemies out of Ukrainian and Western actors and contributed to the efforts of Russian authorities aiming to legitimize the occupation (Leichtova, 2016). Thus, the enmification identified in the analysed news programmes cannot be explained by the logic of international law.

Similarly, other possible causes of non-strategic and non-politically motivated enmification also do not apply in the analysed media. Some of those causes have been conceptualised in the first part of this book (for details, see the chapter The Role of the Media in Constructing Enemies). The first of those causes is that the market pressure on commercial media outlets may result in the broadcasting of a "catchy negative", leading to systematic negative evaluations of particular political actors. The coverage of the events of interest by the analysed channels is, indeed, based on predominately negative evaluations. However, the market pressure on the state-controlled Channel One Russia and RT is not as strong as that on the purely commercial media outlets, and the financial sustainability of the analysed channels does not directly depend on the number of viewers (Vartanova & Zassoursky, 2003; Wright et al., 2020).

Another possible cause of non-strategic and non-politically motivated enmification is failed gatekeeping—situations when enmifying messages voiced by external speakers are broadcast without suitable framing by anchors and journalists (Wettstein et al., 2018; Jacobs & van Spanje, 2020). The analysis shows that failed gatekeeping is also not the root of enmification on Channel One Russia and RT: anchors and journalists of those channels are, themselves, responsible for the majority of detected negative evaluations. The share of evaluations made by invited experts is also relatively high—especially on RT—and those evaluations also cannot be explained by failed gatekeeping: many of the expert enmifying evaluations are made by the same experts who are repeatedly invited to comment on the conflict. If anchors and journalists wanted to keep the enmifying evaluations voiced by those experts out of the gates, they would not invite them over and over again.

The last cause to be discussed here is that common negative stereotypes towards some social groups or political actors may be reflected in the media coverage of events in which those groups or actors take part. Consequently, such stereotypes may cause negative depiction of the groups or actors. If that were the case for Channel One Russia and RT, systematic negative evaluations detected in the coverage would mirror the negative stereotypes widespread among the public. But this mirroring was not the case, at least when it came to the attitude of Russians towards Ukraine. Negative evaluations of Ukrainian actors on Channel One Russia were the most frequent among all evaluations detected during the analysis.

In contrast, polls showed that at the beginning of the events of interest, in January 2014, the majority of Russians (66%) had a very positive or mostly positive view of Ukraine (Levada Center, 2015). Thus, by depicting Ukrainian actors in a negative light, Channel One Russia did not follow widespread stereotypes; it instead opposed the existing positive attitudes. As people typically prefer information that reflects their pre-existing beliefs (Yan & Liu, 2016), by covering Ukrainian actors negatively, Channel One Russia would probably have risked losing its audience if there had been other popular information sources available to the public. A year later—by January 2015—the predominant view of Ukraine among Russians had turned negative: 64% of Russians had very negative or mostly negative attitudes towards Ukraine (Levada Center, 2015). Therefore, enmification of Ukrainian actors on Channel One Russia during the analysed time frame did not mirror existing negative attitudes but contributed to the appearance of new ones.

An exhaustive list of causes of non-strategic and non-politically motivated enmification taking place in the media has not yet been theorised. Nevertheless, even combining existing ideas with the analysed data shows that the identified enmification does not align with (1) a wish to negatively evaluate political actors in line with current international regulations, (2) a gatekeeping failure, (3) a by-product of commercialization or stereotyping.

The more likely reasons for enmification identified in the analysed news programmes are rooted in the peculiarities of media performance in the state-controlled media environment. In line with the official reasoning, Channel One Russia and RT evaluated Russia positively even when its actions qualified as violating international law. Additionally, they negatively evaluated political actors whose rights were infringed by this violation, and thus helped to justify Russia's actions. Channel One Russia—an internal TV channel that should act as a watchdog—did not criticize Russian authorities for anything they did during the analysed period. Among 2,392 non-dismissed evaluation acts identified in the channel's coverage, two acts included a negative evaluation of Russia, accounting for 0.08%. Sheen (2021) argues that absence of criticism of state authorities is typical when citizens obtain information about policy-making from one source of information, and access to other sources is not available or limited. In such a situation, this "the only" media outlet will no longer be a watchdog of the government but will turn into a "yes man" supporting state authorities (Sheen, 2021, p. 345).

Channel One Russia and RT silenced events that could have led to a negative evaluation of Russian or Russia-affiliated actors, as well as events that could have led to a positive evaluation of their opponents. For example, the channels did not pay attention to the torture or the first deaths of Euromaidan Protesters in January 2014 because the news story devoted to them might have included negative evaluations of the pro-Russian Ukrainian authorities.[30] Silencing even happened to particularly "inappropriate" evaluations voiced on the air — in a couple of cases, such evaluations were cut from the news programmes that had been broadcast on RT at EU prime time and were then not included in the news programme broadcast later in the day (at US prime time). For instance, on December 8, 2013, in RT's weekly news broadcast at EU prime time, RT's journalist Irina Galushko voiced a positive evaluation of Euromaidan Protesters, saying that they were predominately peaceful: "The idea [...] is to show that Ukrainians are ready to be part of Europe and they can protest in a peaceful European manner. Of course, the majority of the people are trying to keep it civil, are keeping it peaceful" (December 8, 2013, RT1, 3:06:02–3:06:12). This particular fragment was cut from the journalist's speech and the news programme broadcast and not included in the US prime time broadcast.

The mentioned patterns of enmification identified on Channel One Russia and RT are in line with the existing studies scrutinizing the channels' dependence on Russian authorities and describing the channels' politically motivated coverage (Borcher, 2011; Khaldarova & Pantti, 2016; Ramsay & Robertshaw, 2019; Elswah & Howard, 2020). In turn, strategic and politically driven enmification

---

30 Use of force in the policing of demonstrations. Prohibition of torture and inhuman or degrading treatment (Article 3) (p. 9). (2021). European Court of Human Rights. https://www.echr.coe.int/Documents/FS_Force_demonstrations_ENG.pdf

campaigns are typical of autocracies where the state-controlled media environment turns the media into an effective regime-supporting tool (Siebert et al., 1984; Dukalskis & Patane, 2019).

***

Many more negative evaluations than positive ones were detected both on Channel One Russia and on RT. This higher negative frequency indicates that the analysed channels applied a negativistic approach when covering the conflict: the internal TV channel specifically focused on delegitimation of political actors confronting the Russian ruling elites (Dukalskis & Patane, 2019), while the analysed international broadcaster tried to incite its audience "to hate the enemies of Russia" instead of trying to persuade them "to love Russia" (Rawnsley, 2015; Połońska-Kimunguyi & Gillespie, 2016). Who were those enmified opponents and confronters? I address this question in more detail on the following pages.

Even though successful enmification has general political effects, when implemented, it should be concrete and narrowly focused, i.e. directed at particular actors (Rieber & Kelly, 1991). In the Channel One Russia and RT coverage, two groups of political actors were depicted as enemies: Ukrainian actors were depicted worst, followed by less negatively depicted Western actors. The particular negative features and the degree of enmity attributed to those groups are discussed in the next chapter of the book in more detail. Suffice it to say here that the much higher intensity of negative evaluations towards Ukrainian actors already permits the conclusion that they were the channels' main target of enmification (Dillon et al., 1977; Wanta et al., 2004).

Notably, this conclusion does not align with the widespread labelling of the analysed events of interest as a confrontation between Russia and the West. There is political and scientific consensus that the Russia vs. the West confrontation is definitely a part of the confrontation during Euromaidan, occupation of Crimea and the first months of the war in Donetsk and Luhansk regions of Ukraine. However, there is ambivalence on whether this confrontation is the core one.

If the analysed media had followed this Russia vs. the West logic, it would have ignored the influence of Ukrainian actors and would have created a cleavage between "most positive Russia" and "most negative West" (or "most negative USA"). A similar approach is widespread in the communication by Russian officials, social scientists, and beyond. For example, Piskulov (2015) frames the analysed time frame as a "US-provoked crisis in Ukraine" (p. 4). In his paper "Russia and the West: Conflict of Interests or a new Cold War", Ivanov (2017) writes that the USA orchestrated a crisis in Ukraine to weaken Russia. China-based Neuwirth and Svetlicinii (2016) also call the events happening in Ukraine during the analysed period an "international conflict over Ukraine" (p. 237). Therefore, Ukraine itself is seen by many as an object of global struggle happening on or even over its territory, rather than as a fully-fledged actor.

Scholars analysing media coverage of the events of interest also discovered similar narratives in the Russian state-controlled media: Hinck and colleagues (2018) conclude that Russian media depict Postmaidan Ukrainian Authorities as no more than "'fascist' and illegitimate, put in place by the West to undermine the nation's solidarity with Russia" (p. 34). In their study, Khaldarova and Pantti (2016) reveal the negative depiction of Western actors broadcast by Channel One Russia while pointing to the negative depiction of Ukrainian actors as another significant element of the coverage.

The current enmification analysis makes it possible to rank the importance of those two elements (enmification of Ukrainian actors and of Western actors) for the overall picture of enmity constructed by the analysed media. The list of the top five actors with the most negative evaluation balance does not include the West or NATO. Although it does include the USA and the EU, neither of them is in top position. This enmification structure in the Russian state-controlled media would have been different if the Russian authorities had seen the conflict primarily as a struggle between Russia and the West over Ukraine: it seems contradictory to devote more negative evaluations to "the satellite" of the main enemy than to the main enemy itself. The enmification of the USA, which is second on the list of negatively depicted actors, and enmification of other Western actors are significant elements of the coverage and should by no means be downplayed. However, they are not the most significant elements when it comes to enmification on Channel One Russia and RT in the analysed period.

Such conclusions can be explained by the peculiarities of the coding process, in particular by the separate coding of negative evaluations about the West, the USA, the EU, NATO, etc. and suggest that negativity towards all of them should be coded under one category. The possible argument could be that, by framing conflict as Russia vs. the West, Russian authorities simultaneously refer to all of those actors, and therefore they have to be coded together. But even when negative evaluations of all these Western actors are calculated together, the number of negative evaluations about them is still smaller than the number of negative evaluations of just one most negatively depicted Ukrainian actor — the Postmaidan Ukrainian Authorities.

Similarly, Russian officials and some Russian scholars state that Maidan was orchestrated by the West, especially by the EU, which is considered the main beneficiary of the Association Agreement. In particular, protests on Maidan are often framed by those officials and scholars as "attempts [...] to influence president [Yanukovych] in order to make him change position and sign the agreement that is enslaving Ukraine. As a result, Brussels should have, in fact, obtained the right to control Ukraine economically and politically" (Svechnikov & Filyukov, 2014, p. 24).[31] If they had simply been an anti-Ukrainian tool in the hands of the EU, the protesters would probably have attracted much less negative media attention than the EU itself. However, the number of negative evaluations in the analysed media about those two actors does not support this conclusion: Maidan protesters were negatively evaluated more often than was the EU.

Thus, a comparison of the knowledge on typical Russian narratives with the insights on enmification in the Russian state-con-

---

31   All translations from non-English language sources are my own.

trolled media reveals a principal difference between them and potentially contributes to a fuller picture of the Russian communication strategy on the events of interest. While Russian officials, scholars, and media (including the analysed outlets) argue that the Maidan protesters and Postmaidan Ukrainian Authorities are fully dependent on external hostile powers, the structure of enmification identified in the analysed broadcasts shows that those Ukrainian actors were treated as enemies of full value. As the communication functions of narratives and of enmification differ, such a distinction is easy to explain.

Using strategic narratives, Russia could frame events in Ukraine in accordance with its communication goals: to depict Russia as a great power confronting Western attempts to undermine its influence in Ukraine — the primordial territory of Russian interests (Miskimmon & O'Loughlin, 2017). Ukrainian actors themselves could not be called enemies in such a scheme as it would require granting them at least some degree of sovereignty. Additionally, framing its actions in Crimea and in the Donetsk and Luhansk regions of Ukraine as challenging the West but not Ukraine, Russia aims to challenge the political actor of higher international status and consequently to raise its own status (Wolf, 2019). Enmification, however, serves another goal: to construct hostile attitudes toward a full spectrum of actors confronting Russia, and, according to the analysed media coverage, Ukrainian actors appeared to be at the top of the "blacklist".

Unlike most Ukrainian and Western actors including the EU, neither Germany nor France was on the "blacklist", at least not on Channel One Russia. In this aspect, the structure of enmification echoes Russian strategic narratives. One of those narratives is about the possibility of the "Common European Home" from Lisbon to Vladivostok with Russia as its main power. Such a "Home" from the Atlantic to the Pacific would please Russian officials much more than the existence of the EU, not least because the EU strengthens the Euro-Atlantic geopolitical hegemony (Darczewska, 2014; Casier, 2018). In line with this, the actual and potential EU enlargement in eastern Europe has been seen and communicated by Russia in analogy to the actual and potential enlargement of NATO — as an action challenging Russian international aspiration (Miskimmon & O'Loughlin, 2017). However, for Germany and France, there was hope of softer politics towards Russia. Additionally, not everything was (is) lost for Russia in regard to the relations of Germany and France with the EU, especially in light of pro-Russian Eurosceptic political parties gaining some degree of public support in both countries (Golosov, 2020; Snegovaya, 2021).

A further similarity between enmification and Russian narratives also manifests itself in the enmity networks identified in the analysed media broadcasts. The strongest of the identified networks reflected in the data relate to the EU-US pair and deepen the Russian "International System Narrative"[32] on the hostile Euro-Atlantic hegemony (Gerber & Zavisca, 2016). The pair USA–Postmaidan Ukrainian Authorities is also a noticeable one, especially on Channel One Russia; that is in line with the Russian "Issue narrative" on the dependence of Ukraine on the USA and the West (Khaldarova & Pantti, 2016).

In contrast, positive networks detected in the data do not fully correspond to the Russian narratives and to the cleavage between the "positive Russia" and the "negative West". The analysed coverage showed that many of collective positive actions were made by Russia together with Germany, France, the United Kingdom and sometimes even with the EU or the USA, e.g. when it came to the attempts to "calm tensions" in Ukraine. In the situation when events in Ukraine lead to the increasing isolation of Russia both economically and politically (Engle, 2014), the construction of such networks could support Russia's claim that Russia was not putting itself behind the iron curtain; instead, it was actively trying to stop the violence in Ukraine. In addition, the channels rarely praise Russia for actions taken together with Russia-affiliated actors, possibly because that praise could undermine Russia's international prestige in the viewers' eyes. For example, a potential spreading of a fictional message such as[33] "Cuba, North Korea, Syria, Venezuela and

---

32 For a classification of narratives, see Roselle et al., 2014.
33 This fictional message is of my creation, but it includes real examples of countries that recognized the results of the sham referendum in Crimea in March

other countries supporting Russian actions in Crimea are the only ones who see the situation on the peninsula in all its historical fullness and therefore support the Annexation" would probably not be beneficial for the Russian authorities because of the limited influence and the controversial image those Russia-affiliated actors have in the international arena.

The identified structure of enmification could serve as an additional argument in favour of framing the analysed conflict as Russian-Ukrainian rather than Russian-Western. Even though the covered events definitely include the global confrontation between Russia and the West, the analysis of the Russian state-controlled media shows that, throughout the whole period, neither the collective West nor any Western actors were seen as the main enemy. This finding is supported, not least, by the fact that when it comes to the analysed data, the Russian state-controlled media invested most of its time and effort in enmifying Ukrainian actors.

Furthermore, this analysis adds to the theoretical knowledge on enemy construction and related topics. For example, the empirical study at hand deepens the theoretical understanding of the enmification concept itself. Rieber and Kelly (1991) stated that enmification is always detailed and focused on particular actor(s). By analysing well-structured and systematic enmification campaigns such as those performed by traditional media outlets, scholars may not only define particular actors that were the main targets of the enmification but also define the intensity of each actor's hostile communication.

A further empirically informed theoretical point is the existence of ties between a state's strategic narratives and state-controlled enmification. If the knowledge from the two is combined, it may help reveal insights on what is silenced by the dominating narratives. For instance, when a state seeks the status of a great power, it requires enemies of appropriate international status (Wolf, 2019). However, the political actors challenging interests of this state are

---

2014. This fictional message aims to illustrate how different the enmity networks created by the analysed channels could have been compared to the actual ones.

not necessarily of that desired status. In such cases, a state's strategic narratives would not correspond to state-controlled enmification. In short, if theorists of strategic narratives paid attention to enmification, they could address in more depth all types of international confrontations. The practical question arising from the findings, indicating that Ukraine was the primary target of Russia's hostile communication as early as 2013-2014, is whether Russian aggression against Ukraine was ever about NATO, the USA, or the EU, or if it was always about Ukraine being an independent state determining its internal and international politics.

And, last but not least: the constructivist approach to international relations (Wendt, 1995; Onuf, 2013) as well as to journalistic performance (Pörksen et al., 2011) implies that there are multiple ways of covering each particular international issue in the media. Theorists of securitization add that no situation is problematic by itself and, analogically, no actor or action is negative by definition (Buzan et al., 1998). Therefore, political actors enmified in the analysed news stories could have received opposite assessments if the Russian communication goals had been different.

So far, most of the discussed patterns of enmification were true both for Channel One Russia and RT, but the circumstances in which the two were operating differed in many aspects. The next section addresses those aspects in detail and focuses on the way they influenced the enmification identified in the analysed broadcasts.

Differences in Enmification on Channel One Russia and RT

The two analysed channels constitute the pair of internal mass media and the international broadcaster. Therefore, peculiarities of enmification identified in the analysed broadcasts should mirror the more general and universal peculiarities of the respective media types. As discussed in the first part of the book, independent internal mass media and international broadcasters generally differ in their goals and audiences. In contrast, the goals of state-controlled mass media and international broadcasters mostly overlap — to fulfil a government's communication needs (Wood, 1994; Fuchs, 2018). In earlier studies, Channel One Russia is unequivocally referred to as the state-controlled media outlet (e.g. Hansen, 2015; Khaldarova & Pantti, 2016). In line with this, the goals of the analysed channels are expected to be similar, unlike their viewers. Therefore, differences in enmification identified on Channel One Russia and RT are expected to be rooted in differences between the channels' audiences. Both channels have to make their coverage appropriate for their recipients because, by making their news programmes as widely watched and trusted as possible, the channels maximize their usefulness to the Russian regime.

The identified differences in enmification are listed and discussed in line with the proposed audience-centred approach. Standardized content analysis revealed significant differences in the following aspects of enmification identified on Channel One Russia and RT:

- Actors of enmification. On Channel One Russia, journalists were the main actors of enmification, followed by anchors of the news programme. On RT, the situation was the opposite. Additionally, on RT, experts played a significantly more important role in enmification than on Channel One Russia;
- Targets of enmification. RT was significantly more critical towards Western actors than was Channel One Russia;
- Pluralism of evaluations. Channel One Russia offered its audience less pluralistic coverage than did RT. Consequently, on Channel One Russia, a smaller number of evaluations were dismissed.

Actors of Enmification. Systematic negative evaluations voiced by journalists and anchors of Channel One Russia and RT constitute a similar enmification structure, i.e. identified differences in enmification on the two channels do not seem to be content-related. In contrast, even a glance at the analysed weekly news programmes reveals the noticeable differences in the programmes' formats, which influence the roles of journalists and anchors. Therefore, detected differences in enmification may also be rooted in the peculiarities of the programmes' formats, making the programmes better suited to the channels' respective target audiences.

To a great extent, Channel One Russia follows the Soviet style of news reporting while RT's news reporting is in a more Western style. News programmes on Channel One Russia are well planned and structured; most of the elements are prepared in advance to enable control of the content (Evans, 2016). Even though each period of Soviet and Russian news reporting can be linked with the most known and respected anchor, formally, the role of the anchor in the news programme is limited to announcing what the next news story will be about. It leaves anchors less space for enmification than, for example, journalists have.

Unlike those of the anchors, journalists' statements are directly included in the news stories they create. News stories broadcast on Channel One Russia are often quite long; basically, many of them are pre-made short films lasting for more than 10 minutes. Such a news reporting format contributes to the intense presence of journalists on the air and makes journalists of Channel One Russia responsible for half of all evaluations detected in the respective broadcasts. The long duration of news stories enables repetitions of the main messages during a particular news story and beyond.

Additionally, to watch a whole weekly news programme of Channel One Russia, one has to devote more than an hour of Sunday evening, something scholars studying the history of news broadcasting in the post-Soviet region identify as typical. Such a habit goes back to Soviet times, when people planning TV programming for the weekend treated Sunday as "the second day of rest, when viewers are able, after some time to unwind, to devote a large part of their leisure time to expanding their worldview and deepening their knowledge" (Evans, 2016, pp. 74–75). A weekly news programme on Channel One Russia is not a classic educational programme, but it definitely contributes to the viewers' political education in a way that is fruitful for the ruling political regime (Lukyanova, 2018).

Compared to Channel One Russia, RT has much less in common with the news reporting of the Soviet style, at least in the format of its news programmes. RT, like CGTN — a Chinese international broadcaster — successfully made their news broadcasting look Western:

> [they] have adopted familiar [for the Western viewer] news formats, conventions and protocols that help attract audiences and make them feel comfortable. While wishing to present an alternative to CNN, Al-Jazeera and the BBC, RT and CCTV-N [CGTN] have appropriated their characteristics, even employing foreign reporters, anchors and commentators to reinforce their respectability and legitimacy. (Rawnsley, 2015, p. 284)

In line with the more flexible Western style of news reporting, RT's anchors are more visible during the news programme than Channel One Russia anchors. On RT, anchors play the central role in the news programme; they directly participate in content-creating by revealing the news in detail, interviewing experts, communicating with the channel's journalists, with most reporting happening live. Furthermore, RT journalists regularly prepare on-scene coverage and analytical pieces, making them responsible for a considerable part of the enmifying messages voiced on RT.

As stated above, not only do the roles of journalists and anchors differ on Channel One Russia and RT but also the role of invited experts, who are more noticeable in the RT broadcasts. Merkley (2020) indicates that the main task of experts in news programmes includes revealing background knowledge on the issue and helping journalists interpret the covered event. At the same time, by inviting experts, channels partly give up responsibility for the voiced statements and thus make the channels appear more impartial than if similar statements had been voiced by the channel's anchors or journalists (Albæk, 2011). Sharing responsibility could be an even more fruitful approach when it comes to negative evaluations. Invited experts are presented as professionals in the field and should be seen as objective commentators. Therefore, criticism towards any political actors voiced by experts seems more reliable, and the channels that include such critical comments in their programmes may avoid being blamed for bias.

Coverage of the Russian-Ukrainian conflict on Channel One Russia and RT was predefined by the communication needs of Russian elites. Therefore, the channels' need of help from independent experts in making sense of covered events was, most likely, relatively low. Instead, sharing with experts the responsibility for criticism towards actors confronting Russia could be an attractive strategy, especially when it comes to broadcasting in Western countries, where RT does not enjoy the reliability that Channel One Russia enjoys among its viewers. A closer look at the evaluations made by experts on RT supports such an interpretation: the majority of all evaluations voiced by experts are negative statements about Western actors. They help RT be as critical towards Western actors as needed but appear a bit more impartial so as not to dissuade Western recipients from watching RT news.

Targets of Enmification. Despite some differences in the enmification structure identified on Channel One Russia and RT, its base remains unchanged for both channels and serves as the fundament on which the channels build audience-targeted, nuanced coverage of the Euromaidan, occupation of Crimea and the first months of the war in Donetsk and Luhansk regions of Ukraine. Therefore, before addressing the differences, the common features should be briefly mentioned again. These features include the intense enmification of Ukrainian actors and the less intense enmification of Western ones and a contrasting of negative evaluations of Ukrainian and Western actors with a positive depiction of Russian and Russia-affiliated actors. Within this common frame, enmification of Western actors is more considerable on RT than on Channel One Russia. This aspect is now discussed in more detail.

As stated above, the predominance of negative evaluations about Ukrainian and Western actors and the much smaller share of positive evaluations about Russian and Russia-affiliated actors on RT is sufficient for the conclusion that the Russian international broadcaster applies the negativistic strategy of public diplomacy (i.e. "to hate our enemies") while covering the events of interest. Furthermore, the details of how RT evaluates Western actors while broadcasting for the Western audience is a considerable addition to the understanding of this strategy.

The citizens of "Western countries" are the target audience of RT's weekly news programmes going live at EU and US prime time. Therefore, by enmifying Western actors such as the USA, the EU, NATO, Barack Obama, Angela Merkel, etc., RT can potentially decrease public support of Western politicians or even of whole political entities confronting Russia in the course of the analysed events.

Pluralism of Evaluations. The analysis showed that RT's coverage was more pluralistic than the coverage on Channel One Russia, i.e. on RT there were more evaluations that opposed the dominant patterns. For example, in the analysed coverage, the Russian international broadcaster was more critical toward Russia than the internal TV channel. In democratic settings, the situation should be opposite (Zöllner, 2006; Gilboa, 2008).

Previous studies have shown RT as dependent on Russian elites and on fulfilling their communication goals (e.g. Borcher, 2011; Geniets, 2013; Elswah & Howard, 2020). Thus, some critical statements about Russian authorities broadcast on RT do not seem to reflect the unbiased coverage that the channel wishes to suggest to its audience. In fact, it might even be fruitful for Russian elites that, occasionally, RT lets the negative evaluations of Russian actors be voiced because, in doing so, RT looks more balanced. Such an approach can increase the chances that RT's viewers would consider dominant strategic negative evaluations of Ukrainian and Western actors as being trustworthy, i.e. some degree of criticism towards Russia might make RT's hostile communication about Russia's opponents more successful.

The analysis of the dismissed evaluations revealed that there could be other communication needs requiring RT to criticize Russia. While the Russian internal media environment is under state control, Western viewers of RT live in pluralistic media environments. Therefore, the RT audience is most likely aware of widespread accusations against Russia. As a result, unlike Channel One Russia, RT has to react to the accusations most known to its audience.

Indeed, almost all *dismissed* evaluations identified in RT's broadcast are positive evaluations about Ukrainian and Western actors and negative ones about Russia and Russia-affiliated actors.

Such a finding suggests that evaluations criticizing Russia might have been included in the broadcast primarily to be dismissed, i.e. to show that those evaluations are not trustworthy, the same as speakers spreading criticism. A similar strategy may also be used by independent media to dismiss unscientific or stereotypical messages on the topics of high social importance (Brüggemann & Engesser, 2017). However, in the analysed case, RT used this strategy to dismiss evaluations blaming Russia for its actions. This RT strategy can be seen as an attempt to beat the enemy using its own weapon: it took enmifying messages voiced by Western media and Western politicians, framed them according to its needs and used them to weaken enmification of Russia and to challenge the reliability of the actors spreading those messages among the Western public. Similar approaches were not applied by Channel One Russia on a comparable scale because a controlled media environment prevents unwanted messages from appearing in the public discourse; consequently, there is no need to root them out.

To sum up, differences are visible in the enmification of Ukrainian and Western actors on Channel One Russia and RT. There are also differences in the channels' reactions to popular messages enmifying Russian actors. As both channels are dependent on the Russian ruling elite and help it in achieving its communication goals, those differences may be explained by the channels taking different routes to adapt to their target audiences.

The identified differences are not typical of mass media and international broadcasters and are not widely discussed. The conducted analysis showed that, for state-controlled mass media and a state-controlled international broadcaster, audience matters the most. The audiences can force international broadcasters of autocracies to imitate impartiality and balanced coverage, making the international broadcaster at least slightly more pluralistic and balanced than their internal counterparts. However, generalization of conclusions on this aspect requires more studies comparing internal media and international broadcasters of autocratic states.

Evolution of Enmification Over the Analysed Time Period

Scholars typically divide the analysed time period into three main stages: (1) during the Euromaidan (end of November 2013–February 2014); (2) from the end of the Euromaidan till the occupation of Crimea (end of February 2014–March 2014); (3) from the beginning of the violence in the east of Ukraine (from April 2014) (Roman et al., 2017; Lichtenstein et al., 2019). The current study is focused on the first nine months of these events, which is why the enmification during the third period is analysed until the beginning of September 2014 (until the signing of the First Minsk Agreement).

Even though each of the periods may be further detailed, in this section, the division into three main stages serves as a basis to compare the enmification identified in the coverage of the analysed TV channels. The more nuanced turning points of the conflict are discussed in the next chapter. It is also important to underline that the features discussed in this section in regard to each period are not necessarily the *major* characteristics of enmification in those periods but the *distinctive* features—nuances in which the three periods differ from one another. The other characteristics of enmification that apply to the whole time frame are mentioned above in this chapter.

First Period. Among the distinctive features of the coverage in the first period is that the channels then paid less attention to events happening in Ukraine than during the later periods. Consequently, the number of statements enmifying Ukrainian and Western actors during the mass protests in Kyiv also was much lower than later, when the larger share of the weekly news programmes was devoted to the events of interest.

An earlier study of Russian media has revealed that Russian state-controlled TV channels typically silence anti-government movements and do not cover topics about opposition politicians (Kazun, 2019). During the first period, when mass rallies in Ukraine were confronting the pro-Russian government and the president, the analysed channels seemed to use a similar strategy—they depicted protests as a minor event and paid them little attention.

As argued in the first part of the book, the more attention is paid to a political issue in the media, the more important that issue becomes for the audience's national interests and sense of security (Wanta et al., 2004). In turn, theorists of securitization argue that the more important the issue is for the public, the easier it is to frame this "issue of supreme priority" as a threat and the actors involved as enemies (Buzan et al., 1998, p. 26). In November 2013–February 2014, Russian state-controlled channels did not cover the events of the Euromaidan intensively. Does this suggest that those events were not seen as important and that Russian officials did not perceive them as a threat, at least not to the extent they did with the events of the further periods of interest, which received intense coverage? Despite the limited attention of the channels to the Euromaidan, there are at least three arguments against that assumption.

First, in accordance with the Russian strategic narratives, Panarin[34] also framed the events as a confrontation between Russia and the West. He stated that the Euromaidan was an "anti-Russian campaign artificially planned by the West" and was therefore threatening for Russia (quoted in Darczewska, 2014, p. 17). Second, Putin keeps the Ukrainian events of February 2014 on the agenda and repeatedly reminds the public that in his opinion the then-Ukrainian president Yanukovych has been violently removed from power (Putin, 2021). This repeated reminder makes it hard to explain the cursory attention of Russian state-controlled media to those very events in the time when they were happening. Third, public polls conducted among Russian citizens in the spring of 2014 showed that the removal of Yanukovych from power and the shift of political power in Ukraine to the pro-Maidan authorities were among the major topics of concern for Russians.

Surprisingly, the importance of February's events in the eyes of Russians only grew with time. In accordance with the Levada Center's poll conducted at the end of March 2014, the events in question were sixth in the ranking of the most recollected recent events, way behind the sham referendum in Crimea, the Winter

---

34 Russian scholar, one of the founders of the Information Security Doctrine of the Russian Federation.

Olympics, etc. (Levada Center, 2014a) At the end of April 2014, the Ukrainian February events shifted to seventh place (Levada Center, 2014b). However, in May 2014, February's change of authorities in Kyiv topped the ranking, leaving behind even the "accession"[35] of Crimea to Russia and the Winter Olympics (Levada Center, 2014c). Those polls' results correspond to the finding that the state-controlled Channel One Russia briefly told its viewers about the change of authorities in Ukraine when it happened but paid excessive attention to those events in the following months, thus allowing the enmification based on the events of the Euromaidan to also be in place after the end of the protests.

Instead of focusing on Ukrainian events, in February 2014, the analysed channels were busy covering the Winter Olympics in Russia. At first sight, the Olympics do not seem to be connected to enmification arising from the Euromaidan events, except for attracting the attention of journalists and viewers and distracting the attention from the protests. However, that was not necessarily the case. Scholars call the hosting of sports mega-events, such as the Olympics or FIFA World Cup, the chance to promote the country on the international arena and strengthen the national sentiment among the domestic public (Finlay & Xin, 2010; Grix & Lee, 2013).

Therefore, in February 2014, Russian state-controlled media had valuable support in the task of promoting Russian elites both at home and abroad. However, the strategy of Russian soft power in addressing the mega-event differed from the typical approaches that combine internal and external promotion: Putin's regime focused not on public diplomacy but on cultivating national pride among the domestic public (Grix & Kramareva, 2017). As a result, the Olympics made Russians even more receptive to the enmification of any "others", at the very least because it helped to accentuate the Russian in-group pride (Fuchs, 2018).

Therefore, during the first period of the conflict, when the developments of the Euromaidan protests were hard to predict and when Russian state-media had other strategically important topics

---

35   As the occupation is called in the cited poll.

to report, coverage of the conflict was not the major topic on Channel One Russia or RT. As a result, enmification identified during this period is also less intense than in later stages. Nevertheless, when covered, the events of the Euromaidan served as a basis for a typical black-and-white depiction of political actors involved in the covered events: positive Russia and actors affiliated with it vs. the negative Ukrainian and Western actors.

Importantly, events happening in Ukraine during the first period of the conflict became a traditional topic for blaming and enmifying actors confronting Russia. Russian officials still explain the confrontation of Russia with Ukraine and the West referring to the events of Euromaidan, and this tendency seems set for years to come.

Second Period. The second stage of the events of interest lasted for less than a month, but enmification during this period also has its distinctive features. In the period between the end of Euromaidan and the occupation of Crimea, Russian state-controlled media simultaneously had to react to the rapidly changing political situation and to prepare its audience for the shifts planned by the Russian authorities. Both aspects were addressed with the help of enmification.

The end of the Euromaidan was unfavourable for the Russian regime as it resulted in the removal of the pro-Russian Ukrainian authorities from power. Four days after Yanukovych fled to Russia, Russian Special Operations Forces seized the Crimean parliament. Later that day, deputies of the peninsula's parliament announced the so-called "referendum" on the status of Crimea. As a result of those events, the Crimean Peninsula was illegally annexed by Russia.

Any discussion on the prerequisites of the occupation includes the topics of the Russian sense of security and national interests, such as confrontation with NATO and the question of the Russian Black Sea Fleet, etc. (Delanoe, 2014; Mearsheimer, 2014; Gardner, 2016). In contrast, the issue of Russian national identity is not the typical aspect touched upon when talking about March 2014. There are some exceptions to this rule (Teper, 2016; Forsberg & Pursiainen, 2017), but in general, experts rarely focus on a crisis of Russian self-perception caused by "a loss" of Ukraine as a result of the Euromaidan. Still, this identity crisis was one of the problems Russia tried to influence by annexing Crimea and by enmifying political actors confronting Russia on this course.

The first thing Putin said about Crimea in his post-Annexation speech in order to illustrate that it is a territory imbued with Russian history and pride was that Volodymyr (the Kyivan duke) was baptised in Crimea and, by this, determined the development of Ukrainians, Belarusians, and Russians as orthodox folks (Putin, 2014). A couple of years after the occupation of Crimea, a monument to Volodymyr was erected near the walls of the Kremlin. Those nuances may pass unnoticed, but without them the understanding of enmification performed by Russian state-controlled TV channels in March 2014 cannot be complete.

As mentioned, Russian national identity is built upon the idea that the political power of the medieval Kyivan Rus shifted from Kyiv to Moscow and that there, the state developed into modern-day Russia that should have Ukraine as a part or at least a territory of influence. Therefore, losing control over Ukraine and admitting that Ukraine is a separate national entity, Russia loses the national perception of Russian statehood's history (D'Anieri, 1997). In February 2014, Russia lost the previous degree of control over Ukraine. However, within a month it gained full control over the place where the Russian tradition of Christianity is said to be rooted, a major achievement for Russia especially in light of the growing role of religion in Russian political life (Agadjanian, 2017). At the same time, the Russian authorities never admitted that distancing itself from Russia was a desire of Ukrainians; instead, Euromaidan Protesters, Ukrainian governmental and non-governmental actors confronting Russia were called fascists and said to be fully dependent on the West (Hinck et al., 2018).

The couple of weeks in March 2014 are the rare exception when the Western group of actors got the worst depiction, both on Channel One Russia and RT. Such an approach to enmification applied by those channels corresponds to the above-discussed Russian claim that Ukrainians cannot desire to distance themselves from Russia. Additionally, predominant enmification of Western actors in this short but important period is a way to save face and to argue that Russia is strong enough to react to the Euromaidan outcomes, framed by Russian officials as being orchestrated by the West.

As mentioned in the findings, the two channels did not positively depict the same groups of political actors during this conflict period. On RT, actors such as Crimean self-defence were the most positively evaluated ones, possibly because this channel tried to frame the Crimean events as the initiative of locals. In contrast, on Channel One Russia, Russian actors were the most positively evaluated ones, presumably to assure Russians that the Russian regime was protecting Crimeans from what it called the post-Maidan "junta" (Samokhvalov, 2015; Khaldarova & Pantti, 2016) and was trying to unite the "divided [Russian] nation" at least by bringing back the "compatriots" living in Crimea (Laruelle, 2015, p. 88).

To a great extent, enmification of the second period served to save the face of the Russian regime during the turbulent political conditions. Despite existing challenges, the rankings of the occupation's approval among Russians prove the success of the domestic communication of the issue (Levada Center, 2021). The same cannot be said for RT, but the enmification applied by RT during the second period of the conflict also had a potential to somehow minimize Russia's loses and to blame "others" for the events happening in March 2014; such a strategy could work, at least for RT's western viewers with some degree of Russian sentiment.

Third Period. Unlike during the two previous stages, enmification performed by Channel One Russia and RT after the beginning of the violence in Donbas is predominately based on the evaluation acts with a focus on morality. Such a finding is not surprising, as an earlier study already showed that the Russian media often refer to morality, e.g. when covering the Euromaidan; this trend is especially noticeable in comparison to the coverage of the same events by Western media (Liu, 2020). Therefore, it was predictable that Channel One Russia and RT would intensively use a moral focus in evaluation acts voiced in their weekly news programmes. This trend was noticeable right from the first weeks of Euromaidan, especially in the Channel One Russia coverage. The peculiarity of the third period is that the focus of negative evaluations on morality turned from noticeable to dominant.

Even though the perception of (im)moral actions may differ to some extent depending on an observer's religion or mentality, the main patterns in evaluating (im)moral behaviour are more or less universal because basic moral maxims are common to all mankind (Cohen & Rozin, 2001). In contrast, issues of politics, economics, etc., include rational reasoning and imply that the perception of the information grounded in those issues varies based on a recipient's partisanship. As a result, constructing an enemy based on claims about its immorality is most likely a win-win approach regardless of a viewer's beliefs.

In addition to that comparative advantage, the focus on morality has particular content-related implications in the enmification process. Morality is a perfect tool for in- and out-group categorization, as "morality is the strongest dimension with which individuals define themselves in terms of group membership, [. . .] and belonging" (Pacilli et al., 2016, p. 364). Being based on universal maxims, morality helps to hostilely depict any political actor to whom immoral actions or characteristics are systematically assigned.

Bandura (2002) argues that such moral disengagement leads to the dehumanization of the affected ones, causing further psychological effects: "[o]nce dehumanised, they are no longer viewed as persons with feelings, hopes and concerns but as sub-human objects" (p. 109). Experimental study on the perception of crimes also showed that the level of moral outrage is positively associated with the dehumanization of offenders (Bastian et al., 2013). In line with those scientific conclusions, I assume that attribution of immorality to actors confronting Russia in the analysed conflict could contribute to the dehumanization of those actors and might even be done with such a dehumanizing goal in mind.

The analysis revealed that Ukrainian actors were at the blunt end of more than 80% of the non-dismissed negative evaluations focused on morality and voiced during the third conflict period on Channel One Russia and RT. The conclusion is thus permissible that Ukrainian actors were the main target of this kind of enmification.

The political implications of the aired focus on immorality might differ depending on the channels' audiences. In the eyes of the Russian authorities, the distance of the Western RT viewers from the fight in Donbas meant that the best that those viewers could do was to become supporters of the "(pro-)Russian" side and confronters of the Ukrainian actors (Jones et al., 2002).

In contrast, the *physical fight* against the Ukrainian army and Ukrainian volunteer battalions on the battlefields was among the potential tasks of Russian citizens watching Channel One Russia[36] and of other Russian-speaking viewers of this channel (in this case especially of those based in the east of Ukraine). The focus on the immorality of Ukrainian actors in the analysed news coverage and their dehumanization could help motivate viewers to fight (Bruneau & Kteily, 2017), justify violence (Alleyne et al., 2014), or even make violence against them appear a duty (Giner-Sorolla at al., 2011). Closer attention to the features of Channel One Russia's news coverage having the potential to mobilize the channels' viewers for the physical fight against the Ukrainian army is paid in the next chapter.

To conclude, the findings of this analysis mostly correspond to the findings and conclusions of the earlier studies, first and foremost in the political dependence of both channels on the Russian state: paradigms of media performance of authoritarian states explain tendencies and patterns of enmification identified in the analysed coverage much better than do the paradigms of free media performance.

Western scholars often criticize RT for being unbalanced and for serving the communication goals of the Russian elites. The current comparative study of RT and Channel One Russia details those criticisms. When it came to the coverage of the events of interest and to the enmification of political actors involved in it, the two

---

36 This conclusion from the pre-full-scale invasion period is no longer in question in the days when hundreds of thousands of Russian soldiers are attempting to occupy Ukraine.

channels offered their viewers black-and-white news coverage creating a clear dichotomy between positively depicted Russian and Russia-affiliated actors and negatively depicted Ukrainian and Western actors.

At the same time, the current study shows that, where RT differed from Channel One Russia, RT was significantly more balanced and more critical towards Russian authorities than the country's internal TV channel. However, less extreme enmification identified in the RT coverage is most likely rooted not in the higher degree of independence that RT enjoys compared to Channel One Russia but in the more pluralistic media environment in which RT functions.

In turn, the share of positive and negative evaluations identified on RT allows the conclusion that the channel applies a negativistic strategy of public diplomacy: instead of making the international audience "love Russia", it tries to make the audience "hate Russia's enemies". Even though a similar share of negative evaluations was identified in Channel One Russia, in this particular aspect, the RT case is of greater interest. While Channel One Russia behaves as a typical state-controlled media outlet of an autocracy, RT combines two features – (1) full political dependence on the ruling elites and (2) a negativistic strategy of coverage – making RT a unique communication tool compared to the international broadcasters of other states.

Despite a similar input, the influence of the channels on their audiences was different. The analysis did not address the audiences' perceptions of the coverage. Nevertheless, polls on public attitudes allow an insight into whether the structure of enmification identified in the analysed coverage corresponds to public attitudes. In 2014, Channel One Russia was the main source of news about the events of interest for the vast majority of Russians and was seen by them as a reliable and objective source (Volkov & Goncharov, 2014). Therefore, the 2014 shifts in the Russian public's attitudes towards Ukraine from positive to negative have its roots in the analysed coverage on Channel One Russia, the same as worsening attitudes towards Western actors.

In January 2014, 17% of Russians saw relations between Russia and the USA as tense or hostile; in January 2015, that percentage grew to 79%. For the Russia-EU relations, the same indicator shifted from 10% to 65%; for the Russia-Ukraine relations from 22% to 81% (Levada Center, 2015). When combined with growing support for the Russian regime in the same period, those numbers perfectly match Channel One Russia's depictions of political actors involved in the analysed events and clearly indicate the success of the enmification campaign performed by Channel One Russia.

In general, RT's input into the construction of positive and negative attitudes was similar to that of Channel One Russia, unlike the influence of that input on the public opinion of RT's audiences. Despite RT's efforts, the attitude towards Russia among US citizens and citizens of EU member states worsened in 2014 compared to 2013 (Pew Research Center, 2014). It might be hard to believe, but still nothing is completely lost for Russia regarding its communication abroad even after the beginning of full-scale invasion of Ukraine and news about all the atrocities of the Russian army in Ukraine. With RT being blocked in some of the targeted countries, Russia currently relies on a network of local pro-Kremlin influencers and politicians in those countries to disseminate Kremlin-friendly narratives. Moreover, it regularly manages to win some attention of Western public to those narratives.

The Recipe of Fear and Hatred

Russia's Communication Strategies

The systematic analysis of discourse helped to uncover simple but powerful universal means helping the analysed channels attribute the desired negative features to the actors opposing Russia in its actions against Ukraine. This chapter provides details about them.

Repetitions. The analysed coverage includes dozens of almost identical evaluation acts about political actors involved in the events of interest, first of all about the Postmaidan Ukrainian Authorities and the Right Sector. Most often those repeatable evaluations are based on typical predications and nominations that frame the change of Ukrainian authorities in February 2014 as a "bloody coup" conducted by "Nazis", "fascists", "Russophobes", "anti-semites", "junta", etc. For example, "Nazis came to power" (March 2, 2014, COR2, 05:01–05:03), "Vandals came to power" (March 30, 2014, COR12, 04:23–4:25), "Fascists came to power" (April 13, 2014, COR1, 16:27–16:29), "Junta" (e.g. May 11, 2014, RT2, 8:03:47 or August 31, 2014, COR1, 05:54).

In the following statement voiced on the day of the sham referendum in Crimea the speaker said that under the rule of the neo-fascist Postmaidan Ukrainian Authorities, the life of Ukrainians would be as bad as never before: "The new government in Ukraine consists of right-wingers and neo-fascists, it will oppress the Ukrainian people to such an extent, to which they have not yet been oppressed in their entire history" (March 16, 2014, COR5, 07:22–07:30). It is a strong claim given the history of Ukraine in the 20th century alone, most of which Ukrainians spent under totalitarian rule with artificial communists-made famines starving millions to death and years of Nazi occupation during WWII.

Below, the Russian president shares his thoughts about the change of authorities in Ukraine in February 2014, which were quoted by both analysed channels: "The main perpetrators of the coup were nationalists, neo-Nazis, Russophobes and antisemites, they still define life in Ukraine to a great extent" (March 23, 2014,

COR1, 02:14–02:26). However, the English language translation of predications broadcast by RT differed from the Russian-language original broadcast by Channel One Russia. On RT, the word "Russophobes" was not included in the list of translated predications voiced by Putin: "Who carried on the coup in Ukraine: neo-Nazis, nationalists and antisemites, they still define the country's political agenda" (March 23, 2014, RT1, 3:02:39–3:02:48). Pro-Russian public figures started actively including the notion of "Russophobia" in their communication with Western viewers later, especially after the beginning of Russia's full-scale war against Ukraine causing rapid deterioration of Russia's image abroad. Back in 2014, "Russophobia" was primarily reserved for Russian internal audience, unlike "Nazis", "fascists", and "antisemites" appearing in Russian communication both at home and abroad.

Repetitions of such attributions are to be seen in the channels' news coverage up until the end of the analysed time frame. Importantly, years after the events of interest took place, the Russian president regularly turns to February's change of authorities in Ukraine and continues to frame those events in the way the analysed channels framed them in their news coverage in 2014 (Putin, 2021).

The DHA revealed that the framing of February's events as an "illegal fascistic coup" is at the core of the whole logic of the channels' evaluations of Russian actions against Ukraine in 2014 and thereafter. The same is true about Russia's reasoning behind its full-scale invasion of Ukraine. In such circumstances, an alternative comprehension of the change of the Ukrainian authorities back in 2014 might challenge the whole story told by the analysed channels.

As an element of the black-and-white coverage that the analysed channels offered their audiences, repeated negative evaluations might become simplified "integrated schemas" that were easy to keep in mind (Castano et al., 2016). In other words, repetitive attribution of the same negative features to the same hostilely depicted actors in one-sided coverage might turn those features into elements of case-related cognitive maps helping to keep the audience within the desired framing of the Russia's aggression against Ukraine with its heroes and villains (Herrmann & Fischerkeller,

1995). Those viewers of Channel One Russia and RT who accepted the proposed case-related cognitive map were "protected" from any parallel discourses—they had at their disposal black-and-white, frequently repeated, seemingly coherent and easy to remember contextual information about the events of interest offered by Russian state-controlled TV channels. In that contextual information, Russia could not possibly do anything wrong unlike its opponents.

Historical Analogies. To make the desired comprehension of the Euromaidan, occupation of Crimea and the war in Donbas even more likely, the analysed channels repeatedly turned to certain historical events or periods that were said to be similar to what was happening in Ukraine during the analysed time frame. The channels also reminded their viewers about those events and periods that were said to be crucial for the fuller understanding of Ukrainian events. The former were, primarily, the comparisons of Postmaidan Ukraine with Nazi Germany manifested in attributing features of Nazi leaders to the Postmaidan Ukrainian Authorities, as well as in drawing parallels between the war in Donbas and WWII (Shestopalova, 2023).

In the first fragment, a character in the news story compares the Postmaidan Ukrainian Authorities who came to power in February 2014 and German Nazis who came to power in 1933: "When I saw what is going on in Kiev now [. .]. Nazis came to power. [Today is like in] Germany in 33 and the saddest thing is that Europe supported these fascists" (March 2, 2014, COR2, 04:44–05:09). In the second fragment, an invited expert compares the actions of the Postmaidan Ukrainian Authorities in the Donetsk and Luhansk regions of Ukraine in 2014 with the Siege of Leningrad by the Third Reich in 1941–1942:

> [...] Ukrainian authorities will cut off the Donetsk region from Russia as well. It is the main priority: to cut them off from Russia, to surround them and to crush them in a hunger blockade with the help of shelling. Remember the situation in Leningrad: shelling, hunger, cold, all this led to the death of numerous people. By the design of Hitler, it should have led to the surrender. It is the same situation (July 20, 2014, COR8, 06:56–07:26).

In the third fragment, a Channel One Russia journalist compares the march of the Ukrainian prisoners of war in Donetsk in 2014 with the march of prisoners of war from the German Wehrmacht in Moscow in 1944: "Groups of prisoners of war from the Ukrainian army were brought to Lenin square in Donetsk [. . .].[37] Here the antifascist meeting took place. The historical parallel with the march of captured soldiers of Hitler in Moscow in June of 44 was to be noticed even in the details. [. . .] After the column of prisoners of war left, the same as in 44 in Moscow, the dirt from the pavement was washed away" (August 24, 2014, COR5, 09:57–10:39).

Such historical analogies were also included, for example, in news coverage of the occasion when one of the representatives of the Right Sector—Oleksandr Muzychko—was shot dead while resisting detention by Ukrainian police. In the same news story, representatives of the Right Sector itself were compared to one of the representatives of Nazi Sturmabteilung (SA), Ernst Röhm:

> The current leaders of the 'sturmers' (such as Ernst Röhm in Hitler's time) are of no need for the leaders of the successful revolution. [. . .] Those on Maidan [they] read history textbooks, right? Then they know about the Night of the Long Knives in Germany in 34, when yesterday's associates who became inconvenient were shot by the order of the Führer [. . .] some of them while resisting arrest (March 30, 2014, COR4, 09:05–09:26).

In general, on Channel One Russia, coverage of the events in Ukraine in 2014 was often based on analogies, comparisons and recollections connected to the period of the Great Patriotic War.[38] Interestingly, in accordance with the news coverage by the state-controlled TV channels analysed, it was not just the Postmaidan Ukrainian Authorities, Ukrainian army and other Ukrainian actors that were compared to actors fighting in WWII. Militias of the self-proclaimed Russia-controlled "republics" of Donetsk and Luhansk were also said to have historical ancestors. For example, by covering the battle for one of the strategically important hills in the east

---

37 At the time of the event described, Donetsk was no longer under the control of Ukrainian authorities.
38 This is what the Third Reich-USSR part of WWII is typically called in Russia nowadays.

of the Donetsk region in August 2014, Channel One Russia journalists used a historical allusion that would be unequivocally understood by this channel's audience, based on one of the most popular songs in the USSR about the tragic battle between soldiers of the Red Army and "fascists" who outnumbered them. The song is called "On the Nameless Height"; it includes the line: "Only three of us remain out of the eighteen guys". Therefore, by saying:

> Exactly 71 years ago, in August of 43, SS fascist battalions stormed positions of the Red Army on this very place. [. . .] When 39 tanks of the Ukrainian army approached the foothill of the height, out of the eighteen guys from the militia only seven remain (August 10, 2014, COR5, 02:56–03:29),

the journalist was drawing explicit two-fold historical parallels between, on the one hand, the Ukrainian army and "fascists" and, on the other hand, between soldiers of the Red Army and the militias of the Russia-controlled "republics".

Similar examples are to be found already in the April 2014 coverage from Kharkiv[39] or in news stories about the situation at the time in the Donetsk and Luhansk regions of Ukraine. The reporting of the protests included the following fragment: "Emotions are overwhelming, for example, here people [were] listening to 'Arise, Great Country!'" (April 13, 2014, COR1, 07:21–07:33);[40] while reporting on the situation in Donbas and trying to push Russian fake narrative about the civil war in Ukraine, the journalist says, "Without a declaration of war, they [Postmaidan Ukrainian Authorities] attacked their own country, attacked their own citizens" (April 27, 2014, COR1, 00:59–01:10).[41]

---

39 This second biggest city in Ukraine is not part of Donbas, it remained under the control of Ukrainian authorities during the analysed period of the war. The Russian army tried to occupy it in 2022 but failed. Since then, the Russian army regularly attacks the city causing civilian casualties.
40 "Arise, Great Country!" is the first line of "The Sacred War" – one of the most popular songs in the USSR about the "Great Patriotic War" where the people are motivated to arise and fight "against the fascist dark force, against the cursed horde".
41 For the audience of Channel One Russia, this quote resembles the radio address from June 22, 1941, informing citizens of the USSR about the beginning of war with Nazi Germany "Without a declaration of war, German troops attacked our

Such results support previous research looking into historical frames in Russian media, most of which focus on the frames of "fascism" and the "Great Patriotic War", which are considered to be the most typical examples of recontextualization of history in Russian media and public speeches of Russian politics (Gaufman, 2017; Edele, 2017). These historical frames are so noticeable in the Russian state-controlled news coverage that they have the potential not just to portray actors involved in the analysed events either as fascists or as fighters of fascism, but to present the events in Ukraine as the repetition of the well-known story of WWII (McGlynn, 2020). Importantly, the idea of the "denazification" of Ukraine was one of the main justifications used by Russian officials in the course of the full-scale war that Russia began against Ukraine on February 24, 2022.

Among other historical analogies were numerous recollections about US involvement in violent conflicts all around the world. Sometimes, those enmifying recollections were made in the form of "whataboutism" — an argumentative strategy helping Russia legitimize its aggression against Ukraine based on references to US actions that were said to be much worse than Russia's actions (Barceló Aspeitia, 2020; Gentile, 2020).

An important feature of those recollections is that almost all of them are taken from the post-Cold War era even though it is certainly possible to find examples of US "wrongdoings" in the earlier periods of history. Still, Channel One Russia and RT appear to deliberately choose those recollections because they fall in line with framing of the Cold War as the "good old times" when the USA did not behave so roughly due to the existence of the USSR: in accordance with the analysed coverage, it was after the collapse of the Soviet Union that the USA became the world's hegemon and began to ignore any rules and norms.

For example, it was said that when the world was bipolar with the USSR being one of its poles, the world was better as it was more balanced than nowadays:

---

country, attacked our borders". Many people in post-Soviet states know this fragment by heart.

> Right after the end of the Second World War and until the fall of Berlin Wall in 89, there were at least two points of view about all events. On everything that was going on, the planet was looking using two eyes: the left Soviet one and the right American one, it made the picture fuller. [. . .]. [Nowadays] the world is denied the opportunity to look at what is going on using two eyes (April 27, 2014, COR3, 01:24–01:42; 07:43–07:47).

In the light of the post-2014 developments, especially after the beginning of Russia's full-scale invasion of Ukraine, another mention of the Cold War voiced by the analysed channels looks even more cool-hearted. It was said that during the Cold War, Ukraine was under full control of the Kremlin, meaning that Ukraine did not cause any inconveniences for the gas supply:

> Russia has been sending gas to Europe for decades. I mean, even in the Cold War when we really were enemies, Russia was continuing to be a key supplier of energy to Europe. What's changed is that Ukraine is in the way and the Ukraine is causing all these problems (April 13, 2014, RT1, 3:20:20–3:20:37).

In order to signalize that it does not support violation of international law and aggressive war, EU decreased its import of Russian gas after Russia started its full-scale invasion of Ukraine in 2022, but it did not prevent Russia from continuing its attempts to occupy Ukraine, possibly hoping for business as usual in trade and other spheres in the case of success. It worked with the occupation of almost a quarter of Georgia in 2008, it mostly worked with the occupation of Crimea in 2014, why cannot it work with the occupation of the whole Ukraine or will the help of democratic countries prevent it?

Construction of Causality. The DHA revealed that Channel One Russia and RT repeatedly referred to the events of the Euromaidan long after those events happened and claimed that due to the outcomes of the Euromaidan, ethnic Russians and Russian-speaking people living in Ukraine allegedly faced the risk of violations of their rights. As explained by the channels, to prevent those violations of rights, Russia occupied Crimea while Russian and Russia-backed forces began to capture local administrations in the Donetsk and Luhansk regions of Ukraine. By claiming this, the channels created a causality between the Euromaidan and the violent developments that followed and silenced Russia's role in those violent developments. In other words, the analysis showed that both channels reported that Russia's occupation of Crimea and the beginning of the war in Donbas, with all its civilian casualties (which Russian state-controlled voices try to frame as a "civil war" to hide Russia's involvement in it), were not due to Russia's actions, but due to the Euromaidan. Strategic construction of causality in the context of violent conflict is especially powerful as it is directly linked to the strategic attribution of blame for undesired developments. "Our children will curse Euromaidan, it led to civil war, it destroyed the economy and industry, because of it they, in fact, will not have any future" (August 24, 2014, COR11, 00:52–01:02). "The social and economic situation in Ukraine is rapidly deteriorating. The country is inexorably going towards bankruptcy. Let's remind ourselves what it all began with, it all began with Maidan" (April 13, 2014, COR17, 00:46–01:03).

Aside from justifying Russia's actions in Ukraine, the construction of such a causality has the potential to further strengthen the negative portrayal of the Euromaidan protests as well as that of civil uprisings in general. This assumption is also supported by an analytic piece by Pomerantsev (2021) stating that "[t]he great leitmotif of contemporary Russian and now Chinese propaganda is that the desire for freedom and the fight for rights leads not to prosperity but to misery and bloodshed."

Additionally, after the beginning of the war in Donbas, both of the analysed channels intensively covered human casualties in the Donetsk and Luhansk regions and claimed that they were caused by the actions of Ukrainian authorities coming to power as a result of the Euromaidan, while Channel One Russia even accused the Postmaidan Ukrainian Authorities of the genocide of Russian-speakers in those regions. Years after the beginning of the violent conflict in Donbas, the Russian president continued to say that Ukraine was committing genocide, for example, Putin said so during the joint press conference with the German Chancellor in February 2022. Putin's statements on the matter fell in line with Channel One Russia's and RT's framing of the Russian occupation of Crimea in 2014 as the action preventing genocide there (Gensing, 2022), while the attempt to stop the genocide of Russian-speaking people allegedly performed by the Postmaidan Ukrainian Authorities in other regions of Ukraine was used as one of the pretexts for the full-scale Russian military invasion of Ukraine at the beginning of 2022.

Importantly, the Special Monitoring Mission deployed to the Donetsk and Luhansk regions by the Organization for Security and Co-operation in Europe (OSCE) revealed that in 2017–2021, the number of civilian casualties caused by the fighting in those two regions of Ukraine was decreasing year after year: in 2021, 16 civilians died due to shelling, unexploded ordnance, explosions of mines, etc. compared to 87 civilians in 2017 (OSCE Special Monitoring Mission to Ukraine, 2020, p. 8; OSCE Special Monitoring Mission to Ukraine, 2022). The decrease in the number of civilian casualties did not mean that the violent conflict was over — approximately 7% of Ukrainian territory remained occupied by Russia and Russia-backed forces — but it was not in a hot phase up until hundreds Russian missiles attacked numerous Ukrainian cities while hundred thousand soldiers of Russian occupying army marched into Ukraine from multiple directions in the early morning of February 24, 2022.

Importantly, strategic work with causality in news reporting on various topics includes not just the strategic *construction* of causal relations between actions/events/processes but also the *destruction* of those relations. As mentioned, by claiming that the roots of the Russian occupation of Crimea, of the war in Donbas, and even of the full-scale invasion of Ukraine in 2022 are in the events of the Euromaidan, the analysed TV channels simultaneously contributed to the destruction of causality between Russian aggression and those events.

In fact, the destruction of causality is another politically-relevant feature of the analysed news coverage: if Russian aggression is not to blame for the occupation of Crimea, the anti-Russian sanctions imposed in the context of the occupation are also not justified, and the more people believe this, the less public support politicians proposing to sanction Russia will enjoy. More importantly, the same can be said about military support Ukraine is requesting to defend itself from Russia.

Same Enemies – Different Enmification Patterns

As mentioned in the previous chapter, the general frames of enmification constructed by two of the analysed channels were similar to one another, i.e. the same political actors were glorified and enmified by those channels with similar frequency. Besides similarities, the standardized content analysis helped to capture some of the formal differences between the channels (such as the greater role of invited experts in enmification by RT compared to enmification performed by Channel One Russia) and discuss them in regard to the channels' audiences. In this section, differences in enemy-making between channels are addressed with the help of the findings of the DHA.

Higher Emotionality vs. Higher Impartiality? One of the noticeable differences between the negative portrayal of Western and, especially, of Ukrainian actors by Channel One Russia and RT is that the coverage of the latter channel was much less emotional even when it came to attributing e.g. the Postmaidan Ukrainian Authorities with dehumanizing features. It would not be correct to say that RT's news stories about the analysed conflict were emotionally neutral and balanced, on the contrary, the opposite is shown by researchers studying RT's coverage of various topics, moreover, it is argued that emotional appeals to the audience, which are an especially strong means of information influence, were widely used by RT (Crilley & Chatterje-Doody, 2020; Yablokov & Chatterje-Doody, 2021). Still, a comparison of widely analysed and widely criticized RT (broadcasting for international audience) with Channel One Russia (the TV channel aimed, first of all, at a Russian internal audience) shows that in the pair Channel One Russia and RT, it is RT which offered its viewers noticeably less emotional coverage.

Channel One Russia repeatedly turned to detailed archetypal stories of mothers and their babies who were said to have been killed by the Ukrainian army. In July 2014, this channel also broadcast an archetypal fake story about the public crucifixion of a child in Sloviansk. The authors of the scientific article "Fake News. The narrative battle over the Ukrainian conflict" describe that news story as follows:

> The most scandalous reportage of Channel One is often cited as an illustration of the Russian information war against Ukraine [...]. According to the eyewitness, the Ukrainian soldiers gathered locals on Lenin Square and crucified a three-year-old boy on a bulletin board and left him to bleed out while his mother was forced to watch and then tied to a Ukrainian tank and dragged around the square until she died. (Khaldarova & Pantti, 2016, p. 894)

Insights from the literature about enemies and their construction in violent conflicts of the 20th century (see the first part of this book) allow us to draw some parallels between the emotionality of the Russian information influence against Ukraine in 2014 and, for example, the Entente's atrocity propaganda against the Germans in WWI "where the cutting off of Belgian children's hands was a standard topic" (Koller, 2008, p. 122). However, those parallels with WWI atrocity propaganda are stronger when it comes to the information influence of Channel One Russia than of RT.

Reporters of both channels had access to civilians influenced by the war in Donetsk and Luhansk regions of Ukraine. This is supported by the fact that, similar to journalists from Channel One Russia, RT journalists also made numerous reports from the war zone. Still, while assigning Ukrainian actors with responsibility for alleged atrocities in Donbas, Channel One Russia chose an emotional character-centric approach; in contrast, for RT, emotional reporting on the horrors of war was not an important part of its news coverage. Just like the differences between Channel One Russia and RT discussed in the previous chapter, it would be incorrect to explain the lesser degree of emotionality of RT by its impartiality. Thus, in the case of coverage of the events of interest, RT might have strategically compromised higher emotional influence in order to appeal to Western viewers' expectations of serious journalism, who, unlike Russians, are not used to highly emotional coverage of people's sufferings in news reporting, even when it comes to the coverage of violent conflicts. An earlier study showed that TV channels primarily broadcasting for an internal Russian audience tend to be highly emotional: this is not just the case for Channel One Russia but also for Russia-1, which is another major Russian TV channel (Pasitselska, 2017, p. 598).

Working with the Fears of the Audience as a Basis for Successful Securitization. The analysis of the branch of literature about constructivism in international relations performed in the first part of the book helped to theorize the following chain:

Identity – Interests – Security – Threat – Enemy.

It can be briefly explained as follows: enmity is not objective; on the contrary, an enemy is always the enemy of some actor. This actor has their self-identity and interests that give them a specific understanding of their security and of threats to their security coming from a particular enemy (see e.g. Wendt, 1992; Adler, 1997; Rousseau, 2006; Buzan, 2009; Onuf, 2013).

However, if those performing hostile communication do it strategically and aim to turn a particular political actor into an enemy in the eyes of several social groups with different identities (and therefore different interests, sense of security and threats), communicators have to keep in mind the features of different segments among the recipients of enmifying messages. On a content level, this awareness of communicators can manifest in precise work with the specific fears of different segments of the audience. Some features of enmification performed by Channel One Russia and RT give reasons to say that this might have been the case on the analysed channels. For example, the DHA revealed that Channel One Russia paid noticeably more attention to the threat Russian-speakers face from the Postmaidan Ukrainian Authorities, while RT reported that the "intransigency" of the Postmaidan Ukrainian Authorities on the gas deal with Russia challenged the wellbeing of Europeans because, if Ukraine refused to compromise, Russia could cut off the gas supply to the EU.

Similarly, unlike Channel One Russia, RT compares the person whom the leader of the Right Sector was said to ask for support with Osama bin Laden. Thus, while talking about the Right Sector, RT addresses traumatic associations with bin Laden such as 9/11 among the Western audience of RT, especially its US segment (Burnham, 2007).

In particular, both channels claimed that Dmytro Yarosh — leader of the Right Sector — addressed the terrorists, asking them to take violent action inside Russia: "The appeal of Dmitry Yarosh to the Chechen terrorist Doku Umarov, asking him to support anti-Russian Ukrainian forces [. . .] and begin active measures on the territory of Russia, appeared on the VKontakte page of the grouping [the Right Sector]" (March 2, 2014, COR3, 06:10–06:22).[42] In contrast to the broadcast on Channel One Russia, on RT, the audience was provided with some additional contextual information and comparisons: "The leader of Ukrainian nationalist group Right Sector [. . .] asked Doku Umarov to step up attacks against Russia. Umarov is the leader of the Chechen Islamist movement and an international terrorist, basically, Russia's Osama bin Laden." (March 2, 2014, RT1, 3:13:01–3:13:29). In the same news stories where this information was voiced, both channels reported that Yarosh denied the fact of the appeal by saying that the Right Sector's VKontakte page was hacked. Still, the denial was not framed by the channels as trustworthy. For example, an expert invited by RT to comment on the issue said, "Now they are trying to sort of say that it wasn't them and the website was hacked. It doesn't wash I'm afraid" (March 2, 2014, RT1, 3:15:34–3:15:39).

Besides the above-mentioned comparisons with Osama bin Laden, in another news story on RT reporting that Yarosh was allegedly threatening to blow the transit gas pipeline from Russia to the EU, the Right Sector was compared to the Frankenstein monster threatening Europe:

> the West must be wondering, at least if they have any sense, just what kind of a Frankenstein monster have they created in Ukraine when they encouraged and funded fifty dollars a head per day? [. . .]. [T]he monster that Dr. Frankenstein created quickly got out of control. That's why it's called a monster, and this monstrous threat by the Right Sector is a very grave one for people in Europe because at least a third of the European Union's gas supply

---

42 VKontakte (VK) is the Russian social media platform banned in Ukraine as of 2017.

is coming from Russia, and if the pipelines are blown up [...] then we'll be in very serious trouble indeed (March 16, 2014, RT1, 3:08:34–3:09:38).

As mentioned in the findings, there were also some differences between RT's weekly programmes broadcast at EU and at US prime time that could indicate the channel's targeted attempts to work with the fears of the different segments of its audience: sometimes RT speakers labelled Ukrainian actors as Nazi, neo-Nazi and fascists in their statements voiced at European prime time but the same statements broadcast in the weekly programme from the same date at US prime time did not include such labelling. Several of the above-mentioned studies showed that Russian internal media as well as the Russian international broadcaster actively use the topic of WWII and Nazi-related frames. At the same time, there is a need for more detailed research on this topic, for example looking into differences in usage of this frame for different segments of RT's international audience.

Mobilization *against* the Same Actors but *for* Different Actions. Among the communication advantages of a nuanced construction of enemies is that a different perception of the enemy motivates people for different actions against them. Moreover, if there are no alternative sources of information about the enemy available to the public, the highly targeted and detailed enemy-construction campaign can aim for quite precise social outcomes. In the following paragraphs, this idea is discussed on the basis of the findings of the DHA.

As stated above, the DHA showed that Channel One Russia paid noticeably greater attention than RT to the emotional reporting of what the channels called the atrocities of the Ukrainian army. Even though this book does not include empirical analysis of the audiences of Russian state-controlled channels, the work of regime-critical Russian media outlets (e.g. Meduza, Novaya Gazeta, TVRain) revealed that all the numerous detailed reports of Channel One Russia about "Ukrainian atrocities" had a direct effect on Russians.

For example, in TVRain's documentary devoted to the above-mentioned fake news story about the boy crucified by Ukrainian soldiers in Sloviansk in July 2014, the then-Novaya Gazeta photojournalist said, "I met a man there who voluntarily came from Russia to fight [against Ukrainian soldiers], [while explaining his motives] he was referring exactly to the story about the crucified boy."[43]

In the context of such statements, Channel One Russia's news coverage of events on the ground, to a great extent, resembles atrocity propaganda performed by the media of a country at war in order to mobilize both the public and soldiers for the fight (Robertson, 2014). Moreover, before it was banned, Channel One Russia was widely watched in Ukraine. When looked at from this perspective, propaganda of atrocities of Ukrainian soldiers among Ukrainian viewers had the potential to make locals fear and/or fight the Ukrainian army and the Ukrainian authorities, which would also be fruitful for the Russian political and military goals.

This was not the case on RT, or, at least, not to the same extent as on Channel One Russia. The DHA showed that in comparison to the latter channel, RT paid less attention to the alleged atrocities happening on the ground and more attention to the coverage of Western politicians' thoughts about the events in Ukraine. When those thoughts were critical towards Russia and/or favourable towards Ukraine, they were often dismissed, and the politicians voicing them were often portrayed as unreliable.

Additionally, RT tried to explain to its audience why Ukrainian actors were dangerous not just to some distant Russian-speakers of Ukraine but also to the channel's Western viewers. In other words, RT's enmification was quite detailed and targeted (the same as Channel One Russia's). Therefore, it can be assumed that if successful, it would not just make RT's audience view Ukrainian actors with some hostility but would also encourage RT's viewers to

---

43 For details, see: Istorija 'Raspjatogo Mal'chika': My Nashli Geroinju Glavnogo Fejka Vojny V Donbasse. Jekskljuziv Fake News [The Story of the 'Crucified Boy': We Found the Character of the Main Fake of the War in Donbass. Exclusive Fake News]. (2021, November 4). In Fake News. Quoted fragment: 00:00:12–00:00:20. https://tvrain.ru/teleshow/fake_news/ekskljuziv_fake_news-527992/

doubt the trustworthiness of Western politicians denying Ukrainian inhumanity and enmity.

There are studies looking into the targeting (and microtargeting) of Russian online influence (Ó Fathaigh et al., 2021) including in the context of elections in different countries (Peters, 2017). The detected differences in enmification performed by Channel One Russia and RT give reasons to assume that Russian state-controlled TV channels use similar logic in their performance as they precisely work with the fears of different segments of their audience and propose the most suitable hostile messages to each of them.

The Road to Demonization and its First Fruits

The DHA revealed that, in general, changes in the enmification of political actors involved in the analysed events correspond to the periodization as reflected in the related literature (e.g. Roman et al., 2017; Lichtenstein et al., 2019). In other words, the main changes in the attribution of negative features to actors opposing Russia occur within three periods defined by scholars: Euromaidan; Occupation of Crimea; Violent Conflict in Donbas. However, the findings of the DHA allow us to detail these three periods with the help of more precise information about changes in enmification.

First Period. The analysis showed that enmification of the most negatively depicted actor involved in the Euromaidan — Euromaidan Protesters — can be easily split into two periods: (1) from the beginning of the Euromaidan up until January 26, 2014, (2) from January 26, up until the end of the Euromaidan.

In the weekly news programme broadcast on January 26, the channels acknowledged the dramatic change in the situation on the ground ("It is Maidan 2.0") and paid close attention to the fact that two policemen (supporting the then Ukrainian pro-Russian authorities) were wounded by "angry crowds". RT's weekly news programme broadcast at EU prime time even made this topic their top story, which included comments from those policemen recorded in the hospital where they were treated. Aggression against policemen as well as the storming or taking over of dozens of regional capitals in Ukraine were among the reported manifestations of the change in the behaviour of protesters in that week and became the basis for significant changes in enmification; for example, that was the first time when Euromaidan Protesters were called "neo-Nazi" by RT.

The ability of the DHA to pay attention not just to what was said in the discourse but also to what was *not* said there for some reason allows us to look at the shift happening on January 26, 2014, in a broader context. This can be done with the help of information about other events happening earlier that week, which were not closely reported by Channel One Russia and RT, possibly because the intense coverage of those events could provoke a negative evaluation of the then Ukrainian pro-Russian authorities.

In particular, this concerns the deaths of several Euromaidan Protesters—Yuriy Verbytskyi (a Ukrainian scientist), Serhii Nihoian (a Russian-speaking ethnic Armenian who came to protest in Kyiv from the South-Eastern region of Dnipropetrovsk), and Mikhail Zhyznevski (an ethnic Belarusian who moved out of Belarus for political reasons). As can be expected, the deaths radicalized the protest. However, while reporting the change in behaviour of protesters and some of its outcomes, for example, the fact that some policemen were wounded in clashes with protesters, both of the analysed channels silenced the preceding deaths of protesters, which were the (likely) reason for the radicalization. Therefore, the politically motivated setting of the media agenda meant a fact that could have been presented as the *reaction* of protesters to the actions of security forces was presented as protesters' *action* leading to the escalation.

Certainly, the strategy of setting the media agenda is always somehow discretionary. At the same time, the decision to highlight information about policemen injured by protesters as the top story seems unexpected in the weekly news programme broadcast a couple of days after several protesters were killed. Importantly, silencing the significant part of the story not only helped the analysed channels to ignore the killing of protesters that might provoke a negative evaluation of the then authorities; the silencing also helped RT and Channel One Russia to stay within the constructed frame of the conflict. This would not be likely if the channels had reported the killings of the protesters because the identities of the killed protesters do not fully fall in line with, for example, Channel One Russia's statements that the Euromaidan Protesters were misfits, especially from the west of Ukraine, who were keen on ideas of racial hygiene and the purity of the Ukrainian nation.

The analysis revealed that there were several similar cases when Channel One Russia and RT strategically silenced events which could portray Russian or Russia-affiliated actors negatively and simultaneously intensively covered the reaction of Ukrainian and/or Western actors to those events. As a result, the channels constructed the desired *action-reaction relations* and presented the changes in the behaviour of actors opposing Russia as unpredictable, unexpected, escalating, and, therefore even more undesired (Huang & Kitani, 2014).

A study looking at *action-reaction relations* in the behaviour of sides of violent conflicts underlines that "tit-for-tat" logic plays a significant role in the course of conflicts (Linke et al., 2012). Therefore, reporting the behaviour of both sides is of special importance when it comes to reporting violent events. This was not the case on Channel One Russia and RT as of the first period of the conflict when it had not yet escalated. Moreover, (unexpected) changes in the behaviour of the Euromaidan Protesters at the end of January 2014 were used as justification for even more intense enmification of them. A similar approach was occasionally applied later in the course of the events (for example, towards people protesting in front of the Russian Embassy in Kyiv on June 15, 2014, which was touched upon in the previous chapter).

Second Period. The analysis revealed that the shift from enmification in the context of the Euromaidan to enmification in the context of events in Crimea happened on March 2, 2014. In its turn, enmification in the context of Crimea fully shifted to enmification in regard to the violence in Donbas on April 13, 2014. Unexpectedly, the date of the sham referendum in Crimea — March 16, 2014 — did not mark significant changes in the enmification of actors confronting Russia. The "referendum" itself and its results were reported but the portrayal of each of the various actors challenging the Russian position in Crimea (e.g. the Postmaidan Ukrainian Authorities, the USA, the EU) was quite stable in March and at the beginning of April 2014.

In the weekly news programmes broadcast on March 2, 2014, Channel One Russia and RT reported some involvement of Russia in the events in Ukraine by covering the formal decision of Putin to allow the use of Russian armed forces in Ukraine to "normalize" the situation there; in accordance with the Russian official position, this was not done. As of the same date, the channels intensified their negative coverage of the Postmaidan Ukrainian Authorities and the Right Sector and accused them of having "neo-Nazi" leanings. Also, as of March 2, the analysed channels intensified their negative coverage of the EU and the USA. The most noticeable element of the negative evaluation of those actors, especially of the USA, in the analysed Russian news programmes was based *not* on the actions of this actor performed in the frame of the events of interest in Ukraine, but *earlier in the past* and *outside of Ukraine*. Still, the DHA showed that those historical recollections were used as justification for an even more negative portrayal of the USA prior to Russia's occupation of Crimea.

In its turn, enmification of Ukrainian actors was, to a great extent, based on *potentially* threatening moves those actors could make in future. As quoted above, on March 16, 2014, a statement on Channel One Russia claimed that under the government of neo-fascists, Ukrainians *will be* oppressed to a greater extent than ever before in the entire Ukrainian history.

Thus, predominately, the enmification of both Ukrainian and Western groups of actors carried out in March 2014 was not based on the actions of those actors performed in March 2014. Moreover, the results of the DHA allow us to conclude that the main changes in the enmification of actors opposing Russia in the context of the occupation of Crimea happened in the analysed weekly news programmes broadcast on March 2, 2014, i.e. a couple of weeks before the sham referendum.

This periodization of changes in enmification raises the questions as to why the analysed channels changed their rhetoric in the very first days of March 2014 despite the fact that they did not report on major event(s) happening in and around Crimea at that time, and why the channels did not react to events such as the sham referendum with shifts of enmification helping the Russian-state controlled channels to justify them.

Presumably, the change of rhetoric of both of the analysed channels on March 2, 2014, can be partly explained by the reaction of the channels to the events in Crimea, which they decided NOT to report about in their news coverage.

This concerns Russia taking "effective control" over Crimea weeks before the sham referendum. Up until 2021, the question of whether it took place was a matter of dispute between Ukraine and Russia, including in the European Court of Human Rights. While both Ukraine and Russia agreed on the fact that Russia controlled Crimea at least as of March 18, 2014, the Ukrainian government claimed that Russia had political and military control over Crimea as of February 27, 2014, when Russian forces occupied strategic objects in Crimea; blocked Ukrainian armed forces stationed in Crimea; and seized government buildings in Crimea.

It was the very same day that the Crimean parliament voted to hold the sham referendum (initially scheduled to take place not on the March 16 but at the end of May 2014). In contrast to the Ukrainian position, Russia claimed that "they only exercised jurisdiction in Crimea and Sevastopol after 18 March 2014, when those territories became part of Russia under the 'Treaty of Unification', and not before" (The European Court of Human Rights, 2021, p. 2). In January 2021, the Court "found that there was sufficient evidence for it to conclude that Russia had exercised effective control over Crimea in the period in dispute between the parties, namely from 27 February to 18 March 2014" (The European Court of Human Rights, 2021, p. 4).

I conducted DHA before the court decision of 2021, the analysis also revealed that the analysed channels noticeably intensified the enmification of actors confronting Russian actions in Crimea without reporting the actions themselves. When the changes in enmification happening on March 2, 2014 — in the first weekly news programmes broadcast after February 27, 2014 — are looked at in the context of those silenced events, the detected changes can be seen as the channels' reaction to the beginning of Russia's occupation of

Crimea, despite the fact that they were not covered by any of the analysed channels.

Third Period. The time frame from April 13 up until September 5, 2014, is called "[t]he most active stage of military action" (Taradai, 2019, p. 143) in the pre-2022 period. Still, a closer look at the various events in Donbas in April–September 2014 combined with the findings of the DHA revealed that there were significant shifts in enmification in those several months of 2014.

First, the portrayal of Ukrainian actors (first of all of the Right Sector and the Postmaidan Ukrainian Authorities) significantly worsened on both of the analysed channels as of April 13, 2014, i.e. a day after first local administrations in the Donetsk region were taken over by Russian and pro-Russian forces and on the day when the Postmaidan Ukrainian Authorities decided to begin the so-called "anti-terrorist operation" in Donbas aimed at confronting those developments.

As can be expected, Ukrainian actors were framed as the villains of news stories about those events broadcast by Channel One Russia and RT. In contrast, all who were said to be confronting the fascistic "junta" that came to power after Maidan were framed as heroes. No involvement of Russian military commanders in the seizure of local administrations (e.g. in the Ukrainian town of Sloviansk) was reported by the channels, including in positive evaluations. Among other developments, the channels silenced the involvement of such personalities as Igor Girkin (also known as Igor Strelkov) in the seizure of local administrations and the fact that at the end of April 2014 he was sanctioned by the EU for his actions in Donbas.[44] As mentioned above, both of the analysed channels

---

[44] In the sanctions decision of the EU, Igor Girkin was "[i]dentified as staff of Main Intelligence Directorate of the General Staff of the Armed Forces of the Russian Federation (GRU). He was involved in incidents in Sloviansk. Head of 'Novorossia' public movement. Former 'Minister of Defence' of the so-called 'Donetsk People's Republic'." See: Council Regulation (EU) No 269/2014 of 17 March 2014 Concerning Restrictive Measures in Respect of Actions Undermining or Threatening the Territorial Integrity, Sovereignty and Independence of Ukraine. (2014, p. 20). Official Journal of the European Union. https://eur-lex.europa.eu/legal-content/EN/TXT/?uri=CELEX%3A02014R0269-

framed events beginning in Donbas in April 2014 as "the punitive operation" of the junta/Nazi/neo-Nazi/fascist government and of radicals from the Right Sector against unarmed Russian-speaking locals.

Almost eight years after those events took place as well as after Russia began the full-scale invasion of Ukraine, Russian officials continue to characterize Ukrainian authorities using the frame detected in the news coverage made by Channel One Russia and RT in 2014 despite the fact that in 2022, neither the current Ukrainian parliament nor the president of Ukraine are the same as eight years ago: since April 2014 they have changed twice as a result of competitive democratic elections (Freedom House, 2021).

It is assumed that in the nearest future, the research community will conduct diverse and detailed scientific studies regarding the direct links between, on the one hand, the news coverage of the analysed Ukrainian events by the Russian state-controlled media, and, on the other hand, the Kremlin's attempts to justify its full-scale invasion of Ukraine in February 2022 for an internal and international public. As for now, there are journalistic and analytical pieces making sense of those justifications; typically, authors of those pieces cite the alleged need to "denazify" Ukraine as the main pretext of the Russian invasion (e.g. Gensing et al., 2022). Therefore, it can already be concluded that back in 2014, Channel One Russia and RT performed enmification of Ukrainian actors based on the same messages that were later used by the Kremlin to justify the full-scale war against Ukraine in 2022. Therefore, it can also be assumed that the analysed news coverage of the war in Donbas, to some extent, increased the receptiveness of the audience of Russian state-controlled channels to the Kremlin's official line positioning the attack on Ukraine in February 2022 as a reasonable and necessary "military operation" aimed at liberating Ukrainians from their "fascist" government. Moreover, the frequent social media posts by Russian mothers proud for their sons trying to occupy Ukraine is the continuation of this 2014 development as those mothers often

---

20211213. Later on, Girkin was also said to be involved in the downing of flight MH-17 in July 2014.

believe that the occupying Russian army is trying to liberate Ukrainians from its Nazi authorities.

The analysis revealed that the next shift in the enmification of actors confronting Russia happened in the channels' weekly news programmes broadcast on June 1, 2014. It was the week of a significant battle over Donetsk Airport (which was not closely reported in the analysed news coverage). In June 2014, the analysed coverage remained within the general framing of the violent conflict in Donbas as the fight of locals against (neo)Nazis. At the same time, as of the beginning of June, the analysed channels significantly worsened the portrayal of Ukrainian actors, for example, by claiming that they were committing war crimes. Another worsening of the depiction of Ukrainian actors occurred at the beginning of July when Ukrainian forces began to regain control over captured towns in Donbas (e.g. of Sloviansk). Just as at the beginning of June, the key patterns of enmification introduced to the audience in the earlier periods of the violent conflict remained unchanged. However, compared to the earlier weeks, the analysed channels further raised rates of enmification by closely covering locals' sufferings and deaths allegedly caused by the aggressive Ukraine. The crucified boy from Sloviansk was one of those locals.

Further work with the findings of the DHA in the context of the existing research about the phenomenon of dehumanization showed that Channel One Russia and RT dehumanized and demonized Ukraine by intensively reporting its alleged inhuman actions, and, thus, by portraying it as inhuman aggressor.

An earlier study showed that those communication strategies that include dehumanization of an actor framed as an aggressor help to exaggerate their negative features even more (Rai et al, 2017). The DHA allows to conclude that such a strategy was applied by Channel One Russia and RT in their coverage of the war in Donbas as early as in 2014. Recent statements of Russian officials made after the beginning of the attack on the whole territory of Ukraine show that those officials continue to use the same strategy. For example, on February 24, 2022, Putin referred to the aggressive actions of Ukrainian authorities including the alleged genocide of

Russian-speaking people in Donbas and said that, among other reasons, Russia's "military operation" in Ukraine is "aimed at protecting Donbas" (Lenta.ru, 2022).

In accordance with the results of the DHA, the next shift in the enmification of actors opposing Russia happened right after the downing of flight MH-17 — in the weekly news programme broadcast on July 20, 2014. However, this shift cannot be classified as a separate period of enmification performed by the channels but rather as a reaction of the channels to the particular event. The authors of a study about the Twitter campaign of Russian trolls in the context of the downing of flight MH-17 state that it is typical for Russian digital information operations to praise Russia and to criticize Ukraine; the latter was also the case in the analysed digital operation about MH-17 with its numerous tweets making Ukraine responsible for the tragedy (Vesselkov et al., 2020). Despite the fact that the enmification of the Postmaidan Ukrainian Authorities in the context of the crash of flight MH-17 falls in line with the general patterns of enmification performed by the analysed channels, coverage of this event constitutes a distinct element of the coverage by Russian state-controlled TV, especially by the Russian international broadcaster.

RT's coverage of the downing of flight MH-17 over the Donetsk region is a special case compared to the channel's coverage of other tragic events in Donbas in 2014, at least because this tragedy attracted the very close attention of the Western media and public unlike other events causing human casualties happening in Ukraine in summer 2014. Consequently, the audience of RT was able to find out even the smallest details about this particular event not just from Russian state-controlled media. Moreover, as most of the victims of the crash were citizens of EU member states, this event was closely followed in the EU, especially in the Netherlands. This attention of the Western media and public to the downing of the flight was not the case with any other separate event happening in Ukraine in 2014; consequently, many of the events that did not attract such attention from Western media were intensively covered by RT for its Western audience in line with Russia's communication interests. The DHA revealed that, unlike Channel One Russia, RT rather abstained from the direct and outspoken enmification of Ukrainian actors in the context of the MH-17 tragedy; instead, the channel was underlining that Russia was not responsible for the tragedy and that Russia offered its condolences to the families of victims. Such findings allow us to assume that it is the Western attention to the downing of flight MH-17 that made the Russian international broadcaster apply a defensive strategy, unlike in many other cases when there was not so much attention to an event covered by the channel, as well as unlike in the case of Channel One Russia whose millions of viewers live within the Russian state-controlled information environment and, therefore, tend to accept the information spread by state-controlled TV.

The attention of communication scholars affiliated with Western academic institutions to the different aspects of the downing of flight MH-17 makes this event one of the most-studied events happening in Ukraine in 2013–2022 period (e.g. Oates, 2016; van der Velden et al, 2018; Hartmann et al., 2019; Rietjens, 2019; Sazonov, 2019). In one of the studies about the outcomes of the news coverage of the crash, authors analyse public opinion about the tragedy in the self-proclaimed unrecognized Abkhazia, South Ossetia and Transnistria, in Russia-occupied Crimea as well as in southern and eastern regions of Ukraine and conclude that the "television viewing habits" of respondents are the best predictors of whether the respondent would blame Ukraine or Russia for the tragedy (Toal & O'Loughlin, 2018, p. 882).

The DHA showed that it was repeatedly stated in the analysed news coverage, especially on RT, that no responsibility should be assigned to any political actor before the investigation was complete. Later on, the investigation revealed that the downing of flight MH-17 was carried out by a Russian Buk missile system that returned to Russia afterwards. After the results were made public, Russia continued denying that its Buk was sent to Ukraine in the context of the war in Donbas, and the same was said about any other Russian weaponry, military commanders, soldiers, etc.

Unlike the Western audience of RT, the public in Russia seems to believe the Russian government when it comes to the MH-17 tragedy: in their study, Toal and O'Loughlin refer to the poll by the Levada Center stating that "[m]ore than 4 in 5 respondents [in Russia] explained the crash by blaming the Ukrainian military" (2018, p. 898). In the quoted study, this statement is followed by an explanatory comment by the deputy director of the Levada Center writing "that 94% of Russians get their news from television and that this has created a different reality" (Toal & O'Loughlin, 2018, p. 898).

A couple of weeks after the downing of flight MH-17, both of the analysed channels returned to their standard coverage of the war in Donbas heavily focused on the portrayal of the Postmaidan Ukrainian Authorities as an inhuman aggressor. However, in the weekly news programmes broadcast in the middle of August 2014, another shift in the enmification of actors opposing Russia is noticeable. Back then, the military situation on the ground changed dramatically after Russia intensified its involvement even further. The analysed channels explained these changes by a "counteroffensive" of local pro-Russian forces of Donetsk and Luhansk regions against regular Ukrainian army.

The DHA showed that earlier shifts in enmification (especially at the beginning of July) were connected to the advancements of the Ukrainian army in taking the occupied parts of the Donetsk and Luhansk regions back under Kyiv's control. In the middle of August 2014, both of the analysed channels reported the success of the "counteroffensive" of Russian and pro-Russian forces that, among other developments, led to the death of numerous Ukrainian soldiers including in the green evacuation corridor near the town of Ilovaisk, which was shelled. As mentioned above, the analysed news coverage also includes a report about "the march" of the Ukrainian prisoners of war (POWs) in Donetsk which was held on August 24, 2014, a Ukrainian national holiday — Independence Day.

A Radio Free Europe / Radio Liberty journalist describes this event in the following terms: "When pro-Russian separatists marched captured Ukrainian soldiers at bayonet-point through the streets of Donetsk over the weekend, the crowd jeered, cursed, and hurled refuse at the haggard prisoners" (Schreck, 2014). To my best knowledge, the "parade" of POWs in occupied Donetsk and its coverage by Russian state-controlled TV did not attract much attention from communication scholars. Among a few papers where this event is somehow recalled is one in which the march is said to potentially fall within the jurisdiction of the International Criminal Court as an example of inhuman treatment of Ukrainian POWs (Lachowski, 2015, p. 52). Even though there is definitely a need for further research of this event and its media coverage in the context of the existing research about dehumanization, the results of the DHA allow me to conclude that after the months of intense enmification of Ukrainian actors including the portrayal of them as inhuman aggressors on Channel One Russia, it is no wonder that this enmification campaign might somehow contribute to such treatment of Ukrainian soldiers or even to the public acceptance of such treatment.

This preliminary conclusion is supported by previous studies of dehumanization. For example, earlier studies have shown that dehumanization of an out-group caused a situation when "it no longer feels distressing to inflict pain on others" (Rai et al., 2017, p. 8514) and that dehumanization causes moral outrage (Bastian et al., 2013). Furthermore, in their study looking at the connection between the dehumanization and the torture of prisoners of war, Viki and colleagues (2012) found that the stronger the dehumanization of out-group members, the stronger the willingness to torture them when they become POWs. Moreover, when the out-group is seen as hostile and dangerous, the connection between the dehumanization of this out-group and the readiness to torture its members becomes even stronger (Viki et al., 2012, p. 325).

As can be seen from the DHA, the following was all part of the analysed news coverage of the Euromaidan, occupation of Crimea and the first months of the war in Donbas: (1) positioning of Ukrainian actors as an out-group, (2) portrayal of them as threatening to ethnic Russians and Russian-speakers living in Ukraine as well as to the Western audience of RT, (3) dehumanization of Ukrainian actors based on their alleged inhuman behaviour, (4) repetitive and diverse comparisons of those actors with historical actors performing inhuman actions, etc. In the light of this, the treatment of

Ukrainian prisoners of war in August 2014 in Donetsk is an expected development and might be one of the fruits of the dehumanization efforts of the analysed channels. This statement is especially true for Channel One Russia, as the DHA showed that dehumanization played a greater role in its news coverage than in the coverage of RT, moreover, unlike RT, Channel One Russia was widely watched not just in Russia but also in parts of the Donetsk and Luhansk regions of Ukraine controlled by Russian and pro-Russian forces.

The shift in enmification in the middle of August was the last one detected in the analysed coverage of the events of interest. Therefore, the analysis allows us to conclude that there were four periods marking noticeable shifts in the enmification of actors confronting Russia. To sum up, the first detected period of enmification in the context of the war in Donbas (middle of April – beginning of June 2014) is characterised by the intense portrayal of Ukrainian actors as (neo-)Nazis threatening unarmed Russian-speaking locals of the Donetsk and Luhansk regions. Still, compared to the following periods, this first period of enmification is somewhat lighter. The second period of enmification (beginning of June – beginning of July 2014) reflects the further escalation of the conflict, including in the aspect of the dehumanization of Ukrainian actors on Channel One Russia and on RT. The third period of enmification (beginning of July – middle of August 2014) intensifies the negative portrayal of "inhuman" Ukrainian actors even further by blaming them for numerous sufferings inflicted on the people of Donbas. This period of enmification also includes the coverage of the downing of flight MH-17. Among other factors, the international attention to this event made the analysed channels, especially RT, abstain from the outspoken enmification of the Postmaidan Ukrainian Authorities in the context of the tragedy and instead apply a rather self-defensive strategy. The last of the detected periods of enmification (middle of August – beginning of September 2014) is closely connected to the changes in the military situation on the ground. Unlike previously, in this period, the analysed channels not only framed Ukrainian actors as inhuman aggressors, but also reported event(s) — such as "the march" of Ukrainian POWs in Donetsk — that can be seen as some of the fruits of the dehumanization of previous months. Importantly, all the most noticeable shifts in enmification detected in the news coverage broadcast in April–September 2014 mark changes in the negative portrayal of Ukrainian actors and not of other actors (e.g. Western ones).

In her research about changes in the strategic narratives in Russian TV coverage, Khaldarova (2021) states that the image of Ukrainians transformed from the image of "the (little) brother" of Russians to the image of "the other" in the period from November 1, 2013, to October 31, 2014, which is almost the same time frame as the one analysed in this book. Khaldarova (2021) also claims that the transformation of the portrayal of Ukrainians "began with the narrative of betrayal" (p. 16), however, this narrative was not enough to explain the Euromaidan protests, to justify Russia's occupation of Crimea and its support of the war in Donbas, so, "[f]or that, a specific narrative, which created a sense of threat, was required" (p. 17). The DHA helped to highlight the messages portraying various Ukrainian actors as threatening: it not only allowed to analyse the content of those messages in detail but also to attain a deeper understanding of the communication tactics and strategy of the enemy-making on analysed TV channels.

To sum up this whole chapter:

- The discourse-historical approach revealed that even when it came to the events marking the turning points of the situation on the ground (such as the first killings of the Euromaidan Protesters at the end of January 2014 or taking military control over the Crimean Peninsula at the end of February 2014), both of the analysed channels applied a deliberate strategy while setting their agenda: the selection of those events that were reported by the analysed channels and those that were silenced depended on whether making those events public was in line with Russian communication goals. In a situation where TV channels have the privilege to strategically decide which events are to be covered, setting the media agenda can, to a great extent, replace disinformation. Still, the latter was also applied by Channel One Russia and RT (e.g. Mejias & Vokuev, 2017; Ramsay &

Robertshaw, 2019; Erlich & Garner, 2021). As a result of disinformation and of deliberate agenda-setting, the perception of the channels' audiences of the Euromaidan, occupation of Crimea and war in Donbas, and their understanding of which actors were responsible for the tragic developments, is most likely quite perverse. The same can be said about their understanding of the action-reaction chains and of the causality of different events happening in Ukraine. Moreover, the question of which of the tragic developments reported by the channels happened in reality and which were made up is also a crucial one.

- There were periods when the analysed news coverage of Channel One Russia and RT predominately relied on historical analogies and potential future developments, i.e. the channels turned the (alleged) threats from the *past* and the *future* into the basis for the enmification of actors confronting Russia. These findings are quite surprising as the analysed data purely consists of the news stories that are expected to report most recent events. The same is true about the constant repetitions detected in the analysed coverage: in many cases, those repetitions of (alleged) unfavourable characteristics of actors confronting Russia were not directly connected to the topic of a particular news story, yet they were still included in the broadcast.
- The analysed TV channels referred to the *collective traumatic memories* of their audiences (such as the blockade of Leningrad, mass killings in Belarusian village of Khatyn in 1943, the Nazi occupation during WWII, 9/11, etc.) in order to draw associative lines between those events and events happening in Ukraine in 2013–2014. In all those cases, Ukrainian actors were compared to "the evil" forces of the past. Additionally, the analysed channels, especially Channel One Russia, produced highly emotional news coverage including archetypal frames in order to blame Ukrainian actors for allegedly causing the suffering and death of locals in the Donetsk and Luhansk regions similar to those caused by the Nazis during WWII.

- The findings of the DHA revealed that the analysed channels closely worked with the fears of their audiences and constructed enemies based on detailed knowledge of those fears. Consequently, the enmification performed by Channel One Russia and the two versions of RT noticeably differed in the aspects allowing the channels to make the enmification most appealing to their viewers. *Targeted enmification* helped the channels to enmify the same political actors confronting Russia, but to do so based on different alleged threats coming from those actors. Such an approach was strategically applied and resulted in the construction of quite different portraits of the same enemies for different segments of the audience of Russian state-controlled TV. Moreover, this strategy has the potential to result in mobilizing different segments of the channels' audiences for different actions. As for the audience of Channel One Russia, those actions included the physical fight against the Ukrainian army.
- The discussion of the findings of the DHA in the context of the interdisciplinary research about dehumanization allows concluding that the enmification of Ukrainian actors performed by both of the analysed channels included the *dehumanization* of those actors. This feature was especially strong in the news coverage by Channel One Russia. Several of the above-listed strategies were applied by the latter channel in the context of its dehumanizing efforts including an archetypal fake story about a crucified boy, which is one of the best-known examples of Russian disinformation.

All these strategies contributed to the construction of enemies on Channel One Russia and RT. Moreover, as the analysed time frame includes data from the beginning of the Euromaidan until the signing of the First Minsk Agreement, the critical discourse analysis conducted, in fact, deals with one of the most turbulent periods of Russian TV broadcasting in the post-Soviet period. The analysed nine months were the time when the entire structure of international hostile and friendly networks of Russia was shaken, and these changes were reflected in the analysed data. In some sense, the rhetoric of Russian state-controlled TV changed even more dramatically during the analysed months of 2013 and 2014 than after the beginning of Russia's full-scale war against Ukraine in 2022.

In general, studying the concept of enmification using the example of the particular enmification campaign performed by media outlets helped to award the concept with more practical outlines. Consequently, it also helped to highlight the existing gaps in the comprehension of the concept, such as the lack of systematic attention to the fact that enmification varies depending on the degree of enmity attributed to actor(s) in the process of turning them into enemies in the public eye.

The combination of the findings of the standardized content analysis and discourse-historical approach revealed that a more intense (i.e. more frequent) negative portrayal of an actor does not necessarily mean that this actor was attributed with a higher degree of enmity compared to an actor who was enmified less intensively. Likewise, the similar intensity of the negative coverage of some actors does not necessarily imply a similar degree of enmity attributed to them.

For example, the findings of the standardized content analysis showed that two of the actors confronting Russia — the European Union and the Right Sector — were enmified with similar intensity: the shares of negative evaluations about the two of them were similar. At the same time, the findings of the discourse-historical approach revealed that the features attributed to those two actors were very different: while the EU was repeatedly said to apply double standards and to be "expansionist", "counterproductive", and "inefficient", the Right Sector was repeatedly said to be the main "fighting force" of the "bloody coup", was said to apply "most inhuman tactics", to violate all "moral and human norms", was called a "terrorist", "monstrous" and "neo-Nazi" organization.

While the intensity of enmification is a standardized matter (that can be calculated), the same cannot be said about the degree of enmity. Systematically addressing the latter could be done with the help of a typology of hostile actors where the degree of enmity would be a criterion distinguishing between the types of those actors. As for the Russian state-controlled news coverage of the events happening in Ukraine in 2013–2014, it is clear both from the standardized and from the discursive parts of the research that as early as eight years before the beginning of the full-scale Russian-Ukrainian War, Ukrainian political actors were the main targets of Russian state-controlled enmification compared to other actors including Western ones, and that Ukrainian actors were already being demonized and dehumanized.

Importantly, the findings of this book do not only correspond to the logic of further developments in the Russia's aggression against Ukraine but also have some explanatory potential in regard to those developments: already in 2014, the analysed channels, especially Channel One Russia, were portraying Ukrainian actors as immoral, inhuman, demonized enemies who should be fought.

The findings of this book at least partly explain what exactly happened with Russian public opinion between two polls about the attitude of Russians towards Ukraine that were conducted one year apart (in January 2014 and January 2015) and which revealed opposite results.[45] At least part of the explanation is that during the time between those polls, Russians were exposed to the strategic intense targeted negative portrayal of Ukrainian actors based on (1) one-sided historical recollections, (2) politically motivated causality between the undesired and/or tragic events of the conflict, (3) politically motivated agenda-setting, (4) appeals to fears of the audience and its traumatic experience, and (5) dehumanization, etc. The analysis revealed that these elements of the coverage were part of the news broadcasting on Channel One Russia — one of Russia's most watched national state-controlled TV channels — which were the main sources of news for approximately 90% of Russians (Levada Center, 2017a,b). Those elements, even though in lighter form, were also present in the news coverage by the Russian international broadcaster. Kremlin frames of the events happening in Ukraine in 2013–2014 are definitely not dominant in most of those

---

45 As mentioned in the chapter devoted to the standardized content analysis, the results of the poll conducted in January 2014 showed that 66% of Russians had a predominately positive attitude towards Ukraine, while another poll conducted in January 2015, showed that 64% of Russians had a predominately negative attitude towards Ukraine (Levada Center, 2015).

countries (excluding e.g. Hungary), nevertheless, those frames are still present in Western media and public discourses.

In the morning of February 24, 2022, Putin repeated the same old story about the alleged neo-Nazi leanings of the Ukrainian authorities in his address to Russians. Those leanings were said to be the major reason why Russia began its "special military operation" allegedly aimed at liberating Ukrainians by denazifying their authorities (e.g. Gensing et al., 2022). However, in April 2022, when the world saw the photos of hundreds civilians killed by the occupying Russian army in the Kyiv region, one of the major Russian state-controlled online media outlets RIA Novosti published a column by one of its authors who argued that the "denazification" of Ukraine could not be limited to Ukrainian authorities only, but that it should also be directed at ordinary Ukrainians because, as he claimed, a significant number of them are "passive Nazis". Additionally, the author of the column urged that "Ukronazism is not the smaller but greater threat to the world and to Russia than Hitler's version of German Nazism" (Sergeytsev, 2022). In accordance with the metrics displayed on the RIA Novosti website, by the end of May 2022, this column was read more than 1.5 million times. Therefore, in some aspects, Russian state-controlled coverage of the full-scale invasion of Ukraine mirrors the approaches dating back to 2013–2014, while in other aspects, state-controlled media outlets use the hostile depictions of Ukraine and Ukrainians from a decade ago as the fundament on which an even more extreme portrayal is built.

Conclusion:
Autocracies Learn from Each Other

Due to Russia's full-scale invasion of Ukraine and the pivotal role played by hostile communication, the case I delve into has garnered significant attention from scholars, the expert community, and policymakers alike. From a theoretical standpoint, I examine the state-controlled enmification orchestrated by an autocracy. This case is not entirely unique, given the prevalence of autocratic states worldwide where citizens live within state-controlled information environments.

As autocracies learn from each other, the success or failure of the Russian army and Russian hostile communication in the fight against Ukraine and Ukrainians will form the crux of the broader lesson for other autocracies. To enhance our understanding of state-controlled enmification before it happens, in this last section of the book, I am focusing on drawing general conclusions about how autocracies construct enemies. If Russia's aggression proves successful in some aspects and appears favourable to Russia in the eyes of other autocracies, we can anticipate a proliferation of similar enmifying campaigns in the future with an attempt to repeat Russia's success.

First, my findings imply that in autocracies, enmification is a matter of choice. Earlier expertise in authoritarian communication shows that through control over media, autocratic elites have the power to adjust the balance between legitimization and delegitimization in the mass communication depending on their political goals at a given point. In other words, they can choose whether they and the state-controlled media should focus on the positive portrayal of the authorities or on the negative portrayal of their opponents (Dukalskis & Patane, 2019). As a result, the high degree of control over the media in autocracies allows autocratic elites to decide overnight that enmification might be fruitful for them in the given political circumstances (whatever they are). Right after such a decision is made, state-controlled media will begin the enmification campaign against the listed "enemies". The Right Sector was one of the enemies constructed by Channel One Russia and RT after the end of the Euromaidan. Close attention from the channels to the Right Sector in the analysed news coverage was quite unexpected given the limited influence of this actor in Ukraine during the post-Maidan period. For example, in the parliamentary elections in 2014, the Right Sector Party received 1.81% of the votes, which was not enough to win seats in parliament (The Central Election Commission of Ukraine, 2014). Still, the de-facto irrelevance of the Right Sector for the Ukrainian political agenda did not prevent the Russian channels from turning the previously unknown organization into one of the most intensively enmified political actors. In particular, paying very close attention to the Right Sector and portraying it as an immoral, neo-Nazi organization terrorizing Russian-speakers and allegedly setting the tune in post-Maidan Ukraine helped Channel One Russia and RT to construct a fearsome and dangerous "neo-Nazi" enemy and, therefore, was fruitful for the channel's attempts to justify Russia's aggression against Ukraine in 2014 and thereafter. Where is that mortal enemy now? For a change, Russia created new Ukrainian enemies with similar features.

Second, the state-controlled construction of enemies in an autocracy is likely to lead to the reinforcement of authoritarian tendencies in the country. The results of the research showed that along with lighter types of hostile portrayals, Russian state-controlled TV constructed demonized enemies in the eyes of their audiences. While Oppenheimer (2006) argues that such situations are most likely to occur in non-free information environments, Ivie (2003) underlines that the construction of a diabolical enemy is likely to provoke further limitations of (remaining) freedoms. The latter occurs at least because fighting a diabolical enemy requires extraordinary measures; moreover, if the enmification is successful and the public believes that the enemy is a diabolical one, the public is likely to perceive those extraordinary measures as legitimate and to support them (Floyd, 2015). Those theoretical statements are illustrated by the destruction of the remaining critical (digital) media outlets in Russia that happened right after the beginning of the full-scale Russian-Ukrainian War in 2022. The years-long politically motivated enmification performed by the main Russian TV channels since 2013 was possible due to the state control over this most popular medium. State-controlled enmification helped Russian authorities in their attempts to justify the full-scale aggression against demonized Ukraine. The beginning of the full-scale war against Ukraine made Russian authorities destroy the remaining voices critical towards the Kremlin.

Third, the state-controlled enmification performed for the citizens of an autocracy (internal audience) is likely to be more intense and extreme than the enmification performed under the control of this very autocratic state for the citizens of other states (external audience), especially when the external audiences live in pluralistic media environments. The findings of my research have shown that the enmification performed by state-controlled Channel One Russia was more intense and extreme than the enmification performed by state-controlled RT. As argued, this could be explained by the fact that the Western audience of the latter enjoys the benefits of a free flow of information, therefore, unlike the viewers of Channel One Russia, viewers of RT can easily challenge the enmifying statements of the channel by consuming mainstream media from their countries. This finding about the more one-sided news coverage by an internal TV channel of a country compared to the news coverage by an international broadcaster of the same country appears to be a feature of authoritarian communication, while studies about mass media and international broadcasters of democratic states reveal the opposite results (Zöllner, 2006; Gilboa, 2008). Further comparison of state-controlled communication for an internal audience and for an external audience is needed to show this finding to be true in the examples of other autocracies as well as to detail and deepen the understanding about this finding's practical outcomes.

Fourth, even though not all autocracies have power and resources securing their regional or global information influence (such as Russia's or China's influence), successful enmification performed exclusively for the internal audience, i.e. for the citizens of an autocracy, also increases the risk of conflicts with the constructed enemy, no matter whether this enemy is an internal or an external one. Depending on the particular messages of an enmification campaign, such conflicts might also be violent, up to wars and genocides. Writing about the role of Rwandan media in genocide, Benesch (2004) recalls the examples of the Holocaust and of the genocide of Bosnian Muslims and argues that

> [e]ach modern case of genocide has been preceded by a propaganda campaign transmitted via mass media and directed by a handful of political leaders. If such campaigns could be stopped – or their masterminds deterred – genocide might be averted. (p. 63)

Even though enmifying messages can also be spread by anti-democratic political parties in democratic states (Doerr, 2021), still, the chances that sooner or later the authorities will decide to use enmification for political purposes and that this enmification will be successful are much higher in autocracies due to their state-controlled information environments.

Fifth, Russia is not the only state that is capable of performing state-controlled enmification both for internal and for global audiences. The focus on enmification distinguishes Russian international broadcasting from that of China, which is predominately focused on promoting the positive image of China abroad (Wang, 2020). However, as China is also an authoritarian state where the authorities use media outlets for their political purposes, the literature about enmification would benefit from further research into Chinese state-controlled hostile communication. There are studies analysing the negative stereotypical portrayal of Uyghurs by Chinese media (e.g. Jin et al., 2017) as well as those warning about the genocide of Uyghurs (e.g. Fallon, 2019; Smith Finley, 2021), but, to my best knowledge, there are no systemizing studies putting the hostile portrayal of Uyghurs into the wider scholarly and political context. Importantly, the Chinese authorities use enmification not only in the negative portrayals of national minorities but also to hostilely portray other internal forces challenging the regime, including the Tiananmen square protesters. Dukalskis and Patane (2019) argue that the delegitimation of student protesters included the portrayal of them as "criminals and unpatriotic rivals" and "was meant to marginalize them" and add that Chinese state-controlled media actively blamed foreign forces for attempts to enslave China with the help of protesters (p. 473). The findings reveal that similar enmifying messages were used by Russian state-controlled media to enmify the Euromaidan protesters and that political actors such as the EU and the USA were actively blamed for "orchestrating" protests. State-controlled hostile communication was also applied by the Chinese authorities to enmify Chinese external enemies: Dillon and her colleagues (1977) analyse a shift in the hostile communication of Chinese state-controlled media in 1968–1969, when, in accordance with the change of the political situation,[46] no longer the USA but the USSR was portrayed as China's principal enemy. Therefore, Chinese autocratic authorities also have the means and power as well as diverse experience in the enmification of their political opponents. So far, China does not use this strategy in their international broadcasting (Zhang, 2011; Rawnsley, 2015; Wang, 2020). At the same time, changes in Chinese political interests on the international arena might cause a shift in Chinese strategies of international broadcasting, mirroring the dynamic seen in the case of Russia (Elswah & Howard, 2020). Enmification (including dehumanization and demonization) is a tool available to any autocratic regime exercising control over media.

Autocracies learn from each other. They also support one another. Russian soldiers would never have been able to come so close to Kyiv, as was observed in February and March 2022, if not for the support of the Russia-friendly autocratic Belarusian regime allowing the Russian army to use Belarusian lands for build-up and attack on Ukraine's capital. Russia would never be so successful in systematically attacking Ukraine's energy infrastructure, grain infrastructure and other civilian facilities if not for the help of drones from the Russia-friendly autocratic Iranian regime. Russian pilots would never be so good at bombing their targets in Ukraine (including residential buildings) without all the experience they gath-

---

46   After the invasion of the USSR-lead Warsaw Pact in Czechoslovakia in August 1968.

ered in Syria at the invitation of the Russia-friendly autocratic Syrian regime. Russia would feel way more isolated during the meetings of the UN Security Council devoted to Russia's war against Ukraine if not for the Russia-friendly autocratic Chinese regime. These days, there are discussions about whether the missiles attacking Kharkiv recently have been from the Russia-friendly autocratic North Korean regime. We will soon find out for sure, but the open-source images suggest that this is the case.

The construction of enemies I describe in this book is not an abstract thing: hundreds of thousands of Russian soldiers with the help of autocracies from different parts of the world are trying hard to occupy Ukraine at this very moment. Many of those soldiers and many more of their relatives are proud of this as they do believe that Russia is fighting in a sacred war against Nazism and trying to liberate Ukrainians. As for those who do not believe in it, the story about the sacred war against Nazism told by TV screens and retold by all other types of screens offers a nice and calming excuse. For some, it is an excuse to stay silent when they are told to, for others, it is an excuse to kill Ukrainians when they are told to.

At the end of the day, Russia's state-controlled enmification of Ukraine for internal audience looks successful as no actors inside Russia have been capable of offering the Russian public an appealing framing of Russia's war against Ukraine that would significantly challenge the regime's framing. The Russian public keeps supplying the regime with soldiers to send to battlefields in Ukraine. Some Russians do it with powerlessness, some with pride.

But are democracies strong enough to support each other for as long as needed and learn from each other's experience both when it comes to the Russian army and the Russian hostile communication?

References

Abbott, E. A., & Brassfield, L. T. (1989). Comparing Decisions on Releases by TV and Newspaper Gatekeepers. *Journalism Quarterly, 66*(4), 853–856. https://doi.org/10.1177/107769908906600411

Abraham, L., & Appiah, O. (2006). Framing News Stories: The Role of Visual Imagery in Priming Racial Stereotypes. *Howard Journal of Communications, 17*(3), 183–203. https://doi.org/10.1080/10646170600829584

Abrams, D., & Hogg, M. A. (1988). Comments on the Motivational Status of Self-Esteem in Social Identity and Intergroup Discrimination. *European Journal of Social Psychology, 18*(4), 317–334. https://doi.org/10.1002/Ejsp.2420180403

Aday, S. (2010). Chasing the Bad News: An Analysis of 2005 Iraq and Afghanistan War Coverage on NBC and Fox News Channel. *Journal of Communication, 60*(1), 144–164. https://doi.org/10.1111/J.1460-2466.2009.01472.X

Adler, E. (1997). Seizing the Middle Ground: Constructivism in World Politics. *European Journal of International Relations, 3*(3), 319–363. https://doi.org/10.1177/1354066197003003003

Adorno, T. (1951). *Freudian Theory and the Pattern of Fascist Propaganda*. https://www.semanticscholar.org/paper/Freudian-theory-and-the-pattern-of-fascist-Adorno/a52e0b7698c3b2a55f21328b911e557ec5eeb66a

Agadjanian, A. (2017). Tradition, Morality and Community: Elaborating Orthodox Identity in Putin's Russia. *Religion, State and Society, 45*(1), 39–60. https://doi.org/10.1080/09637494.2016.1272893

Akhvlediani, M. (2009). The Fatal Flaw: The Media and the Russian Invasion of Georgia. *Small Wars & Insurgencies, 20*(2), 363–390. https://doi.org/10.1080/09592310902975497

Albæk, E. (2011). The Interaction Between Experts and Journalists in News Journalism. *Journalism, 12*(3), 335–348. https://doi.org/10.1177/1464884910392851

Allen, C. (2007). Islamophobia and Its Consequences. In S. Amghar, A. Boubekeur, & M. Emerson (Eds.), *European Islam: The Challenges for Society and Public Policy / Samir Amghar, Amel Boubekeur, Michael Emerson (Editors); Chris Allen, ... [Et Al.]* (pp. 144–167). Centre for European Policy Studies.

Alleyne, E., Fernandes, I., & Pritchard, E. (2014). Denying Humanness to Victims: How Gang Members Justify Violent Behavior. *Group Processes & Intergroup Relations, 17*(6), 750–762. https://doi.org/10.1177/1368430214536064

Allison, R. (2008). Russia Resurgent? Moscow's Campaign to 'Coerce Georgia to Peace.' *International Affairs*, *84*(6), 1145–1171. https://doi.org/10.1111/J.1468-2346.2008.00762.X

Alyukov, M. (2021). News Reception and Authoritarian Control in a Hybrid Media System: Russian TV Viewers and the Russia-Ukraine Conflict. *Politics*, 1–20. https://doi.org/10.1177/02633957211041440

Anderson, B. R. O. (2006). *Imagined Communities: Reflections on the Origin and Spread of Nationalism* (Revised Edition). Verso.

Antonenko, O. (2009). Towards a Comprehensive Regional Security Framework in the Black Sea Region After the Russia–Georgia War. *Southeast European and Black Sea Studies*, *9*(3), 259–269. https://doi.org/10.1080/14683850902934275

Aronson, E., & Cope, V. (1968). My Enemy's Enemy Is My Friend. *Journal of Personality and Social Psychology*, *8*(1, Pt.1), 8–12. https://doi.org/10.1037/H0021234

Asdal, K. (2005). Returning the Kingdom to the King: A Post-Constructivist Response to the Critique of Positivism. *Acta Sociologica*, *48*(3), 253–261. https://doi.org/10.1177/0001699305056566

Askerov, A. (2015). The Chechen Wars, Media, and Democracy in Russia. *Innovative Issues and Approaches in Social Sciences*, *8*(2), 8–24.

Åtland, K. (2020). Destined for Deadlock? Russia, Ukraine, and the Unfulfilled Minsk Agreements. *Post-Soviet Affairs*, *36*(2), 122–139. https://doi.org/10.1080/1060586X.2020.1720443

Autocracy. (2022). In *Cambridge Advanced Learner's Dictionary & Thesaurus*. Cambridge University Press. https://Dictionary.Cambridge.Org/Dictionary/English/Autocracy

Badawy, A., Ferrara, E., & Lerman, K. (2018). Analyzing the Digital Traces of Political Manipulation: The 2016 Russian Interference Twitter Campaign. *2018 IEEE/ACM International Conference on Advances in Social Networks Analysis and Mining (ASONAM)*, 258–265. https://doi.org/10.1109/ASONAM.2018.8508646

Baines, P., & Jones, N. (2018). Influence and Interference in Foreign Elections: The Evolution of Its Practice. The *RUSI Journal*, *163*(1), 12–19. https://doi.org/10.1080/03071847.2018.1446723

Balzacq, T. (2005). The Three Faces of Securitization: Political Agency, Audience and Context. *European Journal of International Relations*, *11*(2), 171–201. https://doi.org/10.1177/1354066105052960

Balzacq, T. (Ed.). (2010). *Securitization Theory: How Security Problems Emerge and Dissolve* (1st Ed.). Routledge. https://doi.org/10.4324/9780203868508

Bandura, A. (2002). Selective Moral Disengagement in the Exercise of Moral Agency. *Journal of Moral Education, 31*(2), 101–119. https://doi.org/10.1080/0305724022014322

Barceló Aspeitia, A. A. (2020). Whataboutisms and Inconsistency. *Argumentation, 34*(4), 433–447. https://doi.org/10.1007/S10503-020-09515-1

Bassiouni, M. (1979). International Law and the Holocaust. *California Western International Law Journal, 9*(2), 201–305.

Basso, E. (1978). The Enemy of Every Tribe: 'Bushman' Images in Northern Athapaskan Narratives. *American Ethnologist, 5*(4), 690–709.

Bastian, B., Denson, T. F., & Haslam, N. (2013). The Roles of Dehumanization and Moral Outrage in Retributive Justice. *Plos ONE, 8*(4). https://journals.plos.org/plosone/article?id=10.1371/journal.pone.0061842

Baumgarten, F., & Prescott, D. A. (1928). Why Children Hate. An Experimental Investigation of the Reactions of School Children of Poland to the Enemy Occupation. *Journal of Educational Psychology, 19*(5), 303–312. https://doi.org/10.1037/H0073854

Bayulgen, O., & Arbatli, E. (2013). Cold War Redux in US–Russia Relations? The Effects of US Media Framing and Public Opinion of the 2008 Russia-Georgia War. *Communist and Post-Communist Studies, 46*(4), 513–527. https://doi.org/10.1016/J.Postcomstud.2013.08.003

Bebler, A. (2014). Freezing a Conflict: The Russian–Ukrainian Struggle over Crimea. *Israel Journal of Foreign Affairs, 8*(3), 63–73. https://doi.org/10.1080/23739770.2014.11446603

Becker, J. (2004). Lessons from Russia: A Neo-Authoritarian Media System. *European Journal of Communication, 19*(2), 139–163. https://doi.org/10.1177/0267323104042908

Becker, J. (2014). Russia and the New Authoritarians. *Demokratizatsiya. The Journal of Post-Soviet Democratization, 22*(2), 191–206.

Bednarek, M. (2006). *Evaluation in Media Discourse: Analysis of a Newspaper Corpus*. Continuum.

Belin, L. (2002). The Rise and Fall of Russia's NTV. *Stanford Journal of International Law, 38*(1), 19–42.

Bell, M. (1997). TV News: How Far Should We Go? *British Journalism Review, 8*(1), 7–16. https://doi.org/10.1177/095647489700800102

Bellamy, C. (2001). What Is Information Warfare? In R. Matthews & J. Treddenick (Eds.), *Managing the Revolution in Military Affairs* (pp. 56–75). Palgrave Macmillan UK. https://doi.org/10.1057/9780230294189_4

Benesch, S. (2004). Inciting Genocide, Pleading Free Speech. *World Policy Journal, 21*(2), 62–69.

Bennett, W. L. (1990). Toward a Theory of Press-State Relations in the United States. *Journal of Communication, 40*(2), 103–127. https://doi.org/10.1111/J.1460-2466.1990.Tb02265.X

Besova, A. A., & Cooley, S. C. (2009). Foreign News and Public Opinion: Attribute Agenda-setting Theory Revisited. *Ecquid Novi: African Journalism Studies, 30*(2), 219–242. https://doi.org/10.1080/02560054.2009.9653403

Billig, M., & Tajfel, H. (1973). Social Categorization and Similarity in Intergroup Behaviour. *European Journal of Social Psychology, 3*(1), 27–52. https://doi.org/10.1002/Ejsp.2420030103

Boholm, M. (2009). Risk and Causality in Newspaper Reporting. *Risk Analysis, 29*(11), 1566–1577. https://doi.org/10.1111/J.1539-6924.2009.01296.X

Bojcun, M. (2015). Origins of the Ukrainian Crisis. *Critique, 43*(3–4), 395–419. https://doi.org/10.1080/03017605.2015.1089085

Bonnes, S. (2013). Gender and Racial Stereotyping in Rape Coverage: An Analysis of Rape Coverage in a South African Newspaper, 'Grocott's Mail.' *Feminist Media Studies, 13*(2), 208–227. https://doi.org/10.1080/14680777.2011.623170

Borchers, N. S. (2011). "Do You Really Think Russia Should Pay up for that?": How the Russia-Based TV Channel RT Constructs Russian-Baltic Relations. *Javnost - The Public, 18*(4), 89–106. https://doi.org/10.1080/13183222.2011.11009069

Borgatti, S. P., & Halgin, D. S. (2011). On Network Theory. *Organization Science, 22*(5), 1168–1181. https://doi.org/10.1287/Orsc.1100.0641

Boukala, S. (2016). Rethinking Topos in the Discourse Historical Approach: Endoxon Seeking and Argumentation in Greek Media Discourses on 'Islamist Terrorism.' *Discourse Studies, 18*(3), 249–268. https://doi.org/10.1177/1461445616634550

Bowers, P. J. (2008). Through the Objective Lens: The Ethics of Expression and Repression of High Art in Photojournalism. *American Communication Journal, 10*(Special), 1–27.

Brdar, M., & Vukovic, S. (2006). a Semiotic Analysis of 'Enemy' Management: 'Serbs' in the Western Media. *International Journal for the Semiotics of Law, 19*(4), 435–456.

Brennen, B. (2010). Photojournalism: Historical Dimensions to Contemporary Debates. In the *Routledge Companion to News and Journalism* (pp. 71–81). Routledge.

Brewer, M. B. (1979). In-Group Bias in the Minimal Intergroup Situation: A Cognitive-Motivational Analysis. *Psychological Bulletin, 86*(2), 307–324. https://doi.org/10.1037/0033-2909.86.2.307

Brewer, M. B., & Silver, M. (1978). Ingroup Bias as a Function of Task Characteristics. *European Journal of Social Psychology*, 8(3), 393–400. https://doi.org/10.1002/Ejsp.2420080312

Brüggemann, M. (2014). Between Frame Setting and Frame Sending: How Journalists Contribute to News Frames. *Communication Theory*, 24(1), 61–82. https://doi.org/10.1111/Comt.12027

Brüggemann, M., & Engesser, S. (2014). Between Consensus and Denial: Climate Journalists as Interpretive Community. *Science Communication*, 36(4), 399–427. https://doi.org/10.1177/1075547014533662

Brüggemann, M., & Engesser, S. (2017). Beyond False Balance: How Interpretive Journalism Shapes Media Coverage of Climate Change. *Global Environmental Change*, 42, 58–67. https://doi.org/10.1016/J.Gloenvcha.2016.11.004

Bruneau, E., & Kteily, N. (2017). The Enemy as Animal: Symmetric Dehumanization During Asymmetric Warfare. *PLOS ONE*, 12(7), E0181422. https://doi.org/10.1371/Journal.Pone.0181422

Brzezinski, Z. (2006). *The Grand Chessboard: American Primacy and Its Geostrategic Imperatives* (Repr.). Basic Books.

Bukey, E. B. (2000). *Hitler's Austria: Popular Sentiment in the Nazi Era, 1938-1945*. University of North Carolina Press.

Burnham, J. J. (2007). Children's Fears: A Pre-9/11 and Post-9/11 Comparison Using the American Fear Survey Schedule for Children. *Journal of Counseling & Development*, 85(4), 461–466. https://doi.org/10.1002/J.1556-6678.2007.Tb00614.X

Burrett, T. (2020). Feeling the Bern? Russian Media Reporting on the U.S. Democratic Party's Presidential Primaries. *Russian Analytical Digest (253)*, 12–14. https://doi.org/10.3929/ETHZ-B-000420927

Buzan, B. (1997). Rethinking Security After the Cold War. *Cooperation and Conflict*, 32(1), 5–28. https://doi.org/10.1177/0010836797032001001

Buzan, B. (2009). *People, States & Fear: An Agenda for International Security Studies in the Post-Cold War Era* (2. Ed). ECPR Press.

Buzan, B., Wæver, O., & Wilde, J. De. (1998). *Security: A New Framework for Analysis*. Lynne Rienner Pub.

Buzgalin, A. (2015). Ukraine: Anatomy of a Civil War. *International Critical Thought*, 5(3), 327–347. https://doi.org/10.1080/21598282.2015.1065193

Canefe, N. (2008). Turkish Nationalism and the Kurdish Question: Nation, State and Securitization of Communal Identities in a Regional Context: Review Article. *South European Society and Politics*, 13(3), 391–398. https://doi.org/10.1080/13608740802346627

Carter, E. B., & Carter, B. L. (2021). Questioning More: RT, Outward-Facing Propaganda, and the Post-West World Order. *Security Studies, 30*(1), 49–78. https://doi.org/10.1080/09636412.2021.1885730

Casier, T. (2018). Gorbachev's 'Common European Home' and Its Relevance for Russian Foreign Policy Today. *Debater a Europa, 18*, 17–34. https://doi.org/10.14195/1647-6336_18_2

Castano, E., Bonacossa, A., & Gries, P. (2016). National Images as Integrated Schemas: Subliminal Primes of Image Attributes Shape Foreign Policy Preferences: National Images as Integrated Schemas. *Political Psychology, 37*(3), 351–366. https://doi.org/10.1111/Pops.12259

Castano, E., Yzerbyt, V., Paladino, M.-P., & Sacchi, S. (2002). I Belong, Therefore, I Exist: Ingroup Identification, Ingroup Entitativity, and Ingroup Bias. *Personality and Social Psychology Bulletin, 28*(2), 135–143. https://doi.org/10.1177/0146167202282001

Çetinkaya, Y. D. (2014). Atrocity Propaganda and the Nationalization of the Masses in the Ottoman Empire During the Balkan Wars (1912–13). *International Journal of Middle East Studies, 46*(4), 759–778. https://doi.org/10.1017/S0020743814001056

Chin, S. J. (2018). Institutional Origins of the Media Censorship in China: The Making of the Socialist Media Censorship System in 1950s Shanghai. *Journal of Contemporary China, 27*(114), 956–972. https://doi.org/10.1080/10670564.2018.1488108

Chinn, J., & Kaiser, R. (2019). *Russians as the New Minority: Ethnicity and Nationalism in the Soviet Successor States.* Routledge.

Cohen, A. B., & Rozin, P. (2001). Religion and the Morality of Mentality. *Journal of Personality and Social Psychology, 81*(4), 697–710. https://doi.org/10.1037/0022-3514.81.4.697

Combs, D. J. Y., Powell, C. A. J., Schurtz, D. R., & Smith, R. H. (2009). Politics, Schadenfreude, and Ingroup Identification: The Sometimes Happy Thing about a Poor Economy and Death. *Journal of Experimental Social Psychology, 45*(4), 635–646. https://doi.org/10.1016/J.Jesp.2009.02.009

Constitution of the United Nations Educational, Scientific and Cultural Organization. (1945). UN Documents: Gathering a Body of Global Agreements. http://un-documents.net/unesco-c.htm

Cook, T. E. (1998). *Governing with the News: The News Media as a Political Institution.* University of Chicago Press.

Correa, T. (2009). Does Class Matter? the Effect of Social Class on Journalists' Ethical Decision Making. *Journalism & Mass Communication Quarterly, 86*(3), 654–672. https://doi.org/10.1177/107769900908600312

Crilley, R., & Chatterje-Doody, P. N. (2020). Emotions and War on YouTube: Affective Investments in RT's Visual Narratives of the Conflict in Syria. *Cambridge Review of International Affairs, 33*(5), 713–733. https://doi.org/10.1080/09557571.2020.1719038

Cwicinskaja, N. (2017). The Annexation of Crimea and International Law: Review of Thomas D Grant's "Aggression Against Ukraine: Territory, Responsibility and International Law." *Israel Law Review, 50*(2), 211–225. https://doi.org/10.1017/S0021223717000036

Czuperski, M., Herbst, J., Higgins, E., Polyakova, A., & Wilson, D. (2015). *Hiding in Plain Sight: Putin's War in Ukraine* (M. Czuperski, Ed.). The Atlantic Council of the United States.

D'Anieri, P. (1997). Nationalism and International Politics: Identity and Sovereignty in the Russian-Ukrainian Conflict. *Nationalism and Ethnic Politics, 3*(2), 1–28. https://doi.org/10.1080/13537119708428500

Dahl, R. A. (1992). The Problem of Civic Competence. *Journal of Democracy, 3*(4), 45–59. https://doi.org/10.1353/Jod.1992.0048

Darczewska, J. (2014). *Anatomia Rosyjskiej Wojny Informacyjnej: Operacja Krymska. Studium Przypadku [The Anatomy of Russian Information Warfare: The Crimean Operation, a Case Study]*. Ośrodek Studiów Wschodnich Im. Marka Karpia.

Declaration on Principles of International Law Concerning Friendly Relations and Co-Operation Among States in Accordance with the Charter of the United Nations. 2625 (XXV). (1970). United Nations General Assembly. http://un-documents.net/a25r2625.htm

Deibert, R. J., Rohozinski, R., & Crete-Nishihata, M. (2012). Cyclones in Cyberspace: Information Shaping and Denial in the 2008 Russia–Georgia War. *Security Dialogue, 43*(1), 3–24. https://doi.org/10.1177/0967010611431079

Delanoe, I. (2014). After the Crimean Crisis: Towards a Greater Russian Maritime Power in the Black Sea. *Southeast European and Black Sea Studies, 14*(3), 367–382. https://doi.org/10.1080/14683857.2014.944386

Demeritt, D. (2002). What Is the 'Social Construction of Nature'? A Typology and Sympathetic Critique. *Progress in Human Geography, 26*(6), 767–790. https://doi.org/10.1191/0309132502ph402oa

Dillon, L. D., Burton, B., & Soderlund, W. C. (1977). Who Was the Principal Enemy?: Shifts in Official Chinese Perceptions of the Two Superpowers, 1968-1969. *Asian Survey, 17*(5), 456–473. https://doi.org/10.2307/2643290

Dimitrova, D. V., & Strömbäck, J. (2005). Mission Accomplished? Framing of the Iraq War in the Elite Newspapers in Sweden and the United States. *Gazette (Leiden, Netherlands), 67*(5), 399–417. https://doi.org/10.1177/0016549205056050

Dobre, T. (2015). Mass-Mediated Ukrainian Conflict. *Europolity – Continuity and Change in European Governance*, 9(1), 45–63.

Doerr, N. (2021). The Visual Politics of the Alternative for Germany (Afd): Anti-Islam, Ethno-Nationalism, and Gendered Images. *Social Sciences*, 10(1), 20. https://doi.org/10.3390/Socsci10010020

Dukalskis, A. (2017). The *Authoritarian Public Sphere: Legitimation and Autocratic Power in North Korea, Burma, and China* (1st Ed.). Routledge. https://doi.org/10.4324/9781315455532

Dukalskis, A., & Patane, C. (2019). Justifying Power: When Autocracies Talk about Themselves and Their Opponents. *Contemporary Politics*, 25(4), 457–478. https://doi.org/10.1080/13569775.2019.1570424

Dunham, Y., Baron, A. S., & Carey, S. (2011). Consequences of 'Minimal' Group Affiliations in Children: Minimal Group Affiliations in Children. *Child Development*, 82(3), 793–811. https://doi.org/10.1111/J.1467-8624.2011.01577.X

Edele, M. (2017). Fighting Russia's History Wars: Vladimir Putin and the Codification of World War II. *History and Memory*, 29(2), 90. https://doi.org/10.2979/Histmemo.29.2.05

Ehala, M. (2009). The Bronze Soldier: Identity Threat and Maintenance in Estonia. *Journal of Baltic Studies*, 40(1), 139–158. https://doi.org/10.1080/01629770902722294

Ehrkamp, P. (2006). "We Turks Are No Germans": Assimilation Discourses and the Dialectical Construction of Identities in Germany. *Environment and Planning A: Economy and Space*, 38(9), 1673–1692. https://doi.org/10.1068/A38148

Eicher, V., Pratto, F., & Wilhelm, P. (2013). Value Differentiation Between Enemies and Allies: Value Projection in National Images. *Political Psychology*, 34(1), 127–144. https://doi.org/10.1111/J.1467-9221.2012.00930.X

Eisenberg, L. (1995). The Social Construction of the Human Brain. *American Journal of Psychiatry*, 152(11), 1563–1575. https://doi.org/10.1176/Ajp.152.11.1563

El-Nashar, M., & Nayef, H. (2022). 'Cooking the Meal of Terror' Manipulative Strategies in Terrorist Discourse: A Critical Discourse Analysis of ISIS Statements. *Terrorism and Political Violence*, 34(1), 155–175. https://doi.org/10.1080/09546553.2019.1676238

Elswah, M., & Howard, P. N. (2020). 'Anything that Causes Chaos': The Organizational Behavior of Russia Today (RT). *Journal of Communication*, 70(5), 623–645. https://doi.org/10.1093/Joc/Jqaa027

Engle, E. (2014). A New Cold War—Cold Peace Russia, Ukraine, and NATO. *Saint Louis University Law Journal*, 59(1), 97–174.

Entman, R. M. (1992). Blacks in the News: Television, Modern Racism and Cultural Change. *Journalism Quarterly, 69*(2), 341–361. https://doi.org/10.1177/107769909206900209

Entman, R. M. (2010). Improving Newspapers' Economic Prospects by Augmenting Their Contributions to Democracy. The *International Journal of Press/Politics, 15*(1), 104–125. https://doi.org/10.1177/1940161209352371

Eriksson, E. A. (1999). Viewpoint: Information Warfare: Hype or Reality? *The Nonproliferation Review, 6*(3), 57–64. https://doi.org/10.1080/10736709908436765

Eriksson, J., & Giacomello, G. (2006). The Information Revolution, Security, and International Relations: (IR)Relevant Theory? *International Political Science Review, 27*(3), 221–244. https://doi.org/10.1177/0192512106064462

Erk, J. (2003). Federalism and Mass Media Policy in Germany. *Regional & Federal Studies, 13*(2), 106–126. https://doi.org/10.1080/13597560308559429

Erlich, A., & Garner, C. (2021). Is Pro-Kremlin Disinformation Effective? Evidence from Ukraine. The *International Journal of Press/Politics*, 1–24. https://doi.org/10.1177/19401612211045221

Evans, C. E. (2016). *Between Truth and Time: A History of Soviet Central Television*. Yale University Press.

Fallon, J. (2019). China's Crime Against Uyghurs Is a Form of Genocide. *Fourth World Journal, 18*(1), 76–88.

Farwell, J. P. (2014). The Media Strategy of ISIS. *Survival, 56*(6), 49–55. https://doi.org/10.1080/00396338.2014.985436

Fawzi, N. (2019). Untrustworthy News and the Media as 'Enemy of the People?' How a Populist Worldview Shapes Recipients' Attitudes Toward the Media. The *International Journal of Press/Politics, 24*(2), 146–164. https://doi.org/10.1177/1940161218811981

Feinman, S. (Ed.). (1992). *Social Referencing and the Social Construction of Reality in Infancy*. Springer-Verlag New York.

Feng, G. C. (2015). Mistakes and How to Avoid Mistakes in Using Intercoder Reliability Indices. *Methodology, 11*(1), 13–22. https://doi.org/10.1027/1614-2241/A000086

Ferguson, C. K., & Kelley, H. H. (1964). Significant Factors in Overevaluation of Own-Group's Product. The *Journal of Abnormal and Social Psychology, 69*(2), 223–228. https://doi.org/10.1037/H0046572

Ferguson, D. P. (1998). From Communist Control to Glasnost and Back?: Media Freedom and Control in the Former Soviet Union. *Public Relations Review*, 24(2), 165–182. https://doi.org/10.1016/S0363-8111(99)80049-6

Ferrara, E. (2017). Contagion Dynamics of Extremist Propaganda in Social Networks. *Information Sciences*, 418–419, 1–12. https://doi.org/10.10 16/J.Ins.2017.07.030

Fiedler, A., & Frère, M.-S. (2016). "Radio France Internationale" and "Deutsche Welle" in Francophone Africa: International Broadcasters in a Time of Change. *Communication, Culture & Critique*, 9(1), 68–85. https://doi.org/10.1111/Cccr.12131

Field, A. P. (2006). Watch Out for the Beast: Fear Information and Attentional Bias in Children. *Journal of Clinical Child & Adolescent Psychology*, 35(3), 431–439. https://doi.org/10.1207/S15374424jccp3503_8

Fierke, K. M. (2015). *Critical Approaches to International Security* (Second Edition). Polity Press.

Finkel, S. E. (1993). Reexamining the 'Minimal Effects' Model in Recent Presidential Campaigns. *The Journal of Politics*, 55(1), 1–21. https://doi.org/10.2307/2132225

Finlay, C. J., & Xin, X. (2010). Public Diplomacy Games: A Comparative Study of American and Japanese Responses to the Interplay of Nationalism, Ideology and Chinese Soft Power Strategies Around the 2008 Beijing Olympics. *Sport in Society*, 13(5), 876–900. https://doi.org/10.1080/17430431003651115

Fischer, R., & Derham, C. (2016). Is In-Group Bias Culture-Dependent? A Meta-Analysis Across 18 Societies. *SpringerPlus*, 5(1). https://doi.org/10.1186/S40064-015-1663-6

Flowerdew, J., & Richardson, J. E. (Eds.). (2018). The *Routledge Handbook of Critical Discourse Studies*. Routledge.

Floyd, R. (2015). Extraordinary or Ordinary Emergency Measures: What, and Who, Defines the 'Success' of Securitization? *Cambridge Review of International Affairs*, 29(2), 677–694. https://doi.org/10.1080/09557571.2015.1077651

Forchtner, B. (2011). Critique, the Discourse-Historical Approach, and the Frankfurt School. *Critical Discourse Studies*, 8(1), 1–14. https://doi.org/10.1080/17405904.2011.533564

Forsberg, T., & Pursiainen, C. (2017). The Psychological Dimension of Russian Foreign Policy: Putin and the Annexation of Crimea. *Global Society*, 31(2), 220–244. https://doi.org/10.1080/13600826.2016.1274963

Forster, H. (1917). Are Native American Enemy Sympathizers Subject to Court-Martial? the *Central Law Journal (1874-1927)*, 85(8), 132–134.

Freedom in the World 2021. Ukraine. (2021). Freedom House. https://Freedomhouse.Org/Country/Ukraine/Freedom-World/2021

Fuchs, C. (2018). Authoritarian Capitalism, Authoritarian Movements and Authoritarian Communication. *Media, Culture & Society, 40*(5), 779–791. https://doi.org/10.1177/0163443718772147

Gamson, W. A., & Modigliani. (1989). Media Discourse and Public Opinion on Nuclear Power: A Constructionist Approach. *American Journal of Sociology, 95*(1), 1–37.

García Orosa, B., Gallur Santorun, S., & López García, X. (2017). Use of Clickbait in the Online News Media of the 28 EU Member Countries. *Revista Latina De Comunicación Social, 72*, 1261–1277. https://doi.org/10.4185/RLCS-2017-1218en

Gardner, H. (2016). The Russian Annexation of Crimea: Regional and Global Ramifications. *European Politics and Society, 17*(4), 490–505. https://doi.org/10.1080/23745118.2016.1154190

Gaufman, E. (2015). Memory, Media, and Securitization: Russian Media Framing of the Ukrainian Crisis. *Journal of Soviet and Post-Soviet Politics and Society, 1*(1), 141–174.

Gaufman, E. (2017). Fascism and the Ukraine Crisis. In *Security Threats and Public Perception* (pp. 103–123). Springer International Publishing. https://doi.org/10.1007/978-3-319-43201-4_5

Geddes, B., & Zaller, J. (1989). Sources of Popular Support for Authoritarian Regimes. *American Journal of Political Science, 33*(2), 319. https://doi.org/10.2307/2111150

Gehlbach, S. (2010). Reflections on Putin and the Media. *Post-Soviet Affairs, 26*(1), 77–87. https://doi.org/10.2747/1060-586X.26.1.77

Gendron, S. (2012). Exploiting the Hutu/Tutsi Divide: The Relationship Between Extremist Propaganda and Genocide in Rwanda. In M. Vuorinen (Ed.), *Enemy Images in War Propaganda* (pp. 89–106). Cambridge Scholars.

Geniets, A. (2013). The *Global News Challenge: Market Strategies of International Broadcasting Organizations in Developing Countries*. Routledge.

Gensing, P. (2022). Angeblicher Genozid als Vorwand? *Tagesschau. Faktenfinder. Desinformation zur Ukraine.* https://www.tagesschau.de/faktenfinder/russland-ukraine-medien-101.html

Gensing, P., Reisin, A., & Reveland, C. (2022). "Entnazifizierung" als Vorwand. *Tagesschau. Faktenfinder. Putins Krieg gegen die Ukraine.* https://www.tagesschau.de/faktenfinder/russland-propaganda-ukraine-101.html

Gentile, M. (2020). How to Lose the Information War – Russia, Fake News and the Future of Conflict: By Nina Jankowicz. *Eurasian Geography and Economics*, 1–3. https://doi.org/10.1080/15387216.2020.1825982

Gerber, T. P., & Zavisca, J. (2016). Does Russian Propaganda Work? the *Washington Quarterly*, 39(2), 79–98. https://doi.org/10.1080/0163660X.2016.1204398

Ghanem, S. I., McCombs, M., & Chernov, G. (2009). Agenda Setting and Framing. In *21st Century Communication: A Reference Handbook* (pp. 516–524). SAGE Publications, Inc. https://doi.org/10.4135/9781412964005.N57

Gilboa, E. (2008). Searching for a Theory of Public Diplomacy. The *ANNALS of the American Academy of Political and Social Science*, 616(1), 55–77. https://doi.org/10.1177/0002716207312142

Giner-Sorolla, R., Leidner, B., & Castano, E. (2011). Dehumanization, Demonization, and Morality Shifting: Paths to Moral Certainty in Extremist Violence. In M. A. Hogg & D. L. Blaylock (Eds.), *Extremism and the Psychology of Uncertainty* (pp. 165–182). Wiley-Blackwell. https://doi.org/10.1002/9781444344073.Ch10

Glisk, P. (2005). Choice of Scapegoats. In J. F. Dovidio, P. S. Glick, & L. A. Rudman (Eds.), *On the Nature of Prejudice: Fifty Years After Allport* (pp. 244–261). Blackwell Pub.

Goble, P. (2016). Russian National Identity and the Ukrainian Crisis. *Communist and Post-Communist Studies*, 49(1), 37–43. https://doi.org/10.1016/J.Postcomstud.2015.12.006

Goldschmidt, W., Foster, G., & Essene, F. (1939). War Stories from Two Enemy Tribes. The *Journal of American Folklore*, 52(204), 141–154. https://doi.org/10.2307/535469

Golosov, G. V. (2020). Useful, but Not Necessarily Idiots: The Ideological Linkages Among the Putin-Sympathizer Parties in the European Parliament. *Problems of Post-Communism*, 67(1), 53–63. https://doi.org/10.1080/10758216.2018.1530941

Golovchenko, Y., Hartmann, M., & Adler-Nissen, R. (2018). State, Media and Civil Society in the Information Warfare over Ukraine: Citizen Curators of Digital Disinformation. *International Affairs*, 94(5), 975–994. https://doi.org/10.1093/Ia/Iiy148

Götz, E. (2016). Russia, the West, and the Ukraine Crisis: Three Contending Perspectives. *Contemporary Politics*, 22(3), 249–266. https://doi.org/10.1080/13569775.2016.1201313

Graumann, C., & Kallmeyer, W. (2002). Perspective and Perspectivation in Discourse. An Introduction. In C. F. Graumann & W. Kallmeyer (Eds.), *Perspective and Perspectivation in Discourse* (pp. 1–11). J. Benjamins Pub. Co.

Green, D. M., & Bogard, C. J. (2012). The Making of Friends and Enemies: Assessing the Determinants of International Identity Construction. *Democracy and Security*, *8*(3), 277–314. https://doi.org/10.1080/17419166.2012.715469

Green, M. C., Brock, T. C., & Kaufman, G. F. (2004). Understanding Media Enjoyment: The Role of Transportation into Narrative Worlds. *Communication Theory*, *14*(4), 311–327. https://doi.org/10.1111/J.1468-2885.2004.Tb00317.X

Gregg, B. G. (2012). *Human Rights as Social Construction*. Cambridge University Press.

Gregory, B. (2008). Public Diplomacy: Sunrise of an Academic Field. The *ANNALS of the American Academy of Political and Social Science*, *616*(1), 274–290. https://doi.org/10.1177/0002716207311723

Grix, J., & Kramareva, N. (2017). The Sochi Winter Olympics and Russia's Unique Soft Power Strategy. *Sport in Society*, *20*(4), 461–475. https://doi.org/10.1080/17430437.2015.1100890

Grix, J., & Lee, D. (2013). Soft Power, Sports Mega-Events and Emerging States: The Lure of the Politics of Attraction. *Global Society*, *27*(4), 521–536. https://doi.org/10.1080/13600826.2013.827632

Grusky, D. B., & Szelényi, S. (Eds.). (2011). The *Inequality Reader: Contemporary and Foundational Readings in Race, Class, and Gender* (2nd Ed). Westview Press.

Gunn, T. J. (2003). Shaping an Islamic Identity: Religion, Islamism, and the State in Central Asia. *Sociology of Religion*, *64*(3), 389–410. https://doi.org/10.2307/3712492

Hacking, I. (1999). The *Social Construction of What?* Harvard University Press.

Hallin, D. C. (1984). The Media, the War in Vietnam, and Political Support: A Critique of the Thesis of an Oppositional Media. The *Journal of Politics*, *46*(1), 2–24. https://doi.org/10.2307/2130432

Hallin, D. C., & Mancini, P. (2004). *Comparing Media Systems: Three Models of Media and Politics*. Cambridge University Press.

Hansen, F. S. (2015). Framing Yourself into a Corner: Russia, Crimea, and the Minimal Action Space. *European Security*, *24*(1), 141–158. https://doi.org/10.1080/09662839.2014.993974

Harle, V. (1994). On the Concepts of the "Other" and the "Enemy." *History of European Ideas*, *19*(1–3), 27–34. https://doi.org/10.1016/0191-6599(94)90193-7

Härtel, A. (2019). The EU Member States and the Crisis in Ukraine: Towards an Eclectic Explanation. *Romanian Journal of European Affairs*, *19*(2), 87–106.

Hartmann, M., Golovchenko, Y., & Augenstein, I. (2019). *Mapping (Dis-)Information Flow about the MH17 Plane Crash.* https://doi.org/10.48550/ARXIV.1910.01363

Hast, S. (2014). *Spheres of Influence in International Relations: History, Theory and Politics.* Routledge. https://doi.org/10.4324/9781315610344

Hayes, A. F., & Krippendorff, K. (2007). Answering the Call for a Standard Reliability Measure for Coding Data. *Communication Methods and Measures, 1*(1), 77–89. https://doi.org/10.1080/19312450709336664

Heider, F. (1946). Attitudes and Cognitive Organization. The *Journal of Psychology, 21*(1), 107–112. https://doi.org/10.1080/00223980.1946.9917275

Herrmann, R. K., & Fischerkeller, M. P. (1995). Beyond the Enemy Image and Spiral Model: Cognitive-Strategic Research After the Cold War. *International Organization, 49*(3), 415–450. https://doi.org/10.1017/S0020818300033336

Himes, J. S. (1966). The Functions of Racial Conflict. *Social Forces, 45*(1), 1–10. https://doi.org/10.1093/Sf/45.1.1

Hinck, R. S., Kluver, R., & Cooley, S. (2018). Russia Re-Envisions the World: Strategic Narratives in Russian Broadcast and News Media During 2015. *Russian Journal of Communication, 10*(1), 21–37. https://doi.org/10.1080/19409419.2017.1421096

Hjorth, F., & Adler-Nissen, R. (2019). Ideological Asymmetry in the Reach of Pro-Russian Digital Disinformation to United States Audiences. *Journal of Communication, 69*(2), 168–192. https://doi.org/10.1093/Joc/Jqz006

Hoffmann, J., & Hawkins, V. (Eds.). (2015). *Communication and Peace: Mapping an Emerging Field.* Routledge, Taylor & Francis Group.

Hogg, M. A. (2000). Subjective Uncertainty Reduction Through Self-Categorization: A Motivational Theory of Social Identity Processes. *European Review of Social Psychology, 11*(1), 223–255. https://doi.org/10.1080/14792772043000040

Holsti, O. (1967). Cognitive Dynamics and Images of the Enemy. *Journal of International Affairs, 21*(1), 16–39.

Holt, R. R., & Silverstein, B. (1989). On the Psychology of Enemy Images: Introduction and Overview. *Journal of Social Issues, 45*(2), 1–11. https://doi.org/10.1111/J.1540-4560.1989.Tb01539.X

Horbyk, R. (2015). Little Patriotic War: Nationalist Narratives in the Russian Media Coverage of the Ukraine-Russia Crisis: Media Reviews. *Asian Politics & Policy, 7*(3), 505–511. https://doi.org/10.1111/Aspp.12193

Huang, D.-A., & Kitani, K. M. (2014). Action-Reaction: Forecasting the Dynamics of Human Interaction. In D. Fleet, T. Pajdla, B. Schiele, & T. Tuytelaars (Eds.), *Computer Vision – ECCV 2014* (Vol. 8695, pp. 489–504). Springer International Publishing. https://doi.org/10.1007/978-3-319-10584-0_32

Hungary's Orban Vows Defence of "Christian" Europe. (2019). Al Jazeera. https://www.aljazeera.com/news/2019/02/hungary-orban-vows-defence-christian-europe-190210195421238.html

Irvin-Erickson, D. (2021). Raphaël Lemkin, Genocide, Colonialism, Famine, and Ukraine. *East/West: Journal of Ukrainian Studies, 8*(1), 193–215. https://doi.org/10.21226/Ewjus645

Ivanov, A. G. (2017). Russia and the West: Conflict of Interests or a New Cold War? *Historical and Social-Educational Ideas, 9*(5/2), 63–67. https://doi.org/10.17748/2075-9908-2017-9-5/2-63-67

Ivie, R. L. (2003). Evil Enemy Versus Agonistic Other: Rhetorical Constructions of Terrorism. *Review of Education, Pedagogy, and Cultural Studies, 25*(3), 181–200. https://doi.org/10.1080/10714410390225939

Jacobs, L., & Hooghe, M. (2019). Public Television and Anti-Immigrant Sentiments in Europe. a Multilevel Analysis of Patterns in Television Consumption. *Communications, 0*(0). https://doi.org/10.1515/Commun-2019-2025

Jacobs, L., & van Spanje, J. (2020). Prosecuted, yet Popular? Hate Speech Prosecution of Anti-Immigration Politicians in the News and Electoral Support. *Comparative European Politics, 18*(6), 899–924. https://doi.org/10.1057/S41295-020-00215-4

Jin, J., Pei, G., & Ma, Q. (2017). They Are What You Hear in Media Reports: The Racial Stereotypes Toward Uyghurs Activated by Media. *Frontiers in Neuroscience, 11*, 675. https://doi.org/10.3389/Fnins.2017.00675

Johnson-Cartee, K. S., & Copeland, G. (2004). *Strategic Political Communication: Rethinking Social Influence, Persuasion, and Propaganda*. Rowman & Littlefield.

Jones, A., Kovacich, G. L., & Luzwick, P. G. (2002). *Global Information Warfare: How Businesses, Governments, and Others Achieve Objectives and Attain Competitive Advantages*. Auerbach Publications.

Juzefovičs, J., & Vihalemm, T. (2020). Keeping Channels Open or Screening Out? the Digital Practices of Baltic Russian-Speakers During the Russia-Ukraine Conflict. *Russian Journal of Communication, 12*(3), 262–283. https://doi.org/10.1080/19409419.2020.1851454

Kaiser, J., & Kleinen-von Königslöw, K. (2017). The Framing of the Euro Crisis in German and Spanish Online News Media between 2010 and 2014: Does a Common European Public Discourse Emerge? *JCMS: Journal of Common Market Studies, 55*(4), 798–814. https://doi.org/10.1111/jcms.12515

Kallis, A. (2015). Islamophobia in Europe: The Radical Right and the Mainstream. *Insight Turkey, 14*(4), 27–37.

Kalogeropoulos, A., Svensson, H. M., van Dalen, A., De Vreese, C., & Albæk, E. (2015). Are Watchdogs Doing Their Business? Media Coverage of Economic News. *Journalism: Theory, Practice & Criticism, 16*(8), 993–1009.https://doi.org/10.1177/1464884914554167

Kamalipour, Y. R. (Ed.). (1997). *The U.S. Media and the Middle East: Image and Perception*.

Karafoulidis, T. (2012). Audience: A Weak Link in the Securitization of the Environment? in J. Scheffran, M. Brzoska, H. G. Brauch, P. M. Link, & J. Schilling (Eds.), *Climate Change, Human Security and Violent Conflict* (Vol. 8, pp. 259–272). Springer Berlin Heidelberg.

Karami, A., Lundy, M., Webb, F., Turner-McGrievy, G., McKeever, B. W., & McKeever, R. (2021). Identifying and Analyzing Health-Related Themes in Disinformation Shared by Conservative and Liberal Russian Trolls on Twitter. *International Journal of Environmental Research and Public Health, 18*(4), 2159. https://doi.org/10.3390/Ijerph18042159

Kazakov, A., & Shestov, B. (2016). Cognitive Potential of Framing and Attribute Agenda-setting Theories (Exemplified by "Novaya Gazeta" and "The New York Times" Coverage of the Conflict in Southeast Ukraine). *World of Media. Journal of Russian Media and Journalism Studies, 6*, 147–166.

Kazun, A. (2019). To Cover or Not to Cover: Alexei Navalny in Russian Media. *International Area Studies Review, 22*(4), 312–326. https://doi.org/10.1177/2233865919846727

Kelsen, H. (1948). Collective Security and Collective Self-Defense Under the Charter of the United Nations. The *American Journal of International Law, 42*(4), 783. https://doi.org/10.2307/2193350

Kempner, R. M. W. (1940). The Enemy Alien Problem in the Present War. The *American Journal of International Law, 34*(3), 443–458. https://doi.org/10.2307/2192924

Kernan, W. F. (1943). We the People and Foreign Affairs. The *Virginia Quarterly Review, 19*(1), 20–36.

Khaldarova, I. (2021). Brother or 'Other'? Transformation of Strategic Narratives in Russian Television News During the Ukrainian Crisis. *Media, War & Conflict, 14*(1), 3–20. https://doi.org/10.1177/1750635219846016

Khaldarova, I., & Pantti, M. (2016). Fake News: The Narrative Battle over the Ukrainian Conflict. *Journalism Practice, 10*(7), 891–901. https://doi.org/10.1080/17512786.2016.1163237

Knudsen, O. F. (2001). Post-Copenhagen Security Studies: Desecuritizing Securitization. *Security Dialogue, 32*(3), 355–368. https://doi.org/10.1177/0967010601032003007

Ko, K., Lee, H., & Jang, S. (2009). The Internet Dilemma and Control Policy: Political and Economic Implications of the Internet in North Korea. *Korean Journal of Defense Analysis, 21*(3), 279–295. https://doi.org/10.1080/10163270903087204

Koivula, N. (1999). Gender Stereotyping in Televised Media Sport Coverage. *Sex Roles, 41*(7/8), 589–604. https://doi.org/10.1023/A:1018899522353

Koller, C. (2008). The Recruitment of Colonial Troops in Africa and Asia and Their Deployment in Europe During the First World War. *Immigrants & Minorities, 26*(1–2), 111–133. https://doi.org/10.1080/02619280802442639

Kostyuchenko, E. (2015). 'My vse znali, na chto idem i chto mozhet byt' Interv'ju s rossijskim tankistom, kotoryj vmeste so svoim batal'onom byl komandirovan srazhat'sja za Debal'cevo ['We all knew what we were getting into and what could happen' An interview with a Russian trooper who, along with his battalion, was sent to fight for Debaltseve]. *Novaya Gazeta.* https://novayagazeta.ru/articles/2015/03/02/63264-171-my-vse-znali-na-chto-idem-i-chto-mozhet-byt-187

Kotlyarov, I., & Puzyreva, Y. (2014). Grazhdanskaja vojna v Ukraine: mezhdunarodnoe pravo i ugolovnaja otvetstvennost' individov za sovershenie mezhdunarodnyh prestuplenij. *Moskovskij Zhurnal Mezhdunarodnogo Prava* [Civil War in Ukraine: International Law and Criminal Responsibility of Individuals for Committing International Crimes. *Moscow Journal of International Law*], *96*(4), 16–39.

Kozlowska, H. (2014). The Fascists Are Coming, the Fascists Are Coming! *Foreign Policy.* https://foreignpolicy.com/2014/06/02/the-fascists-are-coming-the-fascists-are-coming/

Kragh, M., & Åsberg, S. (2017). Russia's Strategy for Influence Through Public Diplomacy and Active Measures: The Swedish Case. *Journal of Strategic Studies, 40*(6), 773–816. https://doi.org/10.1080/01402390.2016.1273830

La Ferle, C., Edwards, S. M., & Lee, W.-N. (2000). Teens' Use of Traditional Media and the Internet. *Journal of Advertising Research, 40*(3), 55–65. https://doi.org/10.2501/JAR-40-3-55-65

Lachman, R., Lachman, J. L., & Butterfield, E. (2015). *Cognitive Psychology and Information Processing: An Introduction.* Psychology Press

Lachowski, T. (2015). International Criminal Court—The Central Figure of Transitional Justice? Tailoring Post-Violence Strategies, with Special Reference to Ukraine. The *Polish Quarterly of International Affairs, 3*, 39–58.

Lanoszka, A. (2019). Disinformation in International Politics. *European Journal of International Security, 4*(2), 227–248. https://doi.org/10.1017/Eis.2019.6

Lara-Cabrera, R., Gonzalez Pardo, A., Benouaret, K., Faci, N., Benslimane, D., & Camacho, D. (2017). Measuring the Radicalisation Risk in Social Networks. *IEEE Access, 5*, 10892–10900. https://doi.org/10.1109/ACCESS.2017.2706018

Laruelle, M. (2015). Russia as a "Divided Nation," from Compatriots to Crimea: A Contribution to the Discussion on Nationalism and Foreign Policy. *Problems of Post-Communism, 62*(2), 88–97. https://doi.org/10.1080/10758216.2015.1010902

Laruelle, M. (2016). The Three Colors of Novorossiya, or the Russian Nationalist Mythmaking of the Ukrainian Crisis. *Post-Soviet Affairs, 32*(1), 55–74. https://doi.org/10.1080/1060586X.2015.1023004

Lasorsa, D., & Dai, J. (2007). When News Reporters Deceive: The Production of Stereotypes. *Journalism & Mass Communication Quarterly, 84*(2), 281–298. https://doi.org/10.1177/107769900708400206

Lazarsfeld, P. F., Berelson, B., & Gaudet, H. (1968). The *People's Choice: How the Voter Makes up His Mind in a Presidential Campaign* (3. Ed). Columbia Univ. Press.

Lazutin, L. (2015). Nekotorye Voprosy Nemezhdunarodnogo Vooruzhennogo Konflikta Na Primere Grazhdanskoj Vojny Na Ukraine. *Rossijskij Juridiceskij Zurnal* [Some Issues of Non-International Armed Conflict on the Example of the Civil War in Ukraine. *Russian Journal of Law*], *103*(4), 26–29.

Lee, S. C., Muncaster, R. G., & Zinnes, D. A. (1994). The Friend of My Enemy Is My Enemy?: Modeling Triadic Internation Relationships. *Synthese, 100*(3), 333–358. https://doi.org/10.1007/BF01063907

Leichtova, M. B. (2016). Why Crimea Was Always Ours: Legitimacy Building in Russia in the Wake of the Crisis in Ukraine and the Annexation of Crimea. *Russian Politics, 1*(3), 291–315. https://doi.org/10.1163/2451-8921-00103004

Lester, P. M., & Ross, S. D. (Eds.). (2003). *Images that Injure: Pictorial Stereotypes in the Media* (2nd Ed). Praeger.

Levada Center. (2014a). *Samye Zapominajushhiesja Sobytija (Mart 2014) [Most Remembered Events (March 2014)]*. https://www.levada.ru/2014/03/26/samye-zapominayushhiesya-sobytiya-5/

Levada Center. (2014b). *Samye Zapominajushhiesja Sobytija (Aprel' 2014) [Most Remembered Events (April 2014)]*. https://www.levada.ru/2014/04/29/samye-zapominayushhiesya-sobytiya-6/

Levada Center. (2014c). *Samye Zapominajushhiesja Sobytija (Maj 2014) [Most Remembered Events (May 2014)]*. https://www.levada.ru/2014/05/29/samye-zapominayushhiesya-sobytiya-7/

Levada Center. (2015). *Mezhdunarodnye Otnoshenija [International relations]*. https://www.levada.ru/2015/02/09/mezhdunarodnye-otnosheniya/

Levada Center. (2016). *SMI: Vnimanie I Cenzura [Media: Attention and Censorship]*. https://www.levada.ru/2016/06/06/smi-vnimanie-i-tsenzura/

Levada Center. (2017a). *Prosmotr Novostej [Consumption of News]*. https://www.levada.ru/2017/07/28/prosmotr-novostej/

Levada Center. (2017b). *Rossijskij Medialandshaft 2017 [Russian Media Landscape 2017]*. https://www.levada.ru/2017/08/22/16440/

Levada Center. (2021). *Krym*. https://www.levada.ru/2021/04/26/krym/

Levada Center. (2022). The *Conflict with Ukraine*. https://www.levada.ru/en/2022/04/11/the-conflict-with-ukraine/

Leyens, J.-P., Rodriguez-Perez, A., Rodriguez-Torres, R., Gaunt, R., Paladino, M.-P., Vaes, J., & Demoulin, S. (2001). Psychological Essentialism and the Differential Attribution of Uniquely Human Emotions to Ingroups and Outgroups. *European Journal of Social Psychology, 31*(4), 395–411. https://doi.org/10.1002/Ejsp.50

Libicki, M. C. (1995). *What Is Information Warfare*. National Defense University. Center for Advanced Concepts and Technology. Institute for National Strategic Studies. https://apps.dtic.mil/dtic/tr/fulltext/u2/a367662.pdf

Lichtenstein, D., Esau, K., Pavlova, L., Osipov, D., & Argylov, N. (2019). Framing the Ukraine Crisis: A Comparison Between Talk Show Debates in Russian and German Television. *International Communication Gazette, 81*(1), 66–88. https://doi.org/10.1177/1748048518755209

Linke, A. M., Witmer, F. D. W., & O'Loughlin, J. (2012). Space-Time Granger Analysis of the War in Iraq: A Study of Coalition and Insurgent Action-Reaction. *International Interactions, 38*(4), 402–425. https://doi.org/10.1080/03050629.2012.696996

Linz, J. J. (2000). *Totalitarian and Authoritarian Regimes*. Lynne Rienner Publishers.

Lipman, M. (2018). Russia's Nongovernmental Media Under Assault. In P. Rollberg & M. Laruelle (Eds.), *Mass Media in the Post-Soviet World: Market Forces, State Actors, and Political Manipulation in the Informational Environment After Communism* (pp. 41–55). Ibidem-Verlag.

Lipman, M., & McFaul, M. (2001). "Managed Democracy" in Russia. Putin and the Press. *Press/Politics, 6*(3), 116–127.

Litvinenko, A., & Toepfl, F. (2019). The "Gardening" of an Authoritarian Public at Large: How Russia's Ruling Elites Transformed the Country's Media Landscape After the 2011/12 Protests "For Fair Elections." *Publizistik, 64*(2), 225–240. https://doi.org/10.1007/S11616-019-00486-2

Liu, Z. (2020). News Framing of the Euromaidan Protests in the Hybrid Regime and the Liberal Democracy: Comparison of Russian and UK News Media. *Media, War & Conflict*, 175063522095344. https://doi.org/10.1177/1750635220953445

Loane, J. (1965). Treason and Aiding the Enemy. *Military Law Review, 30*, 43–81.

Lorimer, M. (2021). What Do They Talk about when They Talk about Europe? Euro-Ambivalence in Far Right Ideology. *Ethnic and Racial Studies, 44*(11), 2016–2033. https://doi.org/10.1080/01419870.2020.1807035

Lukyanova, G. (2018). Framing in Russian TV News: How to Shape Reality? *SHS Web of Conferences, 50*, 1–6. https://doi.org/10.1051/Shsconf/20185001098

Lysenko, V. V., & Desouza, K. C. (2014). Charting the Coevolution of Cyberprotest and Counteraction: The Case of Former Soviet Union States from 1997 to 2011. *Convergence: The International Journal of Research into New Media Technologies, 20*(2), 176–200. https://doi.org/10.1177/1354856512459716

Mahfouz, I. M. (2018). The Representation of Meghan Markle in Facebook Posts: A Discourse Historical Approach (DHA). *International Journal of Language & Linguistics, 5*(3). https://doi.org/10.30845/Ijll.V5n3p24

Maidan-2013. (2013). Kyiv International Institute of Sociology (KIIS). https://www.kiis.com.ua/?lang=eng&cat=reports&id=216&page=1&y=2013

'Make Our Planet Great Again': Macron Rebukes Trump over Paris Withdrawal – Video. (2017). Reuters.

Malay, V. V., Krupskaya, S. U., Orehova, M. S., Timoshkova, O. A., & Fomichev, N. N. (2018). European Regional Conflicts of the Second Half of the 1930s and the Evolution of the National-Socialist Image of Enemy. *Journal of History Culture and Art Research, 7*(2), 146. https://doi.org/10.7596/Taksad.V7i2.1598

Marxsen, C. (2014). The Crimea Crisis. An International Law Perspective. *Zeitschrift für Ausländisches Öffentliches Recht und Völkerrecht, 74*, 367–391.

Maslow, A. H. (1943). The Authoritarian Character Structure. The *Journal of Social Psychology*, *18*(2), 401–411. https://doi.org/10.1080/00224545.1943.9918794

McCombs, M. E., & Shaw, D. L. (1972). The Agenda-setting Function of Mass Media. *Public Opinion Quarterly*, *36*(2), 176–187. https://doi.org/10.1086/267990

McDonald, M. (2008). Securitization and the Construction of Security. *European Journal of International Relations*, *14*(4), 563–587. https://doi.org/10.1177/1354066108097553

McGlynn, J. (2020). Historical Framing of the Ukraine Crisis Through the Great Patriotic War: Performativity, Cultural Consciousness and Shared Remembering. *Memory Studies*, *13*(6), 1058–1080. https://doi.org/10.1177/1750698018800740

McNair, B. (1996). Television in Post-Soviet Russia: From Monolith to Mafia. *Media, Culture & Society*, *18*(3), 489–499.

McNair, B. (2000). *Journalism and Democracy: An Evaluation of the Political Public Sphere*. Routledge.

McNair, B. (2014). The Media as Political Actors. In *Political Communication* (pp. 289–304). De Gruyter Mouton.

McNair, B. (2018). An *Introduction to Political Communication* (Sixth Edition). Routledge, Taylor & Francis Group.

Mearsheimer, J. (1993). The Case for a Ukrainian Nuclear Deterrent. *Foreign Affairs*, *72*(3), 50–66.

Mearsheimer, J. (2014). Why the Ukraine Crisis Is the West's Fault: The Liberal Delusions that Provoked Putin. *Foreign Affairs*, *93*(5), 77–89.

Mearsheimer, J. J. (2015). Don't Arm Ukraine. The *New York Times*. https://www.nytimes.com/2015/02/09/opinion/dont-arm-ukraine.html?msclkid=f379a1d1bcaa11ec9338045510f260ca

Meer, S. J. (1955). Authoritarian Attitudes and Dreams. The *Journal of Abnormal and Social Psychology*, *51*(1), 74–78. https://doi.org/10.1037/H0044629

Mejias, U. A., & Vokuev, N. E. (2017). Disinformation and the Media: The Case of Russia and Ukraine. *Media, Culture & Society*, *39*(7), 1027–1042. https://doi.org/10.1177/0163443716686672

Merkel Calls for Unity and Tolerance in New Year's Speech. (2018). [YouTube Video]. DW News. https://www.youtube.com/watch?v=aMR6HCP34dc

Merkley, E. (2020). Are Experts (News)Worthy? Balance, Conflict, and Mass Media Coverage of Expert Consensus. *Political Communication*, *37*(4), 530–549. https://doi.org/10.1080/10584609.2020.1713269

Mickiewicz, E. P. (1988). *Split Signals: Television and Politics in the Soviet Union*. Oxford University Press.

Mikkonen, S. (2010). Stealing the Monopoly of Knowledge?: Soviet Reactions to U.S. Cold War Broadcasting. *Kritika: Explorations in Russian and Eurasian History*, 11(4), 771–805. https://doi.org/10.1353/Kri.2010.0012

Miskimmon, A., & O'Loughlin, B. (2017). Russia's Narratives of Global Order: Great Power Legacies in a Polycentric World. *Politics and Governance*, 5(3), 111–120. https://doi.org/10.17645/Pag.V5i3.1017

Moeller, S. D. (1999). *Compassion Fatigue: How the Media Sell Disease, Famine, War, and Death*. Routledge.

Mullen, B., Brown, R., & Smith, C. (1992). Ingroup Bias as a Function of Salience, Relevance, and Status: An Integration. *European Journal of Social Psychology*, 22(2), 103–122. https://doi.org/10.1002/Ejsp.2420220202

Munger, K. (2020). All the News that's Fit to Click: The Economics of Clickbait Media. *Political Communication*, 37(3), 376–397. https://doi.org/10.1080/10584609.2019.1687626

Murray, E. J., & Foote, F. (1979). The Origins of Fear of Snakes. *Behaviour Research and Therapy*, 17(5), 489–493. https://doi.org/10.1016/0005-7967(79)90065-2

'Muslims Are Thirsty for Islamic Caliphate Around the World' Says Militant Leader – BBC News. (2014). [YouTube Video]. BBC News. https://www.youtube.com/watch?v=-TxHWxNnixs

Nassetta, J., & Gross, K. (2020). State Media Warning Labels Can Counteract the Effects of Foreign Disinformation. *Harvard Kennedy School Misinformation Review*. https://doi.org/10.37016/Mr-2020-45

Neuwirth, R. J., & Svetlicinii, A. (2016). The Current EU/US–Russia Conflict over Ukraine and the WTO: A Preliminary Note on (Trade) Restrictive Measures. *Post-Soviet Affairs*, 32(3), 237–271. https://doi.org/10.1080/1060586X.2015.1039330

Nossek, H. (2004). Our News and Their News: The Role of National Identity in the Coverage of Foreign News. *Journalism: Theory, Practice & Criticism*, 5(3), 343–368. https://doi.org/10.1177/1464884904044941

Nye, J. S. (2008). Public Diplomacy and Soft Power. The *ANNALS of the American Academy of Political and Social Science*, 616(1), 94–109. https://doi.org/10.1177/0002716207311699

Ó Fathaigh, R., Dobber, T., Zuiderveen Borgesius, F., & Shires, J. (2021). Microtargeted Propaganda by Foreign Actors: An Interdisciplinary Exploration. *Maastricht Journal of European and Comparative Law*, 28(6), 856–877. https://doi.org/10.1177/1023263X211042471

Oates, S. (2016). Russian Media in the Digital Age: Propaganda Rewired. *Russian Politics*, 1(4), 398–417. https://doi.org/10.1163/2451-8921-00104004

Onuf, N. G. (2013). *World of Our Making: Rules and Rule in Social Theory and International Relations* (Reissued). Routledge.

Oppenheimer, L. (2005). The Development of Enemy Images in Dutch Children: Measurement and Initial Findings. *British Journal of Developmental Psychology, 23*(4), 645–660. https://doi.org/10.1348/026151005X36155

Oppenheimer, L. (2006). The Development of Enemy Images: A Theoretical Contribution. *Peace and Conflict: Journal of Peace Psychology, 12*(3), 269–292. https://doi.org/10.1207/S15327949pac1203_4

Oppenheimer, L. (2010). Are Children's Views of the 'Enemy' Shaped by a Highly-Publicized Negative Event? *International Journal of Behavioral Development, 34*(4), 345–353. https://doi.org/10.1177/0165025409339098

Orleans, L. (1971). The Fallacy of Sino-American Enmity: The View from Moscow. *World Affairs, 134*(3), 261–266.

OSCE Special Monitoring Mission to Ukraine. (2020). *Civilian Casualties in the Conflict-Affected Regions of Eastern Ukraine*. OSCE Special Monitoring Mission to Ukraine. https://www.osce.org/files/f/documents/f/b/469734.pdf

OSCE Special Monitoring Mission to Ukraine. (2022). *2021 Trends and Observations from the Special Monitoring Mission to Ukraine*. OSCE Special Monitoring Mission to Ukraine. https://www.osce.org/files/f/documents/2/a/511327.pdf

Ottosen, R. (1995). Enemy Images and the Journalistic Process. *Journal of Peace Research, 32*(1), 97–112.

Pacilli, M. G., Roccato, M., Pagliaro, S., & Russo, S. (2016). From Political Opponents to Enemies? the Role of Perceived Moral Distance in the Animalistic Dehumanization of the Political Outgroup. *Group Processes & Intergroup Relations, 19*(3), 360–373. https://doi.org/10.1177/1368430215590490

Page, B. I. (1996). The Mass Media as Political Actors. *PS: Political Science and Politics, 29*(1), 20. https://doi.org/10.2307/420185

Pan, Z., & Kosicki, G. (1993). Framing Analysis: An Approach to News Discourse. *Political Communication, 10*(1), 55–75. https://doi.org/10.1080/10584609.1993.9962963

Parry, C. (1941). The Trading with the Enemy Act and the Definition of an Enemy. The *Modern Law Review, 4*(3), 161–182. https://doi.org/10.1111/J.1468-2230.1940.Tb00769.X

Pasitselska, O. (2017). Ukrainian Crisis Through the Lens of Russian Media: Construction of Ideological Discourse. *Discourse & Communication, 11*(6), 591–609. https://doi.org/10.1177/1750481317714127

Patterson, T. (2000). The United States: News in a Free-Market Society. In R. Gunther & A. Mughan (Eds.), *Democracy and the Media: A Comparative Perspective* (pp. 241–265). Cambridge University Press.

Pavković, A. (2017). Sacralisation of Contested Territory in Nationalist Discourse: A Study of Milošević's and Putin's Public Speeches. *Critical Discourse Studies, 14*(5), 497–513. https://doi.org/10.1080/17405904.2017.1360191

Peek, L., & Guikema, S. (2021). Interdisciplinary Theory, Methods, and Approaches for Hazards and Disaster Research: An Introduction to the Special Issue. *Risk Analysis, 41*(7), 1047–1058. https://doi.org/10.1111/Risa.13777

Peters, M. A. (2017). The Information Wars, Fake News and the End of Globalisation. *Educational Philosophy and Theory, 50*(13), 1161–1164. https://doi.org/10.1080/00131857.2017.1417200

Pew Research Center. (2014, July). *Russia's Global Image Negative Amid Crisis in Ukraine.* https://www.pewresearch.org/global/2014/07/09/russias-global-image-negative-amid-crisis-in-ukraine/

Piskulov, Y. (2015). Rossija – Zapad: Obratnaja Storona Konflikta (Razmyshlenija Jekonomista). *Mezhdunarodnaja Jekonomika* [Russia – West: Reverse Side of the Conflict (Thinking Economist). *International Economics*], *1,* 4–8.

Połońska-Kimunguyi, E., & Gillespie, M. (2016). Terrorism Discourse on French International Broadcasting: France 24 and the Case of Charlie Hebdo Attacks in Paris. *European Journal of Communication, 31*(5), 568–583. https://doi.org/10.1177/0267323116669453

Pomerantsev, P. (2021). Memory in the Age of Impunity. *Coda Story.* https://www.codastory.com/disinformation/modern-memory/

Pörksen, B., Koeck, A. R., & Koeck, W. K. (2011). *The Creation of Reality: A Constructivist Epistemology of Journalism and Journalism Education.* Imprint Academic.

Powell, K. A. (2011). Framing Islam: An Analysis of U.S. Media Coverage of Terrorism Since 9/11. *Communication Studies, 62*(1), 90–112. https://doi.org/10.1080/10510974.2011.533599

Pozacherhovi vybory narodnyh deputativ Ukrayiny 26 zhovtnya 2014 roku. Vidomosti pro pidrahunok holosiv vyborciv po zahal'noderzhavnomu bahatomandatnomu vyborchomu okruhu. (2014). Central'na vyborcha komisiya Ukrayiny [The Central Election Commission of Ukraine]. https://web.archive.org/web/20141028181914/http://www.cvk.gov.ua/pls/vnd2014/wp300pt001f01=910.html

Price, M. E., Haas, S., & Margolin, D. (2008). New Technologies and International Broadcasting: Reflections on Adaptations and Transformations. The ANNALS of the American Academy of Political and Social Science, 616(1), 150–172. https://doi.org/10.1177/0002716207312033

Putin Nazval Russkih I Ukraincev Odnim Narodom [Putin Called Russians and Ukrainians One Folk]. (2022). Ria.Ru. https://ria.ru/20220303/narod-1776354059.html?msclkid=7aeb96f2bea111eca96f3c9013c9c59c

Putin Ob'javil O Nachale Voennoj Operacii Po Zashhite Donbassa [Putin Announced the Start of a Military Operation to Protect the Donbass]. (2022, February 24). Lenta.Ru. https://lenta.ru/news/2022/02/24/operation/

Putin, V. (2014). *Obrashhenie Prezidenta Rossijskoj Federacii*. Kremlin.Ru. http://www.kremlin.ru/events/president/news/20603

Putin, V. (2021). *Poslanie Prezidenta Federal'nomu Sobraniyu*. Kremlin.Ru. http://kremlin.ru/events/president/news/65418

Rabbie, J. M., & Horwitz, M. (1969). Arousal of Ingroup-Outgroup Bias by a Chance Win or Loss. *Journal of Personality and Social Psychology*, 13(3), 269–277.

Rabil, R. (2011). *Religion, National Identity, and Confessional Politics in Lebanon: The Challenge of Islamism*. Palgrave Macmillan.

Rai, T. S., Valdesolo, P., & Graham, J. (2017). Dehumanization Increases Instrumental Violence, but Not Moral Violence. *Proceedings of the National Academy of Sciences*, 114(32), 8511–8516. https://doi.org/10.1073/Pnas.1705238114

Raik, K. (2019). The Ukraine Crisis as a Conflict over Europe's Political, Economic and Security Order. *Geopolitics*, 24(1), 51–70. https://doi.org/10.1080/14650045.2017.1414046

Ramsay, G., & Robertshaw, S. (2019). *Weaponising News RT, Sputnik and Targeted Disinformation*. King's College London Centre for the Study of Media, Communication & Power. https://www.kcl.ac.uk/policy-institute/assets/weaponising-news.pdf

Raskin, J. D. (2002). Constructivism in Psychology: Personal Construct Psychology, Radical Constructivism, and Social Constructionism. *American Communication Journal*, 5(3), 1–26.

Rauscher, W., & Suppan, A. (Eds.). (2016). *Österreich zwischen Isolation und Anschluss: 28. September 1937 bis 15. März 1938*. Verlag der Österreichischen Akademie der Wissenschaften.

Rawnsley, G. D. (2015). To Know Us Is to Love Us: Public Diplomacy and International Broadcasting in Contemporary Russia and China. *Politics*, 35(3–4), 273–286. https://doi.org/10.1111/1467-9256.12104

Read, J. M. (1938). Atrocity Propaganda and the Irish Rebellion. *Public Opinion Quarterly*, 2(2), 229. https://doi.org/10.1086/265177

Reisigl, M., & Wodak, R. (2001). *Discourse and Discrimination: Rhetorics of Racism and Antisemitism* (1. Publ). Routledge.

Reporters Without Borders. (2021). *2021 World Press Freedom Index* [Ranking 2021]. Reporters Without Borders (RSF). https://rsf.org/en/ranking/2021

Reporters Without Borders. (2023). *2021 World Press Freedom Index* [Index 2023]. Reporters Without Borders (RSF). https://rsf.org/en/index

Richter, A. (2008). Post-Soviet Perspective on Censorship and Freedom of the Media: An Overview. *International Communication Gazette*, 70(5), 307-324. https://doi.org/10.1177/1748048508094291

Rieber, R. W., & Kelly, R. J. (1991). Substance and Shadow: Images of the Enemy. In *The Psychology of War and Peace: The Image of the Enemy* (pp. 3-39). Plenum Press.

Rietjens, S. (2019). Unraveling Disinformation: The Case of Malaysia Airlines Flight MH17. *The International Journal of Intelligence, Security, and Public Affairs*, 21(3), 195-218. https://doi.org/10.1080/23800992.2019.1695666

Rinder, I. D. (1954). Identification Reaction and Intergroup Conflict. *Phylon (1940-1956)*, 15(4), 365-370. https://doi.org/10.2307/272846

Ritter, H. R. (1975). Hermann Neubacher and the Austrian Anschluss Movement, 1918-40. *Central European History*, 8(4), 348-369. https://doi.org/10.1017/S000893890001801X

Robertson, E. (2014). Propaganda and 'Manufactured Hatred': A Reappraisal of the Ethics of First World War British and Australian Atrocity Propaganda. *Public Relations Inquiry*, 3(2), 245-266. https://doi.org/10.1177/2046147X14542958

Robinson, J. (1945). Transfer of Property in Enemy Occupied Territory. *The American Journal of International Law*, 39(2), 216-230. https://doi.org/10.2307/2192342

Rollberg, P., & Laruelle, M. (Eds.). (2018). *Mass Media in the Post-Soviet World: Market Forces, State Actors, and Political Manipulation in the Informational Environment After Communism*. Ibidem-Verlag.

Roman, N., Wanta, W., & Buniak, I. (2017). Information Wars: Eastern Ukraine Military Conflict Coverage in the Russian, Ukrainian and U.S. Newscasts. *International Communication Gazette*, 79(4), 357-378. https://doi.org/10.1177/1748048516682138

Rose, A. M. (1960). The Comparative Study of Intergroup Conflict. *The Sociological Quarterly, 1*(1), 57–66. https://doi.org/10.1111/J.1533-8525.1960.Tb01460.X

Roselle, L., Miskimmon, A., & O'Loughlin, B. (2014). Strategic Narrative: A New Means to Understand Soft Power. *Media, War & Conflict, 7*(1), 70–84. https://doi.org/10.1177/1750635213516696

Rosenson, B. A. (2015). Media Coverage of State Legislatures: Negative, Neutral, or Positive? *Social Science Quarterly, 96*(5), 1291–1300. https://doi.org/10.1111/Ssqu.12211

Rousseau, D. L. (2006). *Identifying Threats and Threatening Identities: The Social Construction of Realism and Liberalism*. Stanford University Press.

Rubin, M., Badea, C., & Jetten, J. (2014). Low Status Groups Show In-Group Favoritism to Compensate for Their Low Status and Compete for Higher Status. *Group Processes & Intergroup Relations, 17*(5), 563–576. https://doi.org/10.1177/1368430213514122

Saeed, A. (2007). Media, Racism and Islamophobia: The Representation of Islam and Muslims in the Media. *Sociology Compass, 1*(2), 443–462. https://doi.org/10.1111/J.1751-9020.2007.00039.X

Sakwa, R. (2015). The Death of Europe? Continental Fates After Ukraine. *International Affairs, 91*(3), 553–579. https://doi.org/10.1111/1468-2346.12281

Salute to America: President Trump Historic Lincoln Memorial Speech. (2019). [YouTube Video]. FOX 10 Phoenix. https://www.youtube.com/watch?v=ci15wxwva3Y

Samokhvalov, V. (2015). Ukraine Between Russia and the European Union: Triangle Revisited. *Europe-Asia Studies, 67*(9), 1371–1393. https://doi.org/10.1080/09668136.2015.1088513

Samuel-Azran, T. (2013). Al-Jazeera, Qatar, and New Tactics in State-Sponsored Media Diplomacy. *American Behavioral Scientist, 57*(9), 1293–1311. https://doi.org/10.1177/0002764213487736

Sande, G. N., Goethals, G. R., Ferrari, L., & Worth, L. T. (1989). Value-Guided Attributions: Maintaining the Moral Self-Image and the Diabolical Enemy-Image. *Journal of Social Issues, 45*(2), 91–118. https://doi.org/10.1111/J.1540-4560.1989.Tb01544.X

Sanders, K. (2009). *Communicating Politics in the Twenty-First Century*. Palgrave Macmillan.

Sankey, E. R. (2020). Reconsidering Spheres of Influence. *Survival, 62*(2), 37–47. https://doi.org/10.1080/00396338.2020.1739947

Sazonov, V. (2019). Some Notes on Russian Conspiracy Theories as a Part of the Information War in Ukraine: The Case of MH17. *Security Forum, 3*, 45–56. https://doi.org/10.26410/SF_1/19/3

Schäfer, M. S., Scheffran, J., & Penniket, L. (2016). Securitization of Media Reporting on Climate Change? a Cross-National Analysis in Nine Countries. *Security Dialogue*, 47(1), 76–96. https://doi.org/10.1177/0 967010615600915

Schleifer, R. (2012). The Enemy's Image: Propaganda in the Arab-Israeli Conflict. In *Enemy Images in War Propaganda* (pp. 107–126). Cambridge Scholars.

Schorkowitz, D. (2019). Was Russia a Colonial Empire? In D. Schorkowitz, J. R. Chávez, & I. W. Schröder (Eds.), *Shifting Forms of Continental Colonialism* (pp. 117–147). Springer Singapore. https://doi.org/10.1007 /978-981-13-9817-9_5

Schreck, C. (2014). Donetsk POW March: When Is a Parade a War Crime? *Radio Free Europe/Radio Liberty*. https://www.rferl.org/a/ukraine-p ow-march-war-crime/26548667.html

Schreier, M. (2012). *Qualitative Content Analysis in Practice*. SAGE.

Schuilenburg, M. (2015). The *Securitization of Society: Crime, Risk, and Social Order*. New York University Press.

Semetko, H. A., & Valkenburg, P. M. V. (2000). Framing European Politics: A Content Analysis of Press and Television News. *Journal of Communication*, 50(2), 93–109. https://doi.org/10.1111/J.1460-2466.2000.Tb0 2843.X

Sengul, K. (2019). Critical Discourse Analysis in Political Communication Research: A Case Study of Right-Wing Populist Discourse in Australia. *Communication Research and Practice*, 5(4), 376–392. https:// doi.org/10.1080/22041451.2019.1695082

Sengul, K. (2020). 'Swamped': The Populist Construction of Fear, Crisis and Dangerous Others in Pauline Hanson's Senate Speeches. *Communication Research and Practice*, 6(1), 20–37. https://doi.org/10.1080/22041 451.2020.1729970

Sergeytsev, T. (2022, April). Chto Rossija dolzhna sdelat' s Ukrainoj [What should Russia do with Ukraine?]. *Ria.ru*. https://ria.ru/20220403/u kraina-1781469605.html

Sheen, G. C.-H. (2021). Media with Reputational Concerns: Yes Men or Watchdogs? *Political Science Research and Methods*, 9(2), 345–364. https ://doi.org/10.1017/Psrm.2019.42

Shekhovtsov, A., & Umland, A. (2014). Ukraine's Radical Right. *Journal of Democracy*, 25(3), 58–63. https://doi.org/10.1353/Jod.2014.0051

Sherif, M. (1958). Superordinate Goals in the Reduction of Intergroup Conflict. *American Journal of Sociology*, 63(4), 349–356. https://doi.org/10. 1086/222258

Shestopalova, A. (2022). *Forgotten and Potentially Vulnerable: Why the Online Activity of Middle-Aged Women Matters During Global Information Warfare* (pp. 1–23) [Policy Paper]. International Centre for Defence and Security. https://icds.ee//wp-content/uploads/dlm_uploads/2022/04/ICDS_Policy_Paper_Forgotten_and_Potentially_Vulnerable_Alona_Shestopalova_April_2022.pdf

Shestopalova, A. (2023). Constructing Nazis on Political Demand: Agenda-Setting and Framing in Russian State-Controlled TV Coverage of the Euromaidan, Annexation of Crimea and the War in Donbas. *Central European Journal of International and Security Studies*, 17(2), 112–137. https://doi.org/10.51870/FUQI2558

Shevel, O. (2011). Russian Nation-Building from Yel'tsin to Medvedev: Ethnic, Civic or Purposefully Ambiguous? *Europe-Asia Studies*, 63(2), 179–202. https://doi.org/10.1080/09668136.2011.547693

Shirikov, A. (2021). Who Trusts State-Run Media? Source Cues, Bias, and Credibility in Non-Democracies. *SSRN Electronic Journal*, 69. https://doi.org/10.2139/Ssrn.3686299

Shoshani, A., & Slone, M. (2008). The Drama of Media Coverage of Terrorism: Emotional and Attitudinal Impact on the Audience. *Studies in Conflict & Terrorism*, 31(7), 627–640. https://doi.org/10.1080/10576100802144064

Siebert, F. S., Peterson, T., & Schramm, W. (1984). *Four Theories of the Press: The Authoritarian, Libertarian, Social Responsibility, and Soviet Communist Concepts of What the Press Should Be and Do*. University of Illinois Press

Signitzer, B. H., & Coombs, T. (1992). Public Relations and Public Diplomacy: Conceptual Covergences. *Public Relations Review*, 18(2), 137–147. https://doi.org/10.1016/0363-8111(92)90005-J

Silverstein, B. (1992). The Psychology of Enemy Images. In *Psychology and Social Responsibility: Facing Global Challenges* (pp. 145–162). New York University Press.

Silverstein, B., & Flamenbaum, C. (1989). Biases in the Perception and Cognition of the Actions of Enemies. *Journal of Social Issues*, 45(2), 51–72. https://doi.org/10.1111/J.1540-4560.1989.Tb01542.X

Skorkin, K. (2022). Ot Bandery Do 'Azova': Otvechaem Na Glavnye Voprosy Ob Ukrainskom Nacionalizme. Otkuda On Vzjalsja, Kak Vlijaet Na Sovremennuju Ukrainu — I Kakim Ego Izobrazhaet Rossijskaja Propaganda [From Bandera to Azov: Answering the Main Questions about Ukrainian Nationalism. Where Did It Come From, How Does It Affect Modern Ukraine — and How Russian Propaganda Depicts It]. *Meduza*. https://meduza.io/feature/2022/04/17/ot-ban dery-do-azova-otvechaem-na-glavnye-voprosy-ob-ukrainskom-nats ionalizme

Slavtcheva-Petkova, V. (2018). *Russia's Liberal Media: Handcuffed but Free* (1st Ed.). Routledge. https://doi.org/10.4324/9781315300191

Smith Finley, J. (2021). Why Scholars and Activists Increasingly Fear a Uyghur Genocide in Xinjiang. *Journal of Genocide Research, 23*(3), 348–370. https://doi.org/10.1080/14623528.2020.1848109

Smith, G., & Searles, K. (2013). Fair and Balanced News or a Difference of Opinion? Why Opinion Shows Matter for Media Effects. *Political Research Quarterly, 66*(3), 671–684. https://doi.org/10.1177/1065912912 465922

Smith, N. R. (2016). *EU-Russian Relations and the Ukraine Crisis*. Edward Elgar Publishing.

Snegovaya, M. (2021). Fellow Travelers or Trojan Horses? Similarities Across Pro-Russian Parties' Electorates in Europe. *Party Politics*, 135406882199581. https://doi.org/10.1177/1354068821995813

Soroka, S. N. (2006). Good News and Bad News: Asymmetric Responses to Economic Information. The *Journal of Politics, 68*(2), 372–385. https://doi.org/10.1111/J.1468-2508.2006.00413.X

Stabile, C. A., & Kumar, D. (2005). Unveiling Imperialism: Media, Gender and the War on Afghanistan. *Media, Culture & Society, 27*(5), 765–782. https://doi.org/10.1177/0163443705055734

Stets, J. E., & Burke, P. J. (2000). Identity Theory and Social Identity Theory. *Social Psychology Quarterly, 63*(3), 224–237. https://doi.org/10.2307/2695870

Stier, S. (2015). Democracy, Autocracy and the News: The Impact of Regime Type on Media Freedom. *Democratization, 22*(7), 1273–1295. https://doi.org/10.1080/13510347.2014.964643

Strömbäck, J. (2005). In Search of a Standard: Four Models of Democracy and Their Normative Implications for Journalism. *Journalism Studies, 6*(3), 331–345. https://doi.org/10.1080/14616700500131950

Strycharz, D. (2020). Dominant Narratives, External Shocks, and the Russian Annexation of Crimea. *Problems of Post-Communism*, 1–12. https://doi.org/10.1080/10758216.2020.1813594

Sultan, S., & Rapi, M. (2020). Positive Discourse Analysis of the Indonesian Government Spokesperson's Discursive Strategies During the Covid-19 Pandemic. *GEMA Online® Journal of Language Studies*, 20(4), 251–272. https://doi.org/10.17576/Gema-2020-2004-14

Sumner, W. G. (2007). *Folkways: A Study of Mores, Manners, Customs and Morals*. Cosimo Inc.

Svechnikov, N., & Filyukov, A. (2014). Politiko-Pravovoj Analiz Gosudarstvennogo Perevorota Na Ukraine. *Vestnik Penzenskogo Gosudarstvennogo Universiteta* [Political and Legal Analysis of the Coup in Ukraine. Bulletin of The Penza State University], 3(7), 23–27.

Szöcsik, E., & Polyakova, A. (2019). Euroscepticism and the Electoral Success of the Far Right: The Role of the Strategic Interaction Between Center and Far Right. *European Political Science*, 18(3), 400–420. https://doi.org/10.1057/S41304-018-0162-Y

Szostek, J. (2018). News Media Repertoires and Strategic Narrative Reception: A Paradox of Dis/Belief in Authoritarian Russia. *New Media & Society*, 20(1), 68–87. https://doi.org/10.1177/1461444816656638

Tajfel, H. (1970). Experiments in Intergroup Discrimination. *Scientific American*, 223(5), 96–103.

Tajfel, H. (1979). Individuals and Groups in Social Psychology*. *British Journal of Social and Clinical Psychology*, 18(2), 183–190. https://doi.org/10.1111/J.2044-8260.1979.Tb00324.X

Taradai, D. (2019). Who Is Ukraine's Enemy: Narratives in the Military Communication Regarding the War in Donbas. *Russian Journal of Communication*, 11(2), 141–156. https://doi.org/10.1080/19409419.2019.1622196

Tenove, C., Buffie, J., McKay, S., & Moscrop, D. (2018). Digital Threats to Democratic Elections: How Foreign Actors Use Digital Techniques to Undermine Democracy. *SSRN Electronic Journal*. https://doi.org/10.2139/Ssrn.3235819

Teper, Y. (2016). Official Russian Identity Discourse in Light of the Annexation of Crimea: National or Imperial? *Post-Soviet Affairs*, 32(4), 378–396. https://doi.org/10.1080/1060586X.2015.1076959

Terminove Zvernennya Prezydenta Volodymyra Zelens'koho. Ofis Prezydenta Ukrayiny [*Urgent Address of President Volodymyr Zelenskyi*. Office of the President of Ukraine]. *(2019)* [YouTube Video]. https://www.youtube.com/watch?v=zV8HppvAJj8

The European Court of Human Rights. (2021). *Complaints Brought by Ukraine Against Russia Concerning a Pattern of Human Rights Violations in Crimea Declared Partly Admissible. Press Release Issued by the Registrar of the Court*. https://www.refworld.org/cgi-bin/texis/vtx/rwmain/opendocpdf.pdf?reldoc=y&docid=60016c5f4

The Speech that Made Obama President. (2012). [YouTube Video]. https://www.youtube.com/watch?v=OFPwDe22CoY

Thomas, R. (2017). Biting the Hand: Using the Relationship Between ITV and Barclays to Examine Political Economy. *Journalism Studies, 20*(4), 585-607. https://doi.org/10.1080/1461670X.2017.1359654

Thompson, W. R., & Dreyer, D. R. (2012). *Handbook of International Rivalries, 1494-2010*. CQ Press.

Thornton, R. (2015). The Changing Nature of Modern Warfare: Responding to Russian Information Warfare. The *RUSI Journal, 160*(4), 40-48. https://doi.org/10.1080/03071847.2015.1079047

Toal, G., & O'Loughlin, J. (2018). 'Why Did MH17 Crash?': Blame Attribution, Television News and Public Opinion in Southeastern Ukraine, Crimea and the De Facto States of Abkhazia, South Ossetia and Transnistria. *Geopolitics, 23*(4), 882-916. https://doi.org/10.1080/14650045.2017.1364238

Trombetta, M. J. (2010). Rethinking the Securitization of the Environment: Old Beliefs, New Insights. In *Securitization Theory How Security Problems Emerge and Dissolve*. Routledge. https://www.taylorfrancis.com/books/e/9780203868508

Tschötschel, R., Schuck, A., Schwinges, A., & Wonneberger, A. (2021). Climate Change Policy Support, Intended Behaviour Change, and Their Drivers Largely Unaffected by Consensus Messages in Germany. *Journal of Environmental Psychology, 76*, 101655. https://doi.org/10.1016/J.Jenvp.2021.101655

Tupicyna, I., & Nejmatova, B. (2008). Sociokul'turnaja Missija Telekanala Russia Today. *Social'naja Filosofija I Sociologija Kul'tury. Uchenye Zapiski* [Sociocultural Mission of Russia Today TV Channel. *Social Philosophy and Sociology of Culture. Scholarly Notes*], 2, 85-92.

Turlington, E. (1928). Treatment of Enemy Private Property in the United States Before the World War. The *American Journal of International Law, 22*(2), 270-291. https://doi.org/10.2307/2188531

Turner, J. C. (2010). Social Categorization and the Self-Concept: A Social Cognitive Theory of Group Behavior. In *Key Readings in Social Psychology. Rediscovering Social Identity* (pp. 243-272). Psychology Press. https://psycnet.apa.org/record/2010-11535-012

Ukaz Prezydenta Ukrayiny №133/2017 [Decree of the President of Ukraine №133/2017]. (2017). https://www.president.gov.ua/documents/1332017-21850

Unwala, A., & Ghori, S. (2015). Brandishing the Cybered Bear: Information War and the Russia-Ukraine Conflict. *Military Cyber Affairs, 1*(1). https://doi.org/10.5038/2378-0789.1.1.1001

Vallone, R. P., Ross, L., & Lepper, M. R. (1985). The Hostile Media Phenomenon: Biased Perception and Perceptions of Media Bias in Coverage of the Beirut Massacre. *Journal of Personality and Social Psychology*, 49(3), 577–585. https://doi.org/10.1037/0022-3514.49.3.577

van den Driest, S. F. (2015). Crimea's Separation from Ukraine: An Analysis of the Right to Self-Determination and (Remedial) Secession in International Law. *Netherlands International Law Review*, 62(3), 329–363. https://doi.org/10.1007/S40802-015-0043-9

van der Velden, P. G., van der Meulen, E., Lenferink, L. I. M., & Yzermans, J. C. (2018). Media Experiences and Associations with Mental Health Among the Bereaved of the MH17-Disaster: A Latent Profile Analysis. *Scandinavian Journal of Psychology*, 59(3), 281–288. https://doi.org/10.1111/Sjop.12426

van Dijk, T. A. (2015). *Racism and the Press* (1st Ed.). Routledge. https://doi.org/10.4324/9781315682662

Vartanova, E., & Zassoursky, Y. N. (2003). Television in Russia Is the Concept of PSB Relevant? in G. F. Lowe, T. Hujanen, Tampereen Yliopisto, & Yleisradio Oy (Eds.), *Broadcasting & Convergence: New Articulations of the Public Service Remit* (pp. 93–108). NORDICOM.

Veebel, V., & Markus, R. (2016). At the Dawn of a New Era of Sanctions: Russian-Ukrainian Crisis and Sanctions. *Orbis*, 60(1), 128–139. https://doi.org/10.1016/J.Orbis.2015.12.001

Velychenko, S. (2002). The Issue of Russian Colonialism in Ukrainian Thought. Dependency Identity and Development. *Ab Imperio*, 2002(1), 323–367. https://doi.org/10.1353/Imp.2002.0070

Vesselkov, A., Finley, B., & Vankka, J. (2020). Russian Trolls Speaking Russian: Regional Twitter Operations and MH17. *12th ACM Conference on Web Science*, 86–95. https://doi.org/10.1145/3394231.3397898

Vetlesen, A. J. (1994). *Perception, Empathy, and Judgment: An Inquiry into the Preconditions of Moral Performance*. Pennsylvania State University Press.

Vihalemm, T., Juzefovičs, J., & Leppik, M. (2019). Identity and Media-Use Strategies of the Estonian and Latvian Russian-Speaking Populations Amid Political Crisis. *Europe-Asia Studies*, 71(1), 48–70. https://doi.org/10.1080/09668136.2018.1533916

Viki, G. T., Osgood, D., & Phillips, S. (2012). Dehumanization and Self-Reported Proclivity to Torture Prisoners of War. *Journal of Experimental Social Psychology*, 49(3), 325–328. https://doi.org/10.1016/J.Jesp.2012.11.006

Voigt, K. D. (2015). Steps Towards a Pan-European Peace Order: The Role of Russia, East Central Europe and Germany. In A. Zagorskij (Ed.), *Russia and East Central Europe After the Cold War: A Fundamentally Transformed Relationship* (pp. 13–22). Human Rights Publ.

Volkov, D., & Goncharov, S. (2014). *Rossijskij Media-Landshaft: Televidenie, Pressa, Internet [Russian Media Landscape: TV, Press, Internet]*. Levada Center. https://www.levada.ru/2014/07/08/rossijskij-media-landshaft-televidenie-pressa-internet-3/

von Glasersfeld, E. (1982). An Interpretation of Piaget's Constructivism. *Revue Internationale De Philosophie, 36*(142/143 (4)), 612–635.

Vourinen, M. (2012). Introduction: Enemy Images as Inversions of the Self. In M. Vuorinen (Ed.), *Enemy Images in War Propaganda* (pp. 1–13). Cambridge Scholars.

Wæver, O. (1995). Securitization and Desecuritization. In R. Lipschutz (Ed.), on *Security* (pp. 46–86). Columbia University Press. https://www.libraryofsocialscience.com/assets/pdf/Waever-Securitization.pdf

Wagnsson, C. (2022). The Paperboys of Russian Messaging: RT/Sputnik Audiences as Vehicles for Malign Information Influence. *Information, Communication & Society,* 1–19. https://doi.org/10.1080/1369118X.2022.2041700

Wang, J. (2006). Managing National Reputation and International Relations in the Global Era: Public Diplomacy Revisited. *Public Relations Review, 32*(2), 91–96. https://doi.org/10.1016/J.Pubrev.2005.12.001

Wang, X. (2020). *Winning American Hearts and Minds: China's Image Building Efforts in the 21st Century*.

Wanta, W., & Hu, Y.-W. (1993). The Agenda-setting Effect of International News Coverage: An Examination of Different News Frames. *International Journal of Public Opinion Research, 5*(3), 250–264. https://doi.org/10.1093/Ijpor/5.3.250

Wanta, W., Golan, G., & Lee, C. (2004). Agenda Setting and International News: Media Influence on Public Perceptions of Foreign Nations. *Journalism & Mass Communication Quarterly, 81*(2), 364–377. https://doi.org/10.1177/107769900408100209

Warren, C. (1918). What Is Giving Aid and Comfort to the Enemy? the *Yale Law Journal, 27*(3), 331–347. https://doi.org/10.2307/787437

Watanabe, K. (2017). The Spread of the Kremlin's Narratives by a Western News Agency During the Ukraine Crisis. The *Journal of International Communication, 23*(1), 138–158. https://doi.org/10.1080/13216597.2017.1287750

Weir, F. (2014). How a Poll about Nazis Brought a Russian TV Station Under Kremlin Assault. *Csmonitor*. https://www.csmonitor.com/World/Europe/2014/0203/How-a-poll-about-Nazis-brought-a-Russian-TV-station-under-Kremlin-assault#

Wendt, A. (1992). Anarchy Is What States Make of It: The Social Construction of Power Politics. *46*(2), 391–425.

Wendt, A. (1995). Constructing International Politics. *International Security*, *20*(1), 71–81.

Wertsch, J. V., & Karumidze, Z. (2009). Spinning the Past: Russian and Georgian Accounts of the War of August 2008. *Memory Studies*, *2*(3), 377–391. https://doi.org/10.1177/1750698008337566

Wettstein, M., Esser, F., Schulz, A., Wirz, D. S., & Wirth, W. (2018). News Media as Gatekeepers, Critics, and Initiators of Populist Communication: How Journalists in Ten Countries Deal with the Populist Challenge. *The International Journal of Press/Politics*, *23*(4), 476–495. https://doi.org/10.1177/1940161218785979

Wheatley, L. (2019). Resisting Islamophobia: A Young Muslim Male's Experience in a U.S. Public High School. *Religion & Education*, *46*(3), 297–323. https://doi.org/10.1080/15507394.2019.1577792

White, J. D. (1900). Trading with the Enemy. *Law Quarterly Review*, *16(64)*, 397–413.

White, R. K. (1991). Enemy Images in the United Nations-Iraq and East-West Conflicts. In the *Psychology of War and Peace: The Image of the Enemy* (pp. 59–70). Plenum Press.

Wien, C. (2005). Defining Objectivity Within Journalism. *Nordicom Review*, *26*(2), 3–15. https://doi.org/10.1515/Nor-2017-0255

Wilkin, B. (2017). *Aerial Propaganda and the Wartime Occupation of France, 1914-1918* (First Edition). Routledge Taylor & Francis Group.

Wilkinson, C. (2007). The Copenhagen School on Tour in Kyrgyzstan: Is Securitization Theory Useable Outside Europe? *Security Dialogue*, *38*(1), 5–25. https://doi.org/10.1177/0967010607075964

Williams, M. C. (2003). Words, Images, Enemies: Securitization and International Politics. *International Studies Quarterly*, *47*(4), 511–531. https://doi.org/10.1046/J.0020-8833.2003.00277.X

Wittke, C. (2019). The Minsk Agreements – More than "Scraps of Paper"? *East European Politics*, *35*(3), 264–290. https://doi.org/10.1080/21599165.2019.1635885

Wodak, R. (1999). Critical Discourse Analysis at the End of the 20th Century. *Research on Language & Social Interaction*, *32*(1–2), 185–193. https://doi.org/10.1080/08351813.1999.9683622

Wodak, R., & Reisigl, M. (2005). Discourse and Racism. In *The Handbook of Discourse Analysis* (1st ed., pp. 372–397). Wiley. https://doi.org/10.1002/9780470753460

Wodak, R. (2015a). Critical Discourse Analysis, Discourse-Historical Approach. In K. Tracy, T. Sandel, & C. Ilie (Eds.), *The International Encyclopedia of Language and Social Interaction* (1st Ed., pp. 1–14). Wiley. https://doi.org/10.1002/9781118611463

Wodak, R. (2015b). Saying the Unsayable: Denying the Holocaust in Media Debates in Austria and the UK. *Journal of Language Aggression and Conflict*, 3(1), 13–40. https://doi.org/10.1075/jlac.3.1.01wod

Wolf, R. (2019). Taking Interaction Seriously: Asymmetrical Roles and the Behavioral Foundations of Status. *European Journal of International Relations*, 25(4), 1186–1211. https://doi.org/10.1177/1354066119837338

Woo, J. (1994). Journalism Objectivity: In News Magazine Photography. *Visual Communication Quarterly*, 1(3), 9–16. https://doi.org/10.1080/15551393.1994.10387503

Wood, J. (1994). *History of International Broadcasting*. (Paperback Ed). Inst. of Electrical Engineers.

Wright, J. (1999). Trusting Flexible Friends: The Dangers of Flexibility in NATO and the West European Union/European Union. *Contemporary Security Policy*, 20(1), 111–129. https://doi.org/10.1080/13523269908404213

Wright, K., Scott, M., & Bunce, M. (2020). Soft Power, Hard News: How Journalists at State-Funded Transnational Media Legitimize Their Work. *The International Journal of Press/Politics*, 25(4), 607–631. https://doi.org/10.1177/1940161220922832

Yablokov, I., & Chatterje-Doody, P. N. (2021). *Russia Today and Conspiracy Theories: People, Power and Politics on RT*. Routledge.

Yamagishi, T., Jin, N., & Miller, A. S. (1998). In-Group Bias and Culture of Collectivism. *Asian Journal of Social Psychology*, 1(3), 315–328. https://doi.org/10.1111/1467-839X.00020

Yan, Y., & Liu, J. (2016). Effects of Media Exemplars on the Perception of Social Issues with Pre-Existing Beliefs. *Journalism & Mass Communication Quarterly*, 93(4), 1026–1049. https://doi.org/10.1177/1077699016629374

Yanchenko, K., Shestopalova, A., von Nordheim, G., & Kleinen-von Königslöw, K. (2023). "Repressed Opposition Media" or "Tools of Hybrid Warfare"? Negotiating the Boundaries of Legitimate Journalism in Ukraine Prior to Russia's Full-Scale Invasion. *The International Journal of Press/Politics*, 1–20. https://doi.org/10.1177/19401612231167791

Yatsyk, A. (2022). Biopolitical Responses to the COVID-19 Pandemic in Russia, France, Germany, and the UK: The "Post-Truth" Coverage by RT. *Social Sciences*, 11(3), 139. https://doi.org/10.3390/Socsci11030139

Young, R. L., McDowall, D., & Loftin, C. (1987). Collective Security and the Ownership of Firearms for Protection. *Criminology*, 25(1), 47–62. https://doi.org/10.1111/J.1745-9125.1987.Tb00788.X

Yuki, M. (2003). Intergroup Comparison Versus Intragroup Relationships: A Cross-Cultural Examination of Social Identity Theory in North American and East Asian Cultural Contexts. *Social Psychology Quarterly*, 66(2), 166–183.

Yunis, H. (1996). *Taming Democracy: Models of Political Rhetoric in Classical Athens* (1. Publ). Cornell Univ. Press.

Zhang, X. (2011). China's International Broadcasting: A Case Study of CCTV International. In *Soft Power in China* (pp. 57–71). Palgrave Macmillan US. https://doi.org/10.1057/9780230116375_4

Zheng, Y., & Chan, L. S. (2020). Framing Same-Sex Marriage in U.S. Liberal and Conservative Newspapers from 2004 to 2016: Changes in Issue Attributes, Organizing Themes, and Story Tones. The *Social Science Journal*, 1–13. https://doi.org/10.1016/J.Soscij.2019.07.001

Zhu, Y. (2022). China's 'New Cultural Diplomacy' in International Broadcasting: Branding the Nation Through CGTN Documentary. *International Journal of Cultural Policy*, 1–13. https://doi.org/10.1080/10286632.2021.2022651

Zipser, R. A. (1990). The Many Faces of Censorship in the German Democratic Republic, 1949–1989: Part One: A Survey. *The Germanic Review: Literature, Culture, Theory*, 65(3), 111–117. https://doi.org/10.1080/00168890.1990.9934212

Zlobina, T. (2022). Znajoma Vijna. Rosiyu Treba Peremohty Ostatochno. *Ukrayins'ka Pravda* [Familiar War. Russia Must Be Defeated Once and for All. *Ukrainian Pravda*]. https://life.pravda.com.ua/authors/53f79baba51a7/

Zöllner, O. (2006). A Quest for Dialogue in International Broadcasting: Germany's Public Diplomacy Targeting Arab Audiences. *Global Media and Communication*, 2(2), 160–182. https://doi.org/10.1177/1742766506061817

Annex

A) List of weekly news programmes broadcast on RT between November 21, 2013 and September 7, 2014.

Date	Link to the Weekly News Programme (EU Prime Time)	Programme's code	Link to the Weekly News Programme (US Prime Time)	Programme's code
2013-11-24	https://archive.org/details/RT_20131124_200000/start/1440/end/1500	1	https://archive.org/details/RT_20131125_010000/start/1380/end/1440	2
2013-12-01	https://archive.org/details/RT_20131201_200000_Headline_News	1	https://archive.org/details/RT_20131202_010000_Headline_News	2
2013-12-08	https://archive.org/details/RT_20131208_200000_Headline_News/start/1500/end/1560	1	https://archive.org/details/RT_20131209_010000_Headline_News/start/1620/end/1680	2
2013-12-15	https://archive.org/details/RT_20131215_200000/start/0/end/60	1	https://archive.org/details/RT_20131216_010000/start/960/end/1020	2
2013-12-22	https://archive.org/details/RT_20131222_200000/start/1500/end/1560	1	https://archive.org/details/RT_20131223_010000	2
2013-12-29	https://archive.org/details/RT_20131229_200000_News_Weekly	1	https://archive.org/details/RT_20131230_010000_Headline_News	2
2014-01-05	https://archive.org/details/RT_20140105_200000_News_Weekly	1	https://archive.org/details/RT_20140106_010000_Headline_News	2

2014-01-12	https://archive.org/details/RT_20140112_200000_News_Weekly	1	https://archive.org/details/RT_20140113_010000_Headline_News	2
2014-01-19	https://archive.org/details/RT_20140119_200000_News_Weekly	1	https://archive.org/details/RT_20140120_010000_Headline_News	2
2014-01-26	https://archive.org/details/RT_20140126_200000	1	https://archive.org/details/RT_20140127_010000	2
2014-02-02	https://archive.org/details/RT_20140202_200000	1	https://archive.org/details/RT_20140203_010000	2
2014-02-09	https://archive.org/details/RT_20140209_200000	1	https://archive.org/details/RT_20140210_010000	2
2014-02-16	https://archive.org/details/RT_20140216_200000	1	https://archive.org/details/RT_20140217_010000	2
2014-02-23	https://archive.org/details/RT_20140223_200000	1	https://archive.org/details/RT_20140224_010000	2
2014-03-02	https://archive.org/details/RT_20140302_180000_Interviews_Culture_Art_Documentaries_and_Sports	1	https://archive.org/details/RT_20140303_000000_Interviews_Culture_Art_Documentaries_and_Sports	2
2014-03-09	https://archive.org/details/RT_20140309_180000_Interviews_Culture_Art_Documentaries_and_Sports	1	https://archive.org/details/RT_20140310_000000_Interviews_Culture_Art_Documentaries_and_Sports	2
2014-03-16	https://archive.org/details/RT_20140316_180000_Interviews_Cult	1	https://archive.org/details/RT_20140317_000000_Interviews_Cult	2

		ure_Art_Documentaries_and_Sports		ure_Art_Documentaries_and_Sports
2014-03-23	https://archive.org/details/RT_20140323_180000_Interviews_Culture_Art_Documentaries_and_Sports	1	https://archive.org/details/RT_20140324_000000_Interviews_Culture_Art_Documentaries_and_Sports	2
2014-03-30	https://archive.org/details/RT_20140330_180000_Interviews_Culture_Art_Documentaries_and_Sports	1	https://archive.org/details/RT_20140331_000000_Interviews_Culture_Art_Documentaries_and_Sports	2
2014-04-06	https://archive.org/details/RT_20140406_180000_Interviews_Culture_Art_Documentaries_and_Sports	1	https://archive.org/details/RT_20140407_000000_Interviews_Culture_Art_Documentaries_and_Sports	2
2014-04-13	https://archive.org/details/RT_20140413_180000_Interviews_Culture_Art_Documentaries_and_Sports	1	https://archive.org/details/RT_20140414_000000_Interviews_Culture_Art_Documentaries_and_Sports	2
2014-04-20	https://archive.org/details/RT_20140420_180000_Interviews_Culture_Art_Documentaries_and_Sports	1	https://archive.org/details/RT_20140421_000000_Interviews_Culture_Art_Documentaries_and_Sports	2
2014-04-27	https://archive.org/details/RT_20140427_180000_Interviews_Culture_Art_Documentaries_and_Sports	1	https://archive.org/details/RT_20140428_000000_Interviews_Culture_Art_Documentaries_and_Sports	2

2014-05-04	https://archive.org/details/RT_20140504_180000_Interviews_Culture_Art_Documentaries_and_Sports	1
	https://archive.org/details/RT_20140505_000000_Interviews_Culture_Art_Documentaries_and_Sports	2
2014-05-11	https://archive.org/details/RT_20140511_180000_Interviews_Culture_Art_Documentaries_and_Sports	1
	https://archive.org/details/RT_20140512_000000_Interviews_Culture_Art_Documentaries_and_Sports	2
2014-05-18	https://archive.org/details/RT_20140518_180000_Interviews_Culture_Art_Documentaries_and_Sports	1
	https://archive.org/details/RT_20140519_000000_Interviews_Culture_Art_Documentaries_and_Sports	2
2014-05-25	https://archive.org/details/RT_20140525_180000_Interviews_Culture_Art_Documentaries_and_Sports	1
	https://archive.org/details/RT_20140526_000000_Interviews_Culture_Art_Documentaries_and_Sports	2
2014-06-01	https://archive.org/details/RT_20140601_180000_Interviews_Culture_Art_Documentaries_and_Sports	1
	https://archive.org/details/RT_20140602_000000_Interviews_Culture_Art_Documentaries_and_Sports	2
2014-06-08	https://archive.org/details/RT_20140608_180000_Interviews_Culture_Art_Documentaries_and_Sports/start/3660/end/3720	1
	https://archive.org/details/RT_20140609_000000_Interviews_Culture_Art_Documentaries_and_Sports	2
2014-06-15	https://archive.org/details/RT_20140615_190000_Headline_News	1
	https://archive.org/details/RT_20140616_000000_News_Weekly	2

2014-06-22	https://archive.org/details/RT_20140622_190000_Headline_News	1	https://archive.org/details/RT_20140623_000000_News_Weekly	2
2014-06-29	https://archive.org/details/RT_20140629_190000_Headline_News	1	https://archive.org/details/RT_20140630_000000_News_Weekly	2
2014-07-06	https://archive.org/details/RT_20140706_190000_Headline_News	1	https://archive.org/details/RT_20140707_000000_News_Weekly	2
2014-07-13	https://archive.org/details/RT_20140713_190000_Headline_News	1	https://archive.org/details/RT_20140714_000000_News_Weekly	2
2014-07-20	https://archive.org/details/RT_20140720_190000_Headline_News	1	https://archive.org/details/RT_20140721_000000_News_Weekly	2
2014-07-27	https://archive.org/details/RT_20140727_190000_Headline_News	1	https://archive.org/details/RT_20140728_000000_News_Weekly	2
2014-08-03	https://archive.org/details/RT_20140803_190000_Headline_News	1	https://archive.org/details/RT_20140804_000000_News_Weekly	2
2014-08-10	https://archive.org/details/RT_20140810_190000_Headline_News	1	https://archive.org/details/RT_20140811_000000_News_Weekly	2
2014-08-17	https://archive.org/details/RT_20140817_190000_Headline_News	1	https://archive.org/details/RT_20140818_000000_News_Weekly	2
2014-08-24	https://archive.org/details/RT_20140824_190000_Headline_News	1	https://archive.org/details/RT_20140825_000000_News_Weekly	2
2014-08-31	https://archive.org/details/RT_20140831_190000_Headline_News/start/60/end/120	1	https://archive.org/details/RT_20140901_000000_News_Weekly	2
2014-09-07	Not Available		Not Available	

B) **List of weekly news programmes broadcast on Channel One Russia between November 21, 2013 and September 7, 2014 and of news stories about the Russian-Ukrainian conflict from those programmes collected for the analysis.**

Date	Link to the Weekly News Programme[47]	Number of News Stories in the Weekly News Programme (n = 618)	Number of Collected News Stories (n = 328)	Numeration of Collected News Stories on Channel's Website[48]
2013-11-24	https://www.1tv.ru/news/issue/2013-11-24/21:00	12	2	3/12; 5/12
2013-12-01	https://www.1tv.ru/news/20 13-12-01/	11	3	1 (21:00); 2 (21:02); 3 (21:10)
2013-12-08	https://www.1tv.ru/news/issue/2013-12-08/21:00	10	3	2/10; 3/10; 5/10
2013-12-15	https://www.1tv.ru/news/issue/2013-12-15/21:00	9	2	2/9; 3/9
2013-12-22	https://www.1tv.ru/news/issue/2013-12-22/21:00	10	1	3/10

47 Weekly news programmes from December 1, 2013, May 4, 2014, and July 27, 2014, were not available on the channel's website under the sorting of news by programmes. Therefore, when it comes to those dates, links from the column are leading to the lists of all news stories broadcast on the respective dates on Channel One Russia. All collected news stories are included in those lists.

48 Numeration of collected news stories broadcast on December 1, 2013, May 4, 2014, and July 27, 2014, was absent on channel's website. Thus, in this table they are numerated in accordance with the order in which they were broadcast on the respective date as of 21:00 (usual time when the weekly news programme began). To make the process of awarding news stories with those numbers more transparent and their search on the website more convenient for the reader, the particular time when broadcasting of a collected news story begun on Channel One Russia was documented as well.

2013-12-29	https://www.1tv.ru/news/issue/2013-12-29/21:00	12	0	No
2014-01-05	https://www.1tv.ru/news/issue/2014-01-05/21:00	11	0	No
2014-01-12	https://www.1tv.ru/news/issue/2014-01-12/21:00	12	0	No
2014-01-19	https://www.1tv.ru/news/issue/2014-01-19/21:00	11	1	5/11
2014-01-26	https://www.1tv.ru/news/issue/2014-01-26/21:00	10	1	1/10
2014-02-02	https://www.1tv.ru/news/issue/2014-02-02/21:00	10	2	5/10; 6/10
2014-02-09	https://www.1tv.ru/news/issue/2014-02-09/21:00	12	1	5/12
2014-02-16	https://www.1tv.ru/news/issue/2014-02-16/21:00	15	0	No
2014-02-23	https://www.1tv.ru/news/issue/2014-02-23/	14	2	5/14; 6/14
2014-03-02	https://www.1tv.ru/news/issue/2014-03-02/21:00	19	12	1/19; 2/19; 3/19; 4/19; 5/19; 6/19; 7/19; 15/19; 16/19; 17/19; 18/19; 19/19
2014-03-09	https://www.1tv.ru/news/issue/2014-03-09/21:00	13	5	2/13; 3/13; 4/13; 5/13; 6/13
2014-03-16	https://www.1tv.ru/news/issue/2014-03-16/21:00	17	15	1/17; 2/17; 3/17; 4/17; 5/17; 6/17; 7/17; 8/17;

2014-03-23	https://www.1tv.ru/news/issue/2014-03-23/21:00	12	9/17; 10/17; 11/17; 12/17; 13/17; 17/17
			1/12; 2/12; 3/12; 4/12; 5/12; 6/12; 7/12; 8/12; 9/12
2014-03-30	https://www.1tv.ru/news/issue/2014-03-30/21:00	14	1/14; 2/14; 3/14; 4/14; 5/14; 6/14; 7/14; 8/14; 9/14; 10/14; 11/14; 12/14
2014-04-06	https://www.1tv.ru/news/issue/2014-04-06/21:00	13	1/13; 2/13; 3/13; 4/13; 5/13; 6/13; 7/13; 8/13; 9/13
2014-04-13	https://www.1tv.ru/news/issue/2014-04-13/21:00	18	1/18; 2/18; 3/18; 4/18; 5/18; 6/18; 7/18; 8/18; 9/18; 10/18; 11/18;16/18; 17/18; 18/18
2014-04-20	https://www.1tv.ru/news/issue/2014-04-20/21:00	13	2/13; 3/13; 4/13; 5/13; 6/13; 7/13; 8/13
2014-04-27	https://www.1tv.ru/news/issue/2014-04-27/21:00	10	1/10; 2/10; 3/10; 4/10; 5/10; 6/10; 7/10
2014-05-04	https://www.1tv.ru/news/2014-05-04/	18	1 (21:01); 2 (21:07); 3 (21:09) 4 (21:16); 5 (21:20); 6 (21:21); 7 (21:25); 8 (21:26); 9 (21:27); 10 (21:28); 11 (21:29); 12 (21:30); 13 (21:31); 15 (21:36)
2014-05-11	https://www.1tv.ru/news/issue/2014-05-11/21:00	18	1/18; 2/18; 3/18; 4/18; 5/18; 6/18; 7/18; 8/18; 9/18

2014-05-18	https://www.1tv.ru/news/issue/2014-05-18/21:00	15	1/15; 2/15; 3/15; 4/15; 6/15; 7/15; 8/15; 9/15; 10/15; 11/15; 15/15
2014-05-25	https://www.1tv.ru/news/issue/2014-05-25/21:00	14	1/14; 2/14; 3/14; 4/14; 5/14; 6/14; 7/14; 9/14; 10/14; 13/14; 14/14
2014-06-01	https://www.1tv.ru/news/issue/2014-06-01/21:00	17	1/17; 2/17; 3/17; 4/17; 8/17; 9/17; 10/17; 14/17
2014-06-08	https://www.1tv.ru/news/issue/2014-06-08/21:00	15	1/15; 2/15; 3/15; 4/15; 5/15; 6/15; 7/15; 8/15; 9/15
2014-06-15	https://www.1tv.ru/news/issue/2014-06-15/21:00	12	1/12; 2/12; 3/12; 4/12; 5/12; 6/12; 7/12; 8/12; 9/12; 11/12
2014-06-22	https://www.1tv.ru/news/issue/2014-06-22/21:00	17	3/17; 4/17; 5/17; 6/17; 7/17; 8/17; 9/17; 10/17; 11/17; 12/17; 13/17
2014-06-29	https://www.1tv.ru/news/issue/2014-06-29/21:00	14	1/14; 2/14; 3/14; 4/14; 6/14; 7/14;8/14; 9/14;
2014-07-06	https://www.1tv.ru/news/issue/2014-07-06/21:00	15	1/15; 2/15; 3/15; 4/15; 5/15; 6/15; 7/15; 8/15; 9/15; 10/15; 11/15; 12/15; 15/15
2014-07-13	https://www.1tv.ru/news/issue/2014-07-13/21:00	20	1/20; 2/20; 3/20; 4/20; 5/20; 6/20; 7/20; 8/20;

			9/20; 11/20; 12/20; 13/20; 20/20
2014-07-20	https://www.1tv.ru/news/issue/2014-07-20/21:00	13	1/13; 2/13; 3/13; 4/13; 7/13; 8/13; 9/13; 12/13; 13/13
2014-07-27	https://www.1tv.ru/news/2014-07-27/	23	3 (21:04); 4 (21:07); 5 (21:14); 6 (21:17); 7 (21:19); 8 (21:23); 9 (21:26); 10 (21:30); 11 (21:35); 12 (22:01); 13 (22:03); 15 (22:15); 16 (22:20); 17 (22:34); 18 (22:38); 19 (22:40); 20 (22:43); 23 (22:57)
2014-08-03	https://www.1tv.ru/news/issue/2014-08-03/21:00	22	1/22; 2/22; 3/22; 4/22; 5/22; 6/22; 7/22; 8/22; 9/22; 10/22; 11/22; 12/22
2014-08-10	https://www.1tv.ru/news/issue/2014-08-10/21:00	22	1/22; 2/22; 4/22; 5/22; 6/22; 7/22; 9/22; 10/22; 11/22; 12/22; 13/22; 14/22; 15/22
2014-08-17	https://www.1tv.ru/news/issue/2014-08-17/21:00	19	1/19; 2/19; 3/19; 4/19; 5/19; 6/19; 7/19; 8/19; 9/19; 10/19; 11/19; 12/19; 13/19; 14/19
2014-08-24	https://www.1tv.ru/news/issue/2014-08-24/21:00	20	1/20; 2/20; 3/20; 4/20; 5/20; 6/20; 7/20; 8/20;

2014-08-31	https://www.1tv.ru/news/issue/2014-08-31/21:00	19	9/20; 10/20; 11/20; 12/20; 13/20; 14/20; 15/20
		12	1/19; 2/19; 3/19; 4/19; 5/19; 6/19; 7/19; 8/19; 9/19; 10/19; 11/19; 12/19
2014-09-07	https://www.1tv.ru/news/issue/2014-09-07/21:00	17	1/17; 2/17; 3/17; 4/17; 5/17; 6/17; 8/17; 9/17; 10/17; 11/17
		10	

Index

Al Jazeera 68
Atrocity Propaganda 64, 165, 169
Autocracy 52–54, 78, 189–193
BBC World Service 69
Bipolar 160–161
Causality 161–163, 184. 187
Censorship 77–78, 88
China Global Television Network (CGTN) 69–70, 140
CNN International 68–69
Codebook 105, 108
Cognitive Map 17, 156–157
Cold War 24, 37–38, 62–64, 160–161
Colonialism 95–97
Constructivism 17–20, 31, 166
Copenhagen School (CS) 25–31, 46
Crimean Tatars 11
Critical Discourse Analysis (CDA) 111
Degree of Enmity 186
Dehumanization 150–151, 177, 181–185, 193
Delegitimization 52, 62, 189, 192
Democracy 45, 48–52
Demonization 33, 39, 79, 177, 187, 191, 193
Denazification 58, 160, 176, 188
Deutsche Welle (DW) 69
Discourse-Historical Approach (DHA) 111–113, 156, 174, 183–186
Discursive Strategies 112–113

Effective Control 174
Ekho Moskvy 82–83, 85, 86
Emotionality 164–165
Enemy 23–24, 32–36
Enmification 31, 46, 49–52, 71–73, 189
Euromaidan Protesters 130, 148, 170–172, 183
Euromaidan, Maidan 83–84, 98–99, 118, 130, 144–174
European Court of Human Rights 125, 174
Evaluation Act 120–124
Existential Enemy 24, 29
Fake News 106, 165, 168
Federal Republic of Germany 58, 125, 134–135
France 125, 134–135
France 24 69
Gatekeeping 50, 128
German Democratic Republic 58
Girkin, Igor 175–176
Group Categorization 20–23, 53,
Identity 21–25, 27, 29, 53–54, 148, 166
Ilovaisk 101, 180
Imagined Communities 19
Individual Diplomacy 67
Information Warfare 65–68
In-group 21–24, 29, 53, 126
International Broadcaster 59–65, 68–73, 89, 140, 143, 191
Issue of Supreme Priority 26, 72, 145
Kyivan Rus 95–96, 148

Legitimization 52, 62, 189, 192
Lenta.ru 83–85
Malorussian 95
Mass Media 55–61, 71–72, 137
Mearsheimer, John 93–94
Media Environment 48, 50–51, 55, 73, 81–82, 142, 152, 192
Meduza 85–86
MH-17 100, 122, 176, 178–180
Morality 108, 120–121, 149–151
Moscow Principality 95
News Broadcaster 70–71
North Korea 41, 77, 194
Novaya Gazeta 85–86, 169
NTV 78–79, 82
Number One Topic 118–119
Objective Threat 25–30
Occupation of Crimea 127, 147–148, 161–163, 173–174
Organization for Security and Co-operation in Europe (OSCE) 163
Out-group 20–24, 53, 150
Political System 48, 52–53, 69
Postmaidan Ukrainian Authorities 124, 133–135, 155, 157–159, 162, 164, 166, 172–173, 175, 178, 182
Post-Soviet 78, 81, 139, 185
Press Freedom 47, 77
Prisoners of War (POWs) 180–182
Propaganda 33, 42, 61–62, 67, 91, 162, 192
Psychological Warfare 42–43, 66–67

Public Diplomacy 59–63, 67–70, 89–90, 141, 146, 152
Realism 23, 93–94
RIA Novosti 188
Right Sector 84, 155, 158, 166–167, 173, 175–176, 186, 190
Russia Today 68, 87–92
Russian Colonialism 95–97
Russian Public Television (ORT) 87–88
Russian-Chechen War 79–80
Russian-Georgian War 79–80, 89, 161
Russification 95–96
Scapegoating 54–55
Securitization 26–31, 46, 71–72, 166
Securitized Issue 26–27
Sham Referendum 99–100, 122, 145, 155, 172–174
Simonyan, Margarita 91–92
Slavs 95–96
Sloviansk 99, 165, 169, 175, 177
Social Construct 18–20, 22
Social Identity Theory 21
Social Reality 17–18
Socialization 17
Sovereignty 28, 93, 134
Speech Act 26–27, 111
Sphere of Influence 93, 148
Standardized Content Analysis 105–110, 121, 138, 186
Statehood 28–29, 96, 148
Stereotype 40–41, 50, 128–129
Strategic Narrative 83, 134–137, 145, 183

Strategies of Public Diplomacy 67, 141

Target of Enmification 131, 136, 138, 141–142, 151, 187

Targeted Enmification 185

The First Minsk Agreement 101–102

The Second Minsk Agreement 85, 101–102

TVRain 82–83, 85–86, 168–169

Ukrainian Crisis 93, 97

Ukrainian Media 125

USSR, Soviet Regime, Soviet Union 77–78, 81, 83, 88, 95, 159, 160–161, 193

Uyghurs 192

Voice of America (VOA) 69

Vremya Programme 88

Wendt, Alexander 19, 36

Ukrainian Voices

Collected by Andreas Umland

1 Mychailo Wynnyckyj
   Ukraine's Maidan, Russia's War
   A Chronicle and Analysis of the Revolution of Dignity
   With a foreword by Serhii Plokhy
   ISBN 978-3-8382-1327-9

2 Olexander Hryb
   Understanding Contemporary Ukrainian and Russian Nationalism
   The Post-Soviet Cossack Revival and Ukraine's National Security
   With a foreword by Vitali Vitaliev
   ISBN 978-3-8382-1377-4

3 Marko Bojcun
   Towards a Political Economy of Ukraine
   Selected Essays 1990–2015
   With a foreword by John-Paul Himka
   ISBN 978-3-8382-1368-2

4 Volodymyr Yermolenko (ed.)
   Ukraine in Histories and Stories
   Essays by Ukrainian Intellectuals
   With a preface by Peter Pomerantsev
   ISBN 978-3-8382-1456-6

5 Mykola Riabchuk
   At the Fence of Metternich's Garden
   Essays on Europe, Ukraine, and Europeanization
   ISBN 978-3-8382-1484-9

6 Marta Dyczok
   Ukraine Calling
   A Kaleidoscope from Hromadske Radio 2016–2019
   With a foreword by Andriy Kulykov
   ISBN 978-3-8382-1472-6

7 Olexander Scherba
   Ukraine vs. Darkness
   Undiplomatic Thoughts
   With a foreword by Adrian Karatnycky
   ISBN 978-3-8382-1501-3

8 Olesya Yaremchuk
   Our Others
   Stories of Ukrainian Diversity
   With a foreword by Ostap Slyvynsky
   Translated from the Ukrainian by Zenia Tompkins and Hanna Leliv
   ISBN 978-3-8382-1475-7

9 Nataliya Gumenyuk
   Die verlorene Insel
   Geschichten von der besetzten Krim
   Mit einem Vorwort von Alice Bota
   Aus dem Ukrainischen übersetzt von Johann Zajaczkowski
   ISBN 978-3-8382-1499-3

10 Olena Stiazhkina
   Zero Point Ukraine
   Four Essays on World War II
   Translated from the Ukrainian by Svitlana Kulinska
   ISBN 978-3-8382-1550-1

11 *Oleksii Sinchenko, Dmytro Stus, Leonid Finberg (compilers)*
    Ukrainian Dissidents
    An Anthology of Texts
    ISBN 978-3-8382-1551-8

12 *John-Paul Himka*
    Ukrainian Nationalists and the Holocaust
    OUN and UPA's Participation in the Destruction of Ukrainian Jewry, 1941–1944
    ISBN 978-3-8382-1548-8

13 *Andrey Demartino*
    False Mirrors
    The Weaponization of Social Media in Russia's Operation to Annex Crimea
    With a foreword by Oleksiy Danilov
    ISBN 978-3-8382-1533-4

14 *Svitlana Biedarieva (ed.)*
    Contemporary Ukrainian and Baltic Art
    Political and Social Perspectives, 1991–2021
    ISBN 978-3-8382-1526-6

15 *Olesya Khromeychuk*
    A Loss
    The Story of a Dead Soldier Told by His Sister
    With a foreword by Andrey Kurkov
    ISBN 978-3-8382-1570-9

16 *Marieluise Beck (Hg.)*
    Ukraine verstehen
    Auf den Spuren von Terror und Gewalt
    Mit einem Vorwort von Dmytro Kuleba
    ISBN 978-3-8382-1653-9

17 *Stanislav Aseyev*
    Heller Weg
    Geschichte eines Konzentrationslagers im Donbass 2017–2019
    Aus dem Russischen übersetzt von Martina Steis und Charis Haska
    ISBN 978-3-8382-1620-1

18 *Mykola Davydiuk*
    Wie funktioniert Putins Propaganda?
    Anmerkungen zum Informationskrieg des Kremls
    Aus dem Ukrainischen übersetzt von Christian Weise
    ISBN 978-3-8382-1628-7

19 *Olesya Yaremchuk*
    Unsere Anderen
    Geschichten ukrainischer Vielfalt
    Aus dem Ukrainischen übersetzt von Christian Weise
    ISBN 978-3-8382-1635-5

20 *Oleksandr Mykhed*
    „Dein Blut wird die Kohle tränken"
    Über die Ostukraine
    Aus dem Ukrainischen übersetzt von Simon Muschick und Dario Planert
    ISBN 978-3-8382-1648-5

21 *Vakhtang Kipiani (Hg.)*
    Der Zweite Weltkrieg in der Ukraine
    Geschichte und Lebensgeschichten
    Aus dem Ukrainischen übersetzt von Margarita Grinko
    ISBN 978-3-8382-1622-5

22 *Vakhtang Kipiani (ed.)*
    World War II, Uncontrived and Unredacted
    Testimonies from Ukraine
    Translated from the Ukrainian by Zenia Tompkins and Daisy Gibbons
    ISBN 978-3-8382-1621-8

23 Dmytro Stus
Vasyl Stus
Life in Creativity
Translated from the Ukrainian by
Ludmila Bachurina
ISBN 978-3-8382-1631-7

24 Vitalii Ogiienko (ed.)
The Holodomor and the
Origins of the Soviet Man
Reading the Testimony of
Anastasia Lysyvets
With forewords by Natalka
Bilotserkivets and Serhy
Yekelchyk
Translated from the Ukrainian by
Alla Parkhomenko and
Alexander J. Motyl
ISBN 978-3-8382-1616-4

25 Vladislav Davidzon
Jewish-Ukrainian Relations
and the Birth of a Political
Nation
Selected Writings 2013-2021
With a foreword by Bernard-
Henri Lévy
ISBN 978-3-8382-1509-9

26 Serhy Yekelchyk
Writing the Nation
The Ukrainian Historical
Profession in Independent
Ukraine and the Diaspora
ISBN 978-3-8382-1695-9

27 Ildi Eperjesi, Oleksandr
Kachura
Shreds of War
Fates from the Donbas Frontline
2014-2019
With a foreword by Olexiy
Haran
ISBN 978-3-8382-1680-5

28 Oleksandr Melnyk
World War II as an Identity
Project
Historicism, Legitimacy
Contests, and the (Re-)Con-
struction of Political Commu-
nities in Ukraine, 1939–1946
With a foreword by David R.
Marples
ISBN 978-3-8382-1704-8

29 Olesya Khromeychuk
Ein Verlust
Die Geschichte eines gefallenen
ukrainischen Soldaten, erzählt
von seiner Schwester
Mit einem Vorwort von Andrej
Kurkow
Aus dem Englischen übersetzt
von Lily Sophie
ISBN 978-3-8382-1770-3

30 Tamara Martsenyuk,
Tetiana Kostiuchenko (eds.)
Russia's War in Ukraine
During 2022
Personal Experiences of
Ukrainian Scholars
ISBN 978-3-8382-1757-4

31 Ildikó Eperjesi, Oleksandr
Kachura
Shreds of War. Vol. 2
Fates from Crimea 2015–2022
With an interview of Oleh
Sentsov
ISBN 978-3-8382-1780-2

32 Yuriy Lukanov
The Press
How Russia Destroyed Media
Freedom in Crimea
With a foreword by Taras Kuzio
ISBN 978-3-8382-1784-0

33 Megan Buskey
Ukraine Is Not Dead Yet
A Family Story of Exile and
Return
ISBN 978-3-8382-1691-1

34 *Vira Ageyeva*
Behind the Scenes of the Empire
Essays on Cultural Relationships between Ukraine and Russia
With a foreword by Oksana Zabuzhko
ISBN 978-3-8382-1748-2

35 *Marieluise Beck (ed.)*
Understanding Ukraine
Tracing the Roots of Terror and Violence
With a foreword by Dmytro Kuleba
ISBN 978-3-8382-1773-4

36 *Olesya Khromeychuk*
A Loss
The Story of a Dead Soldier Told by His Sister, 2nd edn.
With a foreword by Philippe Sands
With a preface by Andrii Kurkov
ISBN 978-3-8382-1870-0

37 *Taras Kuzio, Stefan Jajecznyk-Kelman*
Fascism and Genocide
Russia's War Against Ukrainians
ISBN 978-3-8382-1791-8

38 *Alina Nychyk*
Ukraine Vis-à-Vis Russia and the EU
Misperceptions of Foreign Challenges in Times of War, 2014–2015
With a foreword by Paul D'Anieri
ISBN 978-3-8382-1767-3

39 *Sasha Dovzhyk (ed.)*
Ukraine Lab
Global Security, Environment, and Disinformation Through the Prism of Ukraine
With a foreword by Rory Finnin
ISBN 978-3-8382-1805-2

40 *Serhiy Kvit*
Media, History, and Education
Three Ways to Ukrainian Independence
With a preface by Diane Francis
ISBN 978-3-8382-1807-6

41 *Anna Romandash*
Women of Ukraine
Reportages from the War and Beyond
ISBN 978-3-8382-1819-9

42 *Dominika Rank*
Matzewe in meinem Garten
Abenteuer eines jüdischen Heritage-Touristen in der Ukraine
ISBN 978-3-8382-1810-6

43 *Myroslaw Marynowytsch*
Das Universum hinter dem Stacheldraht
Memoiren eines sowjet-ukrainischen Dissidenten
Mit einem Vorwort von Timothy Snyder und einem Nachwort von Max Hartmann
ISBN 978-3-8382-1806-9

44 *Konstantin Sigow*
Für Deine und meine Freiheit
Europäische Revolutions- und Kriegserfahrungen im heutigen Kyjiw
Mit einem Vorwort von Karl Schlögel
Herausgegeben von Regula M. Zwahlen
ISBN 978-3-8382-1755-0

45 *Kateryna Pylypchuk*
The War that Changed Us
Ukrainian Novellas, Poems, and Essays from 2022
With a foreword by Victor Yushchenko
Paperback
ISBN 978-3-8382-1859-5
Hardcover
ISBN 978-3-8382-1860-1

46 *Kyrylo Tkachenko*
Rechte Tür Links
Radikale Linke in Deutschland, die Revolution und der Krieg in der Ukraine, 2013-2018
ISBN 978-3-8382-1711-6

47 *Alexander Strashny*
The Ukrainian Mentality
An Ethno-Psychological, Historical and Comparative Exploration
With a foreword by Antonina Lovochkina
Translated from the Ukrainian by Michael M. Naydan and Olha Tytarenko
ISBN 978-3-8382-1886-1

48 *Alona Shestopalova*
From Screens to Battlefields
Tracing the Construction of Enemies on Russian Television
With a foreword by Nina Jankowicz
ISBN 978-3-8382-1884-7

49 *Iaroslav Petik*
Politics and Society in the Ukrainian People's Republic (1917–1921) and Contemporary Ukraine (2013–2022)
A Comparative Analysis
With a foreword by Mykola Doroshko
ISBN 978-3-8382-1817-5

50 *Serhii Plokhy*
Der Mann mit der Giftpistole
Eine Spionageschichte aus dem Kalten Krieg
ISBN 978-3-8382-1789-5

51 *Vakhtang Kipiani*
Ukrainische Dissidenten unter der Sowjetmacht
Im Kampf um Wahrheit und Freiheit
Aus dem Ukrainischen übersetzt von Christian Weise
ISBN 978-3-8382-1890-8

52 *Dmytro Shestakov*
When Businesses Test Hypotheses
A Four-Step Approach to Risk Management for Innovative Startups
With a foreword by Anthony J. Tether
ISBN 978-3-8382-1883-0

53 *Larissa Babij*
A Kind of Refugee
The Story of an American Who Refused to Leave Ukraine
With a foreword by Vladislav Davidzon
ISBN 978-3-8382-1898-4

54 *Julia Davis*
In Their Own Words
How Russian Propagandists Reveal Putin's Intentions
With a foreword by Timothy Snyder
ISBN 978-3-8382-1909-7

55 *Sonya Atlantova, Oleksandr Klymenko*
Icons on Ammo Boxes
Painting Life on the Remnants of Russia's War in Donbas, 2014-21
Translated from the Ukrainian by Anastasya Knyazhytska
ISBN 978-3-8382-1892-2

56 *Leonid Ushkalov*
Catching an Elusive Bird
The Life of Hryhorii Skovoroda
Translated from the Ukrainian by Natalia Komarova
ISBN 978-3-8382-1894-6

57 *Vakhtang Kipiani*
Ein Land weiblichen Geschlechts
Ukrainische Frauenschicksale im 20. und 21. Jahrhundert
Aus dem Ukrainischen übersetzt von Christian Weise
ISBN 978-3-8382-1891-5

58 Petro Rychlo
„Zerrissne Saiten einer überlauten Harfe ..."
Deutschjüdische Dichter der Bukowina
ISBN 978-3-8382-1893-9

59 Volodymyr Paniotto
Sociology in Jokes
An Entertaining Introduction
ISBN 978-3-8382-1857-1

60 Josef Wallmannsberger (ed.)
Executing Renaissances
The Poetological Nation of Ukraine
ISBN 978-3-8382-1741-3

61 Pavlo Kazarin
The Wild West of Eastern Europe
ISBN 978-3-8382-1842-7

62 Ernest Gyidel
Ukrainian Public Nationalism in the General Government
The Case of Krakivski Visti, 1940–1944
With a foreword by David R. Marples
ISBN 978-3-8382-1865-6

63 Olexander Hryb
Understanding Contemporary Russian Militarism
From Revolutionary to New Generation Warfare
With a foreword by Mark Laity
ISBN 978-3-8382-1927-1

64 Orysia Hrudka, Bohdan Ben
Dark Days, Determined People
Stories from Ukraine under Siege
With a foreword by Myroslav Marynovych
ISBN 978-3-8382-1958-5

65 Oleksandr Pankieiev (ed.)
Narratives of the Russo-Ukrainian War
A Look Within and Without
With a foreword by Natalia Khanenko-Friesen
ISBN 978-3-8382-1964-6

66 Roman Sohn, Ariana Gic (eds.)
Unrecognized War
The Fight for Truth about Russia's War on Ukraine
With a foreword by Viktor Yushchenko
ISBN 978-3-8382-1947-9

67 Paul Robert Magocsi
Ukraina Redux
Schon wieder die Ukraine ...
ISBN 978-3-8382-1942-4

68 Paul Robert Magocsi
L'Ucraina Ritrovata
Sullo Stato e l'Identità Nazionale
ISBN 978-3-8382-1982-0

69 Paul Robert Magocsi
From Nowhere to Somewhere
ISBN 978-3-8382-1973-8

70 Vakhtang Kebuladze (Hrsg.)
Die Zukunft, die wir uns wünschen
Ukrainische Intellektuelle zu Herausforderungen der Ukraine und ganzen Welt
ISBN 978-3-8382-1531-0

Book series "Ukrainian Voices"

Coordinator
Andreas Umland, National University of Kyiv-Mohyla Academy

Editorial Board
Lesia Bidochko, National University of Kyiv-Mohyla Academy
Svitlana Biedarieva, George Washington University, DC, USA
Ivan Gomza, Kyiv School of Economics, Ukraine
Natalie Jaresko, Aspen Institute, Kyiv/Washington
Olena Lennon, University of New Haven, West Haven, USA
Kateryna Yushchenko, First Lady of Ukraine 2005-2010, Kyiv
Oleksandr Zabirko, University of Regensburg, Germany

Advisory Board
Iuliia Bentia, National Academy of Arts of Ukraine, Kyiv
Natalya Belitser, Pylyp Orlyk Institute for Democracy, Kyiv
Oleksandra Bienert, Humboldt University of Berlin, Germany
Sergiy Bilenky, Canadian Institute of Ukrainian Studies, Toronto
Tymofii Brik, Kyiv School of Economics, Ukraine
Olga Brusylovska, Mechnikov National University, Odesa
Mariana Budjeryn, Harvard University, Cambridge, USA
Volodymyr Bugrov, Shevchenko National University, Kyiv
Olga Burlyuk, University of Amsterdam, The Netherlands
Yevhen Bystrytsky, NAS Institute of Philosophy, Kyiv
Andrii Danylenko, Pace University, New York, USA
Vladislav Davidzon, Atlantic Council, Washington/Paris
Mykola Davydiuk, Think Tank "Polityka," Kyiv
Andrii Demartino, National Security and Defense Council, Kyiv
Vadym Denisenko, Ukrainian Institute for the Future, Kyiv
Oleksandr Donii, Center for Political Values Studies, Kyiv
Volodymyr Dubovyk, Mechnikov National University, Odesa
Volodymyr Dubrovskiy, CASE Ukraine, Kyiv
Diana Dutsyk, National University of Kyiv-Mohyla Academy
Marta Dyczok, Western University, Ontario, Canada
Yevhen Fedchenko, National University of Kyiv-Mohyla Academy
Sofiya Filonenko, State Pedagogical University of Berdyansk
Oleksandr Fisun, Karazin National University, Kharkiv
Oksana Forostyna, Webjournal "Ukraina Moderna," Kyiv
Roman Goncharenko, Broadcaster "Deutsche Welle," Bonn
George Grabowicz, Harvard University, Cambridge, USA
Gelinada Grinchenko, Karazin National University, Kharkiv
Kateryna Härtel, Federal Union of European Nationalities, Brussels
Nataliia Hendel, University of Geneva, Switzerland
Anton Herashchenko, Kyiv School of Public Administration
John-Paul Himka, University of Alberta, Edmonton
Ola Hnatiuk, National University of Kyiv-Mohyla Academy
Oleksandr Holubov, Broadcaster "Deutsche Welle," Bonn
Yaroslav Hrytsak, Ukrainian Catholic University, Lviv
Oleksandra Humenna, National University of Kyiv-Mohyla Academy
Tamara Hundorova, NAS Institute of Literature, Kyiv
Oksana Huss, University of Bologna, Italy
Oleksandra Iwaniuk, University of Warsaw, Poland
Mykola Kapitonenko, Shevchenko National University, Kyiv
Georgiy Kasianov, Marie Curie-Skłodowska University, Lublin
Vakhtang Kebuladze, Shevchenko National University, Kyiv
Natalia Khanenko-Friesen, University of Alberta, Edmonton
Victoria Khiterer, Millersville University of Pennsylvania, USA
Oksana Kis, NAS Institute of Ethnology, Lviv
Pavlo Klimkin, Center for National Resilience and Development, Kyiv
Oleksandra Kolomiiets, Center for Economic Strategy, Kyiv

Sergiy Korsunsky, Kobe Gakuin University, Japan
Nadiia Koval, Kyiv School of Economics, Ukraine
Volodymyr Kravchenko, University of Alberta, Edmonton
Oleksiy Kresin, NAS Koretskiy Institute of State and Law, Kyiv
Anatoliy Kruglashov, Fedkovych National University, Chernivtsi
Andrey Kurkov, PEN Ukraine, Kyiv
Ostap Kushnir, Lazarski University, Warsaw
Taras Kuzio, National University of Kyiv-Mohyla Academy
Serhii Kvit, National University of Kyiv-Mohyla Academy
Yuliya Ladygina, The Pennsylvania State University, USA
Yevhen Mahda, Institute of World Policy, Kyiv
Victoria Malko, California State University, Fresno, USA
Yulia Marushevska, Security and Defense Center (SAND), Kyiv
Myroslav Marynovych, Ukrainian Catholic University, Lviv
Oleksandra Matviichuk, Center for Civil Liberties, Kyiv
Mykhailo Minakov, Kennan Institute, Washington, USA
Anton Moiseienko, The Australian National University, Canberra
Alexander Motyl, Rutgers University-Newark, USA
Vlad Mykhnenko, University of Oxford, United Kingdom
Vitalii Ogiienko, Ukrainian Institute of National Remembrance, Kyiv
Olga Onuch, University of Manchester, United Kingdom
Olesya Ostrovska, Museum "Mystetskyi Arsenal," Kyiv
Anna Osypchuk, National University of Kyiv-Mohyla Academy
Oleksandr Pankieiev, University of Alberta, Edmonton
Oleksiy Panych, Publishing House "Dukh i Litera," Kyiv
Valerii Pekar, Kyiv-Mohyla Business School, Ukraine
Yohanan Petrovsky-Shtern, Northwestern University, Chicago
Serhii Plokhy, Harvard University, Cambridge, USA
Andrii Portnov, Viadrina University, Frankfurt-Oder, Germany
Maryna Rabinovych, Kyiv School of Economics, Ukraine
Valentyna Romanova, Institute of Developing Economies, Tokyo
Natalya Ryabinska, Collegium Civitas, Warsaw, Poland
Darya Tsymbalyk, University of Oxford, United Kingdom
Vsevolod Samokhvalov, University of Liege, Belgium
Orest Semotiuk, Franko National University, Lviv
Viktoriya Sereda, NAS Institute of Ethnology, Lviv
Anton Shekhovtsov, University of Vienna, Austria
Andriy Shevchenko, Media Center Ukraine, Kyiv
Oxana Shevel, Tufts University, Medford, USA
Pavlo Shopin, National Pedagogical Dragomanov University, Kyiv
Karina Shyrokykh, Stockholm University, Sweden
Nadja Simon, freelance interpreter, Cologne, Germany
Olena Snigova, NAS Institute for Economics and Forecasting, Kyiv
Ilona Solohub, Analytical Platform "VoxUkraine," Kyiv
Iryna Solonenko, LibMod - Center for Liberal Modernity, Berlin
Galyna Solovei, National University of Kyiv-Mohyla Academy
Sergiy Stelmakh, NAS Institute of World History, Kyiv
Olena Stiazhkina, NAS Institute of the History of Ukraine, Kyiv
Dmitri Stratievski, Osteuropa Zentrum (OEZB), Berlin
Dmytro Stus, National Taras Shevchenko Museum, Kyiv
Frank Sysyn, University of Toronto, Canada
Olha Tokariuk, Center for European Policy Analysis, Washington
Olena Tregub, Independent Anti-Corruption Commission, Kyiv
Hlib Vyshlinsky, Centre for Economic Strategy, Kyiv
Mychailo Wynnyckyj, National University of Kyiv-Mohyla Academy
Yelyzaveta Yasko, NGO "Yellow Blue Strategy," Kyiv
Serhy Yekelchyk, University of Victoria, Canada
Victor Yushchenko, President of Ukraine 2005-2010, Kyiv
Oleksandr Zaitsev, Ukrainian Catholic University, Lviv
Kateryna Zarembo, National University of Kyiv-Mohyla Academy
Yaroslav Zhalilo, National Institute for Strategic Studies, Kyiv
Sergei Zhuk, Ball State University at Muncie, USA
Alina Zubkovych, Nordic Ukraine Forum, Stockholm
Liudmyla Zubrytska, National University of Kyiv-Mohyla Academy

Friends of the Series

Ana Maria Abulescu, University of Bucharest, Romania
Łukasz Adamski, Centrum Mieroszewskiego, Warsaw
Marieluise Beck, LibMod—Center for Liberal Modernity, Berlin
Marc Berensen, King's College London, United Kingdom
Johannes Bohnen, BOHNEN Public Affairs, Berlin
Karsten Brüggemann, University of Tallinn, Estonia
Ulf Brunnbauer, Leibniz Institute (IOS), Regensburg
Martin Dietze, German-Ukrainian Culture Society, Hamburg
Gergana Dimova, Florida State University, Tallahassee/London
Caroline von Gall, Goethe University, Frankfurt-Main
Zaur Gasimov, Rhenish Friedrich Wilhelm University, Bonn
Armand Gosu, University of Bucharest, Romania
Thomas Grant, University of Cambridge, United Kingdom
Gustav Gressel, European Council on Foreign Relations, Berlin
Rebecca Harms, European Centre for Press & Media Freedom, Leipzig
André Härtel, Stiftung Wissenschaft und Politik, Berlin/Brussels
Marcel Van Herpen, The Cicero Foundation, Maastricht
Richard Herzinger, freelance analyst, Berlin
Mieste Hotopp-Riecke, ICATAT, Magdeburg
Nico Lange, Munich Security Conference, Berlin
Martin Malek, freelance analyst, Vienna
Ingo Mannteufel, Broadcaster "Deutsche Welle," Bonn
Carlo Masala, Bundeswehr University, Munich
Wolfgang Mueller, University of Vienna, Austria
Dietmar Neutatz, Albert Ludwigs University, Freiburg
Torsten Oppelland, Friedrich Schiller University, Jena
Niccolò Pianciola, University of Padua, Italy
Gerald Praschl, German-Ukrainian Forum (DUF), Berlin
Felix Riefer, Think Tank Ideenagentur-Ost, Düsseldorf
Stefan Rohdewald, University of Leipzig, Germany
Sebastian Schäffer, Institute for the Danube Region (IDM), Vienna
Felix Schimansky-Geier, Friedrich Schiller University, Jena
Ulrich Schneckener, University of Osnabrück, Germany

Winfried Schneider-Deters, freelance analyst, Heidelberg/Kyiv
Gerhard Simon, University of Cologne, Germany
Kai Struve, Martin Luther University, Halle/Wittenberg
David Stulik, European Values Center for Security Policy, Prague
Andrzej Szeptycki, University of Warsaw, Poland
Philipp Ther, University of Vienna, Austria
Stefan Troebst, University of Leipzig, Germany

[Please send requests for changes in, corrections of, and additions to, this list to andreas.umland@stanforalumni.org.]

ibidem.eu